SELECT ESSAYS ON

GOVERNANCE AND ACCOUNTABILITY ISSUES

IN PUBLIC LAW

EDITORS
HENNIE STRYDOM
JOANNA BOTHA

SUN PRESS

Select Essays on Governance and Accountability Issues in Public Law

Published by African Sun Media under the SUN PReSS imprint

This publication was subjected to an independent double-blind peer evaluation by the publisher.

The editors and the publisher have made every effort to obtain permission for and acknowledge the use of copyrighted material. Refer all enquiries to the publisher.

Views reflected in this publication are not necessarily those of the publisher.

First edition 2020

ISBN 978-1-928480-78-5
ISBN 978-1-928480-79-2 (e-book)
https://doi.org/10.18820/9781928480792

Set in Minion Pro 10,5/13

Cover design, typesetting and production by African Sun Media

SUN PReSS is an imprint of African Sun Media. Scholarly, professional and reference works are published under this imprint in print and electronic formats.

This publication can be ordered from:
orders@africansunmedia.co.za
Takealot: bit.ly/2monsfl
Google Books: bit.ly/2k1Uilm
africansunmedia.store.it.si *(e-books)*
Amazon Kindle: amzn.to/2ktL.pkL

Visit africansunmedia.co.za for more information.

CONTENTS

PREFACE

The contributions in this volume emanated from a joint conference and project by the faculties of law of the University of Johannesburg and the Nelson Mandela University. The range of subject matter addressed at the conference justified the publication of two separate volumes, one containing contributions in respect of maritime law and the law of the sea and the current one focusing on topics in public law featuring mostly governance and accountability issues in the seven chapters this volume comprises.

Chapter 1 is devoted to the explicit and implicit 'waymarks' provided by the constitution and considered to be essential for interpreting legislation as an integral part of a reading strategy for the courts to ensure that statutory interpretation is approached with the aim of finding a solution that will fall within constitutional bounds.

Chapter 2 proposes a hate-crime model for the South African context. This issue is the subject of a protracted legislative process whose finalisation is long overdue, given the frequency of this type of crime, the sporadic eruption of xenophobic violence and the harm caused to victims and their communities. The chapter covers issues such as hate crime as a conceptual problem, the different hate-crime models and the regulatory framework that is required in response.

Chapter 3 engages with accountability issues emanating from abuse of power by heads of state, a matter that is known for its fair share of controversy in South Africa and on the African continent. The chapter enlightens the different accountability types at the domestic, regional and international levels for holding heads of state accountable for transgressions of the law.

Chapter 4 deals with an equally problematic topic, namely presidential time limits in Africa and the political turmoil that emanates from their manipulation and abuse by incumbent presidents. The chapter uses Burundi as a case study and, in particular, the country's constitution of 2005 and its interpretation by the constitutional court of Burundi and the East African Court of Justice in the context of the 2015 presidential crisis and the violence that ensued from it.

Chapter 5 examines the options and obstacles in bringing perpetrators of gender-based violence in the context of the Syrian conflict to justice. The Syrian conflict is one of several current armed conflict situations where gross violations of human rights and international humanitarian law are committed with impunity, despite the existence of volumes of incriminating evidence made available by international organisations and other sources. These included the reports of the Independent

International Commission of Inquiry on Syria, which was established in 2011 by the UN Human Rights Council. On 7 July 2020, the Commission published its twentieth report.

Chapter 6 has, as subject matter, what is commonly known as the Life Esidimeni Tragedy which constitutes one of the most serious examples yet of government intransigence and failure to protect the vulnerable, in this instance mental health care users who were removed from existing facilities in a manner and under conditions that were grossly inhumane by all standards. The chapter applies Fineman's vulnerability theory and explores the need for a responsive state and the relevance of the constitution in considering appropriate remedies for the harm done.

Chapter 7 joins a well-known debate on the African continent, namely the role and future of the still to be established African Court of Justice and Human and People's Rights. This institution, which, once operational, will enjoy criminal jurisdiction over a controversially long list of offences by virtue of the Malabo Protocol, is seen by some commentators as a solution to the African Union's discontent with the International Criminal Court. In this chapter, the focus is on considerations of regionalism as an approach to international criminal justice.

The editors would like to express their gratitude for the assistance and advice provided by Mr Wikus van Zyl of African Sun Media in bringing this project to fruition.

PROF HENNIE STRYDOM
University of Johannesburg

PROF JOANNA BOTHA
Nelson Mandela University

THE THEORETICAL (AND CONSTITUTIONAL) UNDERPINNINGS OF STATUTORY INTERPRETATION*

Marius van Staden[**]

1.1 INTRODUCTION

The goal of statutory interpretation is central to the understanding of the theories and methods of statutory interpretation. There is, however, no consensus as to what this goal should be. Historically, the goals of statutory interpretation (and accordingly theories thereof) have been dependent on the views of the interpreter in relation to various factors. These will be the topic of consideration of this chapter. The judicial power of interpretation derives from the Constitution of the Republic of South Africa, 1996 (the Constitution), yet the Constitution does not prescribe a single accepted thesis of interpretation,[1] although it is trite that the South African judiciary has adopted an approach to the interpretation of statutes that seeks to animate and give life to the values and rights in the Constitution.[2]

Following the advent of constitutional democracy, "broad" purposive or teleological interpretation has been established as the dominant mode of statutory interpretation.[3]

---

1   Cross *Theory and Practice of Statutory Interpretation* (2009) 1.

2   See Botha *Waarde-aktiverende Grondwetuitleg: Vergestalting van die Materiële Regstaat* (1996 thesis UNISA).

3   Van Staden "The role of the judiciary in balancing flexibility and security" 2013 *De Jure* 470-476. Teleological interpretation is the primary interpretive method in the Federal Republic of Germany (see Möllers *Legal Methods* (2020)), France (see Vogenauer *Die Auslegung von Gesetzen in England und auf dem Kontinent* (2001) 286) and Spain (see a 3(1) of the Spanish Código Civil). Although there is some authority for teleological interpretation in the United States of America (see section 1-103 of the Uniform Commercial Code), conservative judges of the US Supreme Court have been reluctant to look beyond the text of a legislative provision (see Scalia "Textualism and the Constitution" in Miroff, Seidelman and Swanstrom (eds) *Debating Democracy: A Reader in American Politics* (2010) 288-294). The approach is also becoming more preeminent in England and Wales (see *Pepper (Inspector of Taxes) v Hart* [1992]

---

*   This chapter is an adapted version of a part of my doctoral thesis submitted at the University of Pretoria, titled *Identification of the employment relationship: An appraisal of the teleological interpretation of statutes*. I am indebted to my supervisors, Professors Stefan van Eck and Christo Botha, for their valuable comments and guidance in the preparation of the study.

** Lecturer in Public Law, University of Johannesburg.

However, as the Court in *Qozoleni v Minister of Law and Order*[4] pointed out, "it serves little purpose to characterise the proper approach to constitutional interpretation as liberal, generous, purposive or the like. These labels do not in themselves assist in the interpretation process and carry the danger of introducing concepts or notions associated with them which may not find expression in the Constitution itself."[5] As such, it is of paramount importance to investigate the theoretical (and constitutional) underpinnings that animate such an approach to the interpretation of statutes.

In South Africa, the views that underlie any given theory of statutory interpretation are dependent upon the Constitution. They are considerations of the relevance of the intention of the legislature, the nature and function of language, the role of the judiciary in the interpretation of statutes and the time frame within which statutes operate. An inquiry into questions of this nature must inevitably start with the Constitution.[6] A constitution cannot, however, comprehensively guide the balancing of these underlying notions as cases may test the boundaries between vagueness and precision in language, text and purpose or intent, the role of judges, time-bound or contemporary interpretation and these notions in themselves.[7]

This chapter explores the theoretical underpinnings of a constitutionally appropriate theory of statutory interpretation. It will consider the historic use of theories of statutory interpretation in South Africa. The theoretical underpinnings central to theories of interpretation will consequently be explored. as well as implicit and explicit constitutional waymarks that should inform our understanding of the teleological model of interpretation.

1.2   THEORIES OF STATUTORY INTERPRETATION

Eskridge and Frickey have warned readers not to expect that anybody's theory of statutory interpretation is an accurate statement of what courts actually do.[8] This is so as judges differ on the factors that underlie a theory of statutory interpretation, often blend approaches, may find that a given approach does not work in a given case, or join the opinions of others.[9] All theories have failings. Nevertheless, three theories of statutory interpretation have dominated statutory interpretation in jurisdictions that share the common-law tradition: literalism, intentionalism and purposivism.[10]

UKHL 3). Teleological interpretation also plays a leading role in the European Court of Justice (see Hager *Rechtsmethoden in Europe* (2009) 11).

4   1994 3 SA 625 (E).

5   633G.

6   *Holomisa v Argus Newspapers Ltd* 1996 6 BCLR 836 (W) 863.

7   Solan "Linguistic issues in statutory interpretation" in Tiersma and Solan (eds) *Language and the Law* (2012) 88-89.

8   Eskridge and Frickey "Introduction" in Hart and Sacks (eds) *The legal Process: Basic Problems in the Making and Application of Law* (1994) 1169.

9   Jellum "The theories of statutory construction and legislative process in American jurisprudence" in Araszkiewicz and Płeszka *Logic in the Theory and Practice of Lawmaking* (2015) 193.

10   Above 181-199.

Literalism (or textualism)[11] maintains that meaning must be deduced from the very words of the statute, to the exclusion of other interpretive criteria.[12] The theory is best described by its Afrikaans designation: *letterknegtigheid*, which translates as subservience to the letter. Intentionalism (or "actual specific intent")[13] maintains that meaning must be determined by ascertaining the real, subjective intention of the legislature.[14] Purposivism (or "hypothetical intent")[15] holds that meaning must be deduced through asking what the objective purpose of the law is.[16] It holds the view that the law is designed to solve specific societal problems.[17]

The key difference between purposivism and intentionalism is that, instead of asking what was actually intended, purposivism asks what a reasonable legislature would have reasonably wanted. Both theories reject the notion that meaning can be deduced solely from the words. Although both start with the statutory language, they do not stop there even if the text is clear. They examine other sources of meaning.[18] What they disagree about, however, is what sources may be used and what they seek by examining extra-textual sources of meaning. Intentionalist search for the actual intent of the legislature. Purposivists search for the hypothetical intent of a reasonable legislature, attempting to address a societal problem with a specific remedy. Literalists attack purposivists and intentionlists because, they aver, looking beyond the enacted text raises constitutional concerns associated with the separation of powers. Purposivists and intentionlists argue that literalists misunderstand the nature of language and are wrong to believe that language can constrain meaning.

The debate between advocates of these theories is central to the field of statutory interpretation. It is difficult to pin down what the debate is about, as various

---

11 "Literalism" and "textualism" are often used as synonyms. See Popkin *Statutes in Court: The History and Theory of Statutory Interpretation* (1999) 194. According to the author, the better approach is to refer to literalism as "'spurious' textualism" or "the practice of interpreting a text without adequate attention to the way authors write and audiences understand language". For purposes of this study no such distinction is made as it is incompatible with the South African common-law tradition and as such a distinction can be regarded as a mere semantic exercise or as a distinction without a difference. On this account literalism can be seen as an extreme form of textualism. As Jellum (n 9) 183-184 states, "[t]extualism comes in gradations". There are extreme, moderate and "soft plain meaning" theories of textualism, with various degrees of variance thereof. The use of two distinct binary terms to denote (only two) textualist positions is therefore counterproductive. Importantly, it should be noted that proponents of literalism in South Africa have also advocated different versions thereof and that not all have advocated extreme positions thereof. In this study the two terms are used interchangeably.

12 Du Plessis "Interpretation of the Bill of Rights" in Woolman, Roux and Bishop (eds) *Constitutional Law of South Africa* (2014) 32-29 and Popkin (n 11) 263.

13 Popkin (n 11) 185.

14 Du Plessis (n 12) 32-31.

15 Popkin (n 11) 185.

16 Du Plessis (n 12) 32-35.

17 Purposivism has traditionally been expressed as the so-called mischief rule. According to this rule, a court interpreting a statutory provision must ask four questions: "first, what the common law was before the enactment of the provision; second, what the mischief and defect were for which the common law did not provide; third, what remedy Parliament resolved and appointed 'to cure the disease of the common-wealth'; and, fourth, the true reason for the remedy." See Du Plessis (n 12) 32-31.

18 Jellum (n 9) 190-191.

difficulties must be confronted. The theories are broad churches and there is not necessarily a single position for each of these theories. The boundaries between the theoretical positions are not clear-cut as the advocates find common ground. The debate is often complicated by a reformulation or re-labelling of pre-existing theories of statutory interpretation. Additionally, *bona fide* attempts to acknowledge pragmatic aspects of language have spawned new theories of statutory interpretation, which are not necessarily different to existing theories. It is important to clarify these labels because contemporary debate is phrased in terms thereof.[19]

Du Plessis argues that the South African judiciary has utilised two further theories of statutory interpretation: contextualism and literalism-cum-intentionalism. Contextualism holds that the meaning of legislative provisions should be determined through a consideration of the background conditions and context of the law.[20] It is difficult to normatively justify contextualism as an independent theory. Contextualism does not necessarily challenge literalism.[21] Every action of communication contains different kinds of content. In addition to semantic content, "which is the type of content that is fully determined by the lexical meaning of the words used", there are other types of content that are context dependent. Assertive content "is the content that the speaker actually says or asserts by an occasion of speech in the context of the expression".[22] Assertive content is determined, *inter alia*, by "the semantic content of the sentence uttered, the communicative intentions of the speaker, the shared presuppositions of speaker-hearers, and obvious features of the context of utterances".[23] Implicated content is the content that a speaker is committed to even though they have not said it. There may also be presuppositions that are relied on by speakers and taken for granted in the context of a conversation.[24]

Recall that, in terms of the literalist position, meaning of a legislative provision must be deduced from the very words in which they are couched. Literalists do not only believe that words have semantic content, but also that they have assertive content, that is, context dependent. Context is important as it helps the listener figure out what the communicative intentions of the speaker are.[25] Literalists accept and adopt this view. Scalia has stated that "[i]n textual interpretation, context is everything".[26]

---

19   Jellum (n 9) 181-199.

20   Du Plessis (n 12) 32-35.

21   Jellum (n 9) 183-184.

22   Marmor "Introduction" in Marmor and Soames (eds) *Philosophical Foundations of Language and Law* (2013) 1 6.

23   Above 8.

24   Above 7.

25   Marmor "Textualism in context" 2012 *USC Law Legal Studies Paper No 12-13* 1 7.

26   Scalia "Common-law courts in a civil-law system: the role of United States federal courts in interpreting the constitution and laws" in Gutmann (ed) *A Matter of Interpretation* (1996) 37.

In *Chisom v Edwards*,[27] Scalia J, writing in dissent, stated that interpretation starts by finding the ordinary meaning of the language in its textual context.[28] The Supreme Court of Appeal[29] has approved a similar dictum by Sir Anthony Mason CJ:

> Problems of legal interpretation are not solved satisfactorily by ritual incantations which emphasise the clarity of meaning which words have when viewed in isolation, divorced from their context. The modern approach to interpretation insists that context be considered in the first instance, especially in the case of general words, and not merely at some later stage when ambiguity might be thought to arise.[30]

Contextualism also does not challenge purposivism or intentionalism. It is impossible to determine true or hypothetical intentions without having regard to the background provisions and the legislative history of the adoption of a legislative provision. If interpreters were only to have regard to the text to determine the intention of the legislature, the theory degenerates into literalism (or literalism-cum-intentionalism). In any event, literalists acknowledge that meaning is context-dependent. Similarly, purposivism without contextualism will be an empty theory as we determine purpose of the law from circumstances that brought about the legislation, the mischief it aimed to remedy and from assumptions about what a reasonable legislature would have wanted to achieve.[31] The Supreme Court of Canada in *R v Big M Drug Mart Ltd*[32] illustrated the importance of context to purposive theory:

> The meaning of a right or freedom guaranteed by the Charter was to be ascertained by an analysis of the purpose of such a guarantee; it was to be understood, in other words, in the light of the interests it was meant to protect. In my view this analysis is to be undertaken, and the purpose of the right or freedom in question is to be sought by reference to the character and larger objects of the Charter itself, to the language chosen to articulate the specific right or freedom, to the historical origins of the concepts enshrined, and where applicable, to the meaning and purpose of the other specific rights and freedoms with which it is associated within the text of the Charter. The interpretation should be ... a generous rather than legalistic one, aimed at fulfilling the purpose of the guarantee and securing for individuals the full benefit of the Charter's protection.[33]

---

27   111 S. Ct. 2354 (1991).

28   2369.

29   *Natal Joint Municipal Pension Fund v Endumeni Municipality* 2012 4 SA 593 (SCA) par 18.

30   *K & S Lake City Freighters Pty Ltd v Gordon & Gotch Ltd* 1985 157 CLR 309 315.

31   Marmor (n 25) 4.

32   (1985) 13 C.R.R. 64.

33   103. This passage was endorsed by the Constitutional Court in *Ferreira v Levin; Vryenhoek v Powell* 1996 1 SA 984 (CC) par 46 and 172.

In terms of literalism-cum-intentionalism, the purpose of statutory interpretation is to determine the intention of the legislature. It was, however, presumed that the legislature "encoded" or "couched" its intention within the words of the legislation. But as Du Plessis points out, this was essentially a literalist position as

> it is assumed that there is a grammatical structure that allows for a fixed, 'ordinary effect' of the language" and "that the (most) correct use of the language, in conformity with its grammatical structure and rules, will make for an objective perspicuity in the advantages of which all (reasonable?) users of the language can share.[34]

Du Plessis dismisses the idea that language can have such a fixed effect that the intention of a speaker can be conveyed to the listener. Notions of intention in the literal interpretation of law cannot be underestimated. Legislation is a speech act: "A hearer who wants to grasp what the speaker says aims to grasp what the speaker intended to communicate, legal speech cannot be a kind of striking exception."[35] This position is not contrary to the literalist position. Literalists do not view language as consisting merely of semantic content. The intention of the speaker is important to determine the assertive content of the speech act. Teleological interpretation is a relative of purposivism that can also be labelled as "broad" purposivism.[36]

1.3   THEORETICAL UNDERPINNINGS

1.3.1 The relevance of the intention of the legislature

Legislative intent is of fundamental importance to the interpretation of statutes. Legislation is a speech act that is communicated intentionally.[37] Texts without authors and intended meanings are not texts and texts are only texts in regard to their intended meanings.[38] As Rosen shows, legislators may have various different kinds of intentions.[39] They have lexical intentions ("the intention to use a certain word or construction"),[40] semantic intentions ("the intention to mean this or that by their words"), communicative intentions ("the intention to cause certain beliefs or expectations in their audience in a characteristic way"), and practical intentions ("the intention to cause downstream non-legal effects, e.g., to promote economic

---

34   Du Plessis (n 12) 2C-55.

35   Marmor (n 25) 9.

36   See Le Roux "Directory provisions, section 39(2) of the Constitution and the ontology of statutory law *African Christian Democratic Party v Electoral Commission*" 2006 *SAPR/PL* 382.

37   Marmor (n 25) 3.

38   Alexander and Prakash "'Is that English you're speaking?' some arguments for the primacy of intent in interpretation" 2003 *Public Law and Legal Theory Research Paper Series* 1 13.

39   Rosen "Textualism, intentionalism and the law of contract" in Marmor and Soames (eds) *Philosophical Foundations of Language and Law* (2013) 130 132-133.

40   Above 132.

growth"). Importantly, they have legal intentions ("the intention to bring about certain changes in the law by means of their pronouncements").[41]

There are three distinct conceptions of the relevance of legislative intent.[42] The first, what Popkin labels "actual specific intent", requires that judges ask if the legislature had any specific intent about the facts of the case.[43] "Instead of averring that a provision 'means X or Y', a court will typically assert that 'the legislature intended X or Y'."[44] To find specific intent, intentionalists will start with the text, but they will not stop there.[45] They reject ordinary meaning for a meaning that furthers specific legislative intent. As Popkin states, intentionalism conceived in this way is not workable as "legislatures probably did not think of the issue; legislatures might want to avoid a decision and pass the buck to the court; and change prevents legislatures who adopted the law from appreciating the actual impact of a statute on future events".[46] It has been questioned how a legislature (composed of a body of persons) can have a specific intent. It has also been argued that

> the tools available for courts trying to figure out legislative intent are such that the courts are bound to yield skewed and biased results, mostly favoring the vocal supporters of a law who use strategic manoeuvres to overemphasize their legislative agenda over of the views of the median legislators who formed the majority.[47]

There are constitutional reasons to reject intentionalism. In *Matiso v The Commanding Officer, Port Elizabeth Prison*,[48] it was stated that the intention of the legislature does not apply in a system based on the supremacy of the Constitution, as the Constitution is sovereign and not Parliament.[49] Interpreters who searched for the actual intent of legislatures did so because of the supremacy of Parliament. In a constitutional democracy, the Constitution is binding on all branches of the state and has priority over any rules made by the legislature.[50] Meaning must be determined not with reference to the intent of any legislature but with reference to a supreme constitution. Scalia has said that it is incompatible with democratic government to have meaning determined by the intention of the legislature.[51]

---

41   Above 133.

42   Popkin (n 11) 185.

43   Above.

44   Du Plessis (n 12) 31-32.

45   Jellum (n 9) 190. Such as statements made during he legislative process, early draft versions of the bill and policy documents.

46   Popkin (n 11) 187. See also Marmor "On some pragmatic aspects of strategic speech" in Marmor and Soames (eds) *Philosophical Foundations of Language and Law* (2013) 83 97.

47   Marmor (n 25) 2-3.

48   1994 3 SA 592 (SE).

49   597B-597H.

50   Currie and De Waal *The Bill of Rights Handbook* (2013) 9. See also ss 2 and 8 of the Constitution.

51   Scalia (n 26) 16.

The chief response has been the objectification of legislative intent.[52] The literalist response, what Du Plessis terms "literalism-cum-intentionalism",[53] gives rise to the second conception of the relevance of legislative intent.[54] In England, Lord Diplock has held that "the role of the judiciary is confined to ascertaining from the words that Parliament has approved as expressing its intention what that intention was, and to giving effect to it".[55] In the same case, Lord Scarman held that "[i]f Parliament says one thing but means another, it is not … for the courts to correct it … . We are to be governed not by Parliament's intentions but by Parliament's enactments."[56] Lord Reid has explained that "[w]e are seeking not what Parliament meant but the true meaning of what they said".[57] Scalia has stated that it is the law that governs and not the intention of the legislature.[58] Prior to the advent of constitutional democracy, the dominant theory of statutory interpretation assumed that

> [t]he legislature couches or encodes its intention in the language of the statutory provision to be construed. When the words used for this purpose are clear and unambiguous, their literal, grammatical meaning must prevail and they must be given their ordinary effect. This, it is believed, will disclose and convey, without further ado, the true intention of the legislature and thereby the 'correct' meaning of the provision construed.[59]

The purposivist response ("hypothetical intent") gives rise to the third conception of the relevance of legislative intent.[60] It requires the interpreter to enquire into the objects, purposes or intentions of a hypothetical, reasonable legislature. This response has also been the objectification of legislative intent, but it also rejects the idea that the intention of the legislature can be couched within the words used by the legislature. Purposivism has an advantage over intentionalsm as purposivists can interpret statutes in situations that the legislature did not contemplate. Purposivism allows laws to change with technological, social, legal, and other circumstances.[61] By contrast, intentionalism is unhelpful when a statute is applied to a new circumstance not foreseen by the legislature. Again, the use of hypothetical intent has also been subject to criticism. Although purposivists rely on factors such as text, history,

---

52   Above 17.

53   Du Plessis (n 12) 32-32.

54   Popkin (n 11) 185. It should however be noted that there are literalist positions that reject the relevance of the intention of the legislature outright.

55   *Duport Steels Ltd v SIRS* 1980 1 All ER 529 (HL) 541.

56   Above.

57   *Black-Clawson International Ltd v Papierwerke Waldhof-Aschaffenberg AG* 1975 1 All ER 810 (HL) 814. Refer also to the *Sussex Peerage Case* 1844 8 ER 1034 where Tindal CJ held that "[t]he words themselves alone do, in such case, best declare the intention of the lawgiver".

58   Scalia (n 26) 17.

59   Du Plessis (n 12) 32-32.

60   Popkin (n 11) 185.

61   Jellum (n 9) 194-195.

context, values and legal comparisons to discover purpose,[62] these sources may be inconclusive. The proposed answer is for courts to "presume that legislatures are 'made of reasonable persons pursuing reasonable purposes, reasonably'". Literalists criticise the subjectivity of this approach and point to the fact that there may be competing ideas of how to further the purpose and that statutes often have many (sometimes competing) purposes.[63]

1.3.2 The nature and function of language

If it seems that a provision doesn't have to be interpreted, that is because you have interpreted it already. Interpretive principles are always at work.[64] This is so because a statute is a legal instrument and a legal instrument is, according Endicott, "a normative text with a technical effect" in that "the law itself has techniques for determining the effect of the normative text".[65] This is not to say that legislative provisions may not be more precise than others (or perhaps more vague than others). According to the author, "[a] legal instrument is vague if its language is imprecise, so that there are cases in which its application is unclear".[66]

The central point is that "there is no straightforward, general relation between the language used in a legal instrument to make law, and the law that is made".[67] A paradoxical question that has often been posed is how legislation can be certain while still achieving flexibility. Legal certainty is required by the rule of law, which, in turn, requires predictability of outcome.[68] The Constitutional Court has held that laws must be written in a clear and accessible manner and that impermissibly vague provisions violate the rule of law, a founding value of our Constitution.[69] On the other hand, no two sets of facts are ever exactly the same, requiring that legislation should be sufficiently flexible to cover a multitude of situations.

---

62   Du Plessis (n 12) 32-159.

63   Jellum (n 9) 195.

64   Sunstein *The Partial Constitution* (1993) 104. This presupposition stands in stark contrast to the maxim *clara non sunt interpretanda* (transparent text requires no interpretation).

65   Endicott "The value of vagueness" in Marmor and Soames (eds) *Philosophical Foundations of Language and Law* (2013) 14 15.

66   Above 16.

67   Above 16. In *Combined Developers v Arun Holdings* 2015 3 SA 215 (WCC) it was held that "the nature of language does not always admit to one a clear answer". In *Venter v R* 1907 TS 910 913 it was stated that there is "a difficulty inherent in the nature of language – that no matter how carefully words are chosen, there is a difficulty in selecting language which, while on the face of it expressing generally the idea of the framer of the measure, will not, when applied under certain circumstances, go beyond it, and, when applied under other circumstances, fall short of it".

68   Maley "The language of the law" in Gobbons (ed) *Language and the Law* (1994) 17.

69   *National Credit Regulator v Opperman* 2013 2 SA 1 (CC) par 49. S 1(c) of the Constitution states that the Republic is founded upon the values of "supremacy of the constitution and the rule of law". See also *President of the Republic of South Africa v Hugo* 1997 4 SA 1 (CC) par 102 where the Constitutional Court stated that "[t]he need for accessibility, precision and general application flow from the concept of the rule of law. A person should be able to know of the law, and be able to conform his or her conduct to the law".

Vague language is viewed as "bad", and precise language as "good". Precise legal standards are not necessarily better than vague ones.[70] Rules of interpretation may give a vague effect to a precise term.[71] Similarly, rules of interpretation may give a precise effect to a precise term. Meaning can only be determined through the processes of interpretation. This is contrary to the literalist position, which assumes that there is a fixed and stable ordinary effect of language.[72] Some have described a linguistic turn in legal interpretation where meaning is not discovered from a construable text, but made in dealing with it.[73]

Values are expressed in vague language. This is the concern of those who express a preference for "black letter law".[74] The concern is understandable. The purpose of any provision is to create a norm to which citizens may conform their conduct. When a norm is vague, it is incapable of guiding conduct (nor does it control the conduct of the officers or public officials responsible for applying the norm or resolving a dispute). How then is it possible for individuals to conform their conduct to the norm? Concerns related to the separation of powers are also raised. The task of giving content to a vague norm is transferred first to an applying official but ultimately to the courts. In effect, vague norms open the doors for judicial law making. Even the most adamant defenders of positivism concede this point.[75]

Our legal system consists of vague and precise norms and, it will be argued, that vague norms are not always "bad", but sometimes politically desirable. Legislatures may choose to frame legislative provisions in a vague manner. The effect would be to create a vague norm so that its application is unclear.[76] The judiciary is given discretion to decide for itself what the norm means. Additionally, there may be instances where, although the text of a legislative provision is seemingly precise the technical effect of legal language means that rules of interpretation may give a vague effect to a precise term. This is so because there is no general relation between the language of a provision and the law that is made.

To understand why vagueness can be valuable, the starting point must inevitably be to ask why precision is valuable. Precision has guidance value because a precise standard makes it clear what people's rights and obligations are. Precision has process

---

70   Endicott (n 65) 19.

71   Above 16.

72   Du Plessis (n 12) 32-159.

73   Above 32-44 and Boshoff *Die Interpretasie van Fundamentele Aansprake in 'n Heterogene Samelewing* (2000 thesis Rand Afrikaans University) 157-162.

74   Woolman "True in theory, true in practice: why direct application still matters" in Woolman and Bishop (eds) *Constitutional Conversations* (2008) 135.

75   Raz *Ethics in the Public Domain: Essays in the Morality of Law and Politics* (1994) 332 and Waluchow *Inclusive legal Positivism* (1994) 157. According to Waluchow this is so as the statute in such cases obliges judges to seek guidance from non-legal sources.

76   Endicott (n 65) 16.

value because it directs officials in a legal system.[77] From here, it is easy to formulate the chief points of criticism against the judiciary's reliance on values: the vagueness of values does not make it clear what the obligation of affected parties are. But when a legislature decides to draft a norm vaguely that does not mean to say that this is always a result of poor legislative drafting. It might be useful for the legislature to leave it to the judiciary to give content to a legislative norm. According to Endicott this choice has power allocation value and private ordering value.[78]

Substantively, the effect of vague terms is to delegate to courts the power to determine the content thereof. This is justifiable because judges possess specialised expertise to develop norms and, because the doctrine of precedent will allow them to develop the norm incrementally, to revise general principles through the processes of appeal. The processes of the courts mean that general rules would develop after taking cognisance of parties to a dispute in which the value is deployed. It may be valuable to leave persons affected by a rule uncertain as to its application as parties will have an incentive to come up with creative ways to avoid accountability, which might not have occurred to the legislature. The uncertainty created incentivises parties to avoid the risk of being found to have contravened the value.[79]

It is important to note that what is vague or precise is a contextual matter,[80] and that it would be wrong to describe values as either totally vague or precise. Every communication act contains different kinds of content. In addition to semantic content, communication acts contain assertive content, implicated content. There may be presuppositions that are relied on by speakers and taken for granted in the context of a conversation.[81] It is indisputable that values are vague terms but this does not mean that these terms do not contain at least assertive content. It also does not mean that the interpretive choice of the presiding officer will be as arbitrary as flipping a coin. The judiciary will not have an unfettered discretion. Not any decision will do. The task of the interpreter will be to figure out what the (reasonable) drafter of the Constitution intended to convey through its choice of words and to this end the assertive content, which is context dependent, must be taken into account.

Following from the above, it would be logical to ask how we could determine what the assertive content of a value is. The starting-off point should be to acknowledge that actors in the legal profession constantly partake in this exercise. A decision about the appropriate interpretation of a legislative provision can only be said to be "good" if it is principled (and not arbitrary). The principles on which these cases are determined are not only contained in the legislative provision itself but also in other

---

77   Endicott (n 65) 19.

78   Above 26-28.

79   Above.

80   Saomes "What vagueness and inconsistency tell us about interpretation" in Marmor and Soames (eds) *Philosophical Foundations of Language and Law* (2013) 31 32.

81   Marmor (n 25) 6 and Marmor (n 22) 8.

sources of our legal system. When terms are employed that may be said to be vague, it merely means that the principles outside of the legislative provision are perhaps more important than the provision itself.

The shift in the interpretive approach endorsed by the Constitutional Court (from "the strict legalistic to the substantive")[82] can be illustrated with reference to the way the Court has sought to determine if a statutory provision in peremptory (when statutes require exact compliance and when failure to comply will leave the ensuing act null and void) or directory (when a statute requires substantial compliance only and when non-compliance thereof will not result in ensuing acts being null and void).[83] There were cases in which our courts, even before the advent of constitutionalism, "insisted that the distinction between directory and peremptory provisions does not rest on semantic or textual considerations (alone), but requires reference to extra-textual (or contextual) factors".[84]

Nevertheless in the great bulk of pre-constitutional cases matters of compliance were decided on rules such as the following: a word or words with an imperative or affirmative character indicate a peremptory provision (e.g., "shall" or "must"),[85] permissive words indicate a discretion and are directory (e.g., "may" or "can"),[86] words in negative form are peremptory,[87] positive language is directory,[88] flexible or vague terms are directory,[89] and so on.[90] Due to the shift in interpretive approach by the judiciary, which favours extra-textual factors over textual elements, Du Plessis has questioned the relevance of this distinction:

> It may be that the majority judgment of the Constitutional Court in *African Christian Democratic Party* has dealt the distinction between peremptory and directory provisions a blow, since the court raised the question whether a provision can be ever so peremptory that *eo nomine* compliance with it has to be preferred to realising its purpose, and the court itself, in point of fact, answered this question in the negative. The Supreme Court of Appeal previously also voiced rejection of a categorical distinction between peremptory and directory provisions ... and the ACDP case thus actually confirmed an already existing move away from such a distinction.[91]

In *Steenkamp v Edcon Ltd*, the Constitutional Court had to determine what the consequences of non-compliance with section 189A(2)(*a*) of the LRA is ("an

82   *African Christian Democratic Party v Electoral Commission* 2006 3 SA 305 (CC) par 25.
83   Botha *Statutory Interpretation: An Introduction for Students* (2005) 109.
84   Le Roux (n 36) 389.
85   *Messenger of the Magistrate's Court, Durban v Pillay* 1952 3 SA 678 (A).
86   *Amalgamated Packaging Industries v Hutt* 1975 4 SA 943 (A).
87   *Samuel Thomas Myers v Pretorius* 1944 OPD 144.
88   *R v Sopete* 1950 3 SA 769 (EC).
89   *Leibrandt v SA Railways* 1941 AD 9.
90   Botha (n 83) 111.
91   Du Plessis (n 12) 2C-131.

employer *must* give notice of termination of employment in accordance with the provisions of this section").[92] The employer retrenched over 3,000 employees and gave the employees notices of termination of their contracts of employment. These notices were given prior to the expiry of the periods prescribed by section 189A(8) of the LRA and therefore were in breach of the Act.[93] The Act allows aggrieved parties to strike in the event of non-compliance with the section[94] or to approach the Labour Court for an appropriate order.[95] The Act does not explicitly provide that any dismissal in contravention of the Act would be invalid. The applicants however argued that the 30- to 60-day period allowed under the Act suspends the employer's power to dismiss and relegate the relief available under section 189A(7).[96]

The applicant's arguments were based on the literalistic archetype that the Act used the word "must" and therefore that the employer was obliged to comply with the prescribed procedures before dismissing the employees. Failure to do so, they argued, resulted in an invalid dismissal.[97] Tellingly, the majority of the Court did not utilise the distinction between peremptory and directory provisions to resolve the question as to what the consequences of non-compliance with section 189A(2)(*a*) of the Act was. Rather, it may be argued that the distinction was merely used as a semantic device to frame the distinction after the fact. Instead both the majority[98] and the minority[99] asked what the purpose of the statutory provision was to determine its consequence (although it may be argued that the minority used purpose to determine if the provision was peremptory or directory).

The majority and the minority however disagreed as to what the purpose of the provision is. The minority argued that the purpose of the provision was to "create a dismissal-free zone during which consensus may be sought and alternatives may be explored"[100] and that the purpose of the act would be contravened if this "dismissal-

---

92   2016 37 ILJ 564 (CC) par 6.

93   s 189A(8) reads: "If a facilitator is not appointed (a) a party may not refer a dispute to a council or the Commission unless a period of 30 days has lapsed from the date on which notice was given in terms of section 189(3); and (b) once the periods mentioned in section 64(1)(a) have elapsed (i) the employer may give notice to terminate the contracts of employment in accordance with section 37(1) of the Basic Conditions of Employment Act; and (ii) a registered trade union or the employees who have received notice of termination may (aa) give notice of a strike in terms of section 64(1)(b) or (d); or (bb) refer a dispute concerning whether there is a fair reason for the dismissal to the Labour Court in terms of section 191(11)."

94   s 189A(8) and (9).

95   These orders may include: 189A(13) "an order (a) compelling the employer to comply with a fair procedure; (b) interdicting or restraining the employer from dismissing an employee prior to complying with a fair procedure; (c) directing the employer to reinstate an employee until it has complied with a fair procedure; (d) make an award of compensation, if an order in terms of paragraphs (a) to (c) is not appropriate."

96   par 30.

97   par 43.

98   par 99, 101, 147, 182, 183, 184, 185 and 186.

99   par 20, 23, 26, 33, 36, 46, 60 and 74.

100 par 45.

free zone" was disregarded. As such, the minority found the dismissal to be null and void.[101] The majority disagreed. Instead the majority found that the concept "invalid dismissal" was not part of the Act and that it was therefore inappropriate to import a remedy designed for "unfair dismissals" (reinstatement) for invalid dismissals.[102] The Court found that the dismissal of the employees could have been unfair, but that they had not claimed this. In any event, the Court found that the remedies provided in the section were "adequate" and, as such that "there seems to be no justification for the conclusion that the purpose of the legislation is to visit an act committed in breach of the provision with nullity".[103]

1.3.3 The role of the judiciary in the interpretation of statutes

Considerations of separation of powers, democracy, rule of law, and the role of a judge in a democracy have important consequences for the way that statutes are interpreted.[104] "The theory of statutory interpretation a judge adopts is based, in large part, on that judge's view of the proper power distribution of the judiciary and the legislature – in other words, on that judge's view of separation of powers."[105] One conception of separation of powers is that the principle means that specific functions, duties and responsibilities are allocated to distinctive institutions with defined areas of competence.[106] On this view, which is described as the "airtight compartment approach", judges interpret law, Parliament makes the law and the executive implements it. There should be no overlap.[107] The courts, as Montesquieu stated, are a "mouth that pronounces the words of the law".[108] This approach is invoked as an objection to judges having (too much) discretion in their interpretive tasks, and the approach only allows judges to create law when a statute is vague. The Constitutional Court has rejected a strict separation between the three branches of government.[109] The rejection of such a separation has, however, not prevented the Constitutional Court from acknowledging that each branch has a specific mandate.

---

101 par 60 and 86.

102 par 180 and 188.

103 par 183.

104 Barak *Purposive Interpretation in Law* (2005) 88.

105 Jellum (n 9) 177.

106 Seedorf and Sibanda "Separation of powers" in Woolman, Roux and Bishop (eds) *Constitutional Law of South Africa* (2014) 12.1. In *South African Association of Personal Injury Lawyers v Heath* 2001 1 SA 883 (CC) par 25 it was held that "[t]he separation of the judiciary from the other branches of government is an important aspect of the separation of powers required by the Constitution, and is essential to the role of the courts under the Constitution. Parliament and the provincial legislatures make the laws but do not implement them. The national and provincial executives prepare and initiate laws to be placed before the legislatures, implement the laws thus made, but have no law-making power other than that vested in them by the legislatures.... Under our Constitution it is the duty of the courts to ensure that the limits to the exercise of public power are not transgressed. Crucial to the discharge of this duty is that the courts be and be seen to be independent."

107 Popkin (n 11) 241.

108 Montesquieu *The Spirit of the Laws* (translated by Nugent) (1748) 191.

109 *Ex Parte Chairperson of the Constitutional Assembly: In Re Certification of the Constitution of the Republic of South Africa, 1996* 1996 4 SA 744 (CC) par 112.

In *Minister of Health v Treatment Action Campaign (2)*,[110] the Court clearly made this point when it stated that "although there are no bright lines that separate the roles of the legislature, the executive and the courts from one another, there are certain matters that are pre-eminently within the domain of one or other of the arms of government and not the others. All arms of government should be sensitive to and respect this separation".[111] In *Doctors for Life International v Speaker of the National Assembly*,[112] the Constitutional Court warned that "[c]ourts must be conscious of the vital limits on judicial authority and the Constitution's design to leave certain matters to other branches of government. They too must observe the constitutional limits of their authority. This means that the judiciary should not interfere in the processes of other branches of government unless to do so is mandated by the Constitution."[113]

The Court stressed that separation of powers concerns, although important, "cannot be used to avoid the obligations of a court to prevent the violation of the Constitution".[114] It can be said that the Constitutional Court has instead adopted the conception of separation of powers, referred to as the "checks and balances" approach, that judges do some legislating such as in the case of the judicial review of legislation and invoking the golden rule of statutory interpretation to prevent unjust law.[115] These approaches are rooted in literal modes of statutory interpretation.[116] These modes of interpretation are often defended by separation of powers arguments by literalists or formalists. On their view, judges "create law" when they look beyond the text of the statutory provision and rely on features such as "purpose", "values" or "principles" which they deem to lie outside of the law.

They defend the use of literalist modes of interpretation on four grounds. First, they argued that, should we allow judges to disregard the literal meaning, it is difficult to explain why law is authoritative for judges. The more scope we give judges, the more we permit them to treat legal rules not as "proper" rules but merely as "guides".[117] Second, it is averred that disregarding the literal meaning represents a threat to the rule of law because citizens will be uncertain how the rules will be applied before a

---

110 2002 5 SA 721 (CC).

111 par 199.

112 2006 6 SA 416 (CC).

113 par 37.

114 par 200.

115 Popkin (n 11) 241.

116 Some formalists, such as Schauer "Formalism" 1988 *Yale LR* 509 521 even rejected the idea that judges could reject unjust or absurd interpretations. In South Africa, adherence to the so-called golden rule of statutory interpretation meant that the grammatical and ordinary sense of the words may be modified, so as to avoid the absurdity and inconsistency. As such South African literalism, even at its zenith, was not as formalistic. Nevertheless, meaning was still primarily to be discerned from the very words a provision was couched in.

117 Meyerson *Jurisprudence* (2011) 145.

court has had the opportunity to interpret them.[118] Third, it is argued that judges may make mistakes when trying to do justice based on the teleological approach and therefore subvert Parliament's legislative programs.[119] Fourth, it is reasoned that judges are not accountable to an electorate. They claim that notions of intention or purpose are disguises for judicial law making.[120]

Such formalism, that only text is relevant to interpretation, places the role of the legislature above that of the judiciary,[121] and is rooted in a particular view of the nature of the law.[122] Some positivists, for example, argue that the law consists only of "pedigreed sources" and that courts cannot rely on consideration outside the text.[123] Ethical or democratic positivists put more faith in the legislature than the judiciary and believe that legislatures should assume full responsibility for the making of moral or policy choices.[124] Although ethical positivists believe that it may by possible that there are moral criteria for the validity of law, that moral criteria in law is not morally desirable and that the application thereof should be avoided where possible.[125] On this view, legislation should be drafted in precise and unambiguous language so that judges do not need to rely on moral or political considerations.[126] They believe that judges are under an obligation to apply clear legal rules.[127]

---

118 Above 146. According to Eskridge "Dynamic statutory interpretation" 1987 *University of Pennsylvania Law Review* 1479 1483 "the traditional understanding of the 'rule of law' requires that statutes enacted by the majoritarian legislature be given effect, and that citizens have reasonable notice of the legal rules that govern their behavior."

119 Above 147.

120 Above 147. Scalia (n 26) 17-18 has argued that, "under the guise or even the self-delusion of pursuing unexpressed legislative intents, common-law judges will in fact pursue their own objectives and desires, extending their lawmaking proclivities from the common law to the statutory field".

121 Jellum (n 9) 178.

122 Meyerson (n 117) 147. According to Barak (n 104) 54 there exists an interrelationship between jurisprudential theories and interpretative theories. According to the author "legal philosophy expresses its distinctiveness 'practically' through its treatment of interpretation".

123 An Austinian approach to the interpretation of statutes, for example, would require that only "positive laws" or "laws strictly so called" should be taken into consideration when interpreting a statutory provision. As such only the legislative text, as a sanction-backed command handed down by a sovereign, can be taken into consideration. Matters of 'positive morality' would be deemed irrelevant to the interpretive task. Austin's Command Theory as an aggregate of nothing but rules also does not take societal values and principles or standards such as equity, good faith and reasonableness into account. See Austin "Extract from *The Province of Jurisprudence Determined*" in Freeman (ed) *Lloyd's Introduction to Jurisprudence* (2008). Similarly, Raz *The Authority of Law: Essays on Law and Morality* (1975) 39-40 and 47-48 argued that law necessarily only consists of source-based or pedigreed standards, and that moral value can never be criteria for legal validity. See also Raz "Authority, law and morality" 1985 *The Monist* 295 316. For Raz law is an exercise in authority and "nothing can possibly count as an exercise of authority if its net effect is to leave [a person] in the position of having to figure out the issue for himself". See Waldron "Vagueness and the guidance of action" in Marmor and Soames (eds) *Philosophical Foundations of Language and Law* (2013) 58 68.

124 Above 102-103. See also Campbell *The Legal Theory of Ethical Positivism* (1996) 3; Waldron "Normative and ethical positivism" in Coleman (ed) *Hart's Postscript: Essays on the Postscript to the Concept of Law* (2001) 421 and Dyzenhaus "The genealogy of legal positivism" 2004 *Oxford Journal of Legal Studies* 39 62.

125 Meyerson (n 117) 102.

126 Campbell (n 124) 64.

127 Meyerson (n 117) 103.

The other side of the spectrum, that considerations outside of the law such as purpose and values are more important than the legislative text, places the role of the judiciary above that of the legislature. On this view,

> every statutory interpretation case requires a judge to make a policy choice by adopting one statutory meaning and thereby rejecting at least one other meaning. Further, this choice will affect future cases because of *stare decisis* – the concept that similar cases should be decided similarly. Thus, judges do not simply interpret law; judges act in concert with the legislature to develop law; while legislatures make law, judges inevitably assist them in the process.[128]

Such a view may be justified on several perspectives of the nature of law. Realists argue that legal doctrine is indeterminate and that legal doctrine could be used to support contradictory outcomes.[129] They claim that non-legal factors are more important than legal factors in adjudicating cases.[130] Such a view would have the consequence of untethering interpretation as a field of study as it would mean that judges do not decide cases on legal grounds. Such an approach would lead to unpredictability of the law. It also leaves citizens with no way to determine what conduct is expected of them. In hard cases, Hart argues that courts do go beyond their traditional function of merely interpreting the rules of law and that they "perform a rule producing function":[131]

> In all fields of experience, not only that of rules, there is a limit, inherent in the nature of language, to the guidance which general language can provide. There will be plain cases constantly recurring in similar contexts to which general expressions were clearly applicable ... but there will also be cases where it is not clear whether they apply or not.[132]

---

128 Jellum (n 9) 178.

129 Meyerson (n 117) 190.

130 Meyerson (above) 191. See Holmes *The Common Law* (1923) 1. Similarly, in the postmodernist movement it was argued that it is impossible to achieve finality in interpretation because meaning is endlessly deferred and incapable of being fully determined. See Derrida *Positions* (1981) 41. The author argued that it is only possible to create the illusion of stable meaning through binary options. The Critical Legal Studies movement took the attack further. They claimed that "the law is so full of contradictory values and so obviously the outcome of political conflict that judges can never make fully coherent sense out of it". See Howarth "Making sense out of nonsense" in Gross and Harrison *Jurisprudence: Cambridge Essays* (1992) 30.

131 Hart *The Concept of Law* (1961) 135. Barak "The role of a supreme court in a democracy" 2002 *Hastings Law Journal* 1205 1205-1206, in endorsing this view of law has said that "there are hard cases. In such cases, the law is uncertain. There is more than one meaning to be given to the legal text. There is more than one solution to the legal problem. In such cases, law declaration also involves law creation. Prior to the judicial determination, the law (the constitution, the statute, the common law) spoke-even after all rules of interpretation were used-with a number of voices. After the judicial determination the law speaks with a single voice. The law was changed. A new meaning was created. The creation of a new norm – to be binding on all courts by the rule of precedent – is the main function of the supreme court in a democracy. Such creation involves discretion. The judge of a supreme court is not a mirror, passively reflecting the image of the law. He is an artist, creating the picture with his or her own hands. He is 'legislating' – engaging in 'judicial legislation'."

132 Hart (above) 123.

In hard cases, judges have an unapologetic creative function; they act as political decision makers. The source of this legislative power is "not a reflection of judicial imperialism" but rather "an indication of the uncertainty inherent in the law itself".[133] In these cases, judges rely on their sense of what is best.[134] In easy cases, Hart believes that judges should not stray from the rule as stated, even if they believe that the result is undesirable. Most cases will fall within the core of determinate meaning.[135]

Hart does not believe it to be entirely the function of language whether or not a case falls within the core of easy cases or the penumbra of hard cases. A case can fall within the core because the purpose of the rule is clear.[136] Hart did not consider purposive interpretation of a rule to be a threat to the separation between law and morality because rules may also have an evil (or immoral) purpose.[137] A case can conceivably fall within the core of easy cases because its language is entirely certain.

According to Kelsen, every act of law applying would be regarded as an act of law creating: "The function of laying down the law is a properly constitutive one, it is a making of law in the real sense of the word. ... The judicial decision is itself an individual legal norm."[138] When a norm is applied to a new set of facts, any decision would "add something" that might be significant for future cases. New norms would enter our legal system through the doctrine of precedent.[139]

There are those who deny that judges exercise discretion when they look beyond the text.[140] According to Dworkin, the law comprises rules and principles. Whereas rules either apply or do not apply, principles can be relevant to a given case without being decisive.[141] Principles will always carry some weight but not conclusive weight, and judges will have to decide how much weight a principle will carry (taking into consideration other competing principles) when applied to the circumstances of a given case.[142] This distinction is central to Dworkin's thesis that the law is always determinate, and he avers that although rules cannot always provide clear answers, principles can always supply answers. Judges can therefore go beyond established and explicit rules and still come to a decision according to the law. Judges do not create law when they rely on principles to interpret rules, as these rules are present in the law. In any event, judges are constrained by the fact that a satisfactory interpretation must fit the pre-interpretive legal materials and make the law the best (read "most

---

133 Barak (n 104) 1206.

134 Hart (n 131) 275.

135 Above 123 and 150.

136 Hart *Esays in Jurisprudence and Philosophy* (1983) 106.

137 Hart "Positivism and the Separation of Law and Morals" 1958 *Harvard Law Review* 593.

138 Kelsen "Extract from *The Pure Theory of Law*" in Freeman *Lloyd's Introduction to Jurisprudence* (2008) 331.

139 Patterson "Hans Kelsen and his *Pure Theory of Law*" 1952 *California Law Review* 5 9.

140 Dworkin *Taking Rights Seriously* (1977) concedes that judges will have discretion in the weak sense of the word because principles "cannot be applied mathematically but demand the use of judgment".

141 Above 23.

142 Above 22-28.

morally valuable") it can be.[143] Accordingly, determining what the law *should* be based on the criteria of "fit" and "value" is equal to determining what the law is.[144]

There are also separation of power arguments which, although focusing on the role of the courts, argue that when judges look beyond text, that this allows the courts to legislate without completing the required processes for enactment of legislation.[145] It is argued that it is only the text, and not any general or specific intent, which is adopted through constitutionally appropriate procedures by the legislature.[146] The text is often a compromise between political factions.[147] As such, the text (in being such a compromise) may possibly be narrower or more restrictive than the primary objectives of any real or hypothetical legislature.[148]

1.3.4 The time frame within which statutes operate

Scalia and Garner uses the following example to support their argument that words must be given the meaning they had when the text was adopted:

> Queen Ann is said (probably apocryphally) to have commented about Sir Christopher Wren's architecture at St. Paul's Cathedral that it was 'awful, artificial, and amusing' – by which she meant that it was awe-inspiring, highly artistic, and thought-provoking. All three words have since undergone what linguistics call *pejoration*: Their meanings have degenerated so that they now bear mostly negative connotations. It would be quite wrong for someone to ascribe to Queen Ann's 18th-century words their 21st-century meanings. To do so would be to misunderstand – or misrepresent – her meaning entirely.[149]

Historically, common-law jurisdictions have adopted similar rules.[150] The South African judiciary has also adopted such an approach, in that legislative provisions must be understood in accordance with the usage and linguistic conventions at the time of adoption.[151] This canon of interpretation can be seen as an exception to the

---

143 Dworkin *Law's Empire* (1986) 104.

144 Dworkin *Justice in Robes* (2006) 145.

145 Chomsky "Unlocking the mysteries of Holy Trinity: Spirit, letter, and history in statutory interpretation" 2000 *Columbia Law Review* 901 951.

146 Above. See s 73 of the Constitution.

147 Above.

148 Above.

149 Scalia and Gardner *Reading Law: The Interpretation of Legal Texts* (2012) 78.

150 Scalia and Gardner (above) 79 refer to the earliest statute directed to statutory interpretation which made it an offence to argue the opposite of the rule. The Scottish Parliament in 1427 adopted an act titled "That nane interpreit the Kingis statutes wrangeouslie". It read: "Item, The King of deliverance of councel, the manner of statute forbiddis, that na man interpreit his statutes utherwaies, then the statute beares, and to the intent and effect, that they were maid for, and as the maker of them understoode: and quha so dois the contrarie, shall be punished at the Kingis will." Similar approaches were advocated by Coke *The Fourth Part of the Institutes of the Laws of England* (1797) 324-325, Lock *An Essay Concerning Human Understanding* (1801) 133 and Blackstone *Commentaries on the Laws of England* (1770) 60.

151 *Finbro Furnishers Pty Ltd v Registrar of Deeds, Bloemfontein* 1985 4 SA 773 (A) 804D; *Minister of Water Affairs and Forestry v Swissborough Diamond Mines Pty Ltd* 1999 2 SA 345 (T) 352A-B. Refer however to *Golden China TV Game Centre v Nintendo Co Ltd* 1997 1 SA 405 (A) par 13 where it was found that the

canon that "language of a legislative instrument must be understood in its ordinary signification" – the so-called "ordinary-meaning" rule.[152] Du Plessis has suggested that the canon be reformulated as follows: "The interpreter must observe usage and the conventions of the natural language ... in which the text (a statute or the Constitution) has been drafted."[153]

Intentionalism is innately originalist as, in terms thereof, the paramount rule is that the real intention of the legislature at the time of adoption, once discerned, must be given full effect. This rule was therefore, even prior to the advent of constitutional democracy, criticised because it encouraged excessive over-the-shoulder peering that is based upon a wrong construction of an historic legislature's thoughts.[154] But it is not true that all originalist arguments are intentionalist and such criticism fails to effectively deal with textualist arguments that words must be given the meaning they had when the text was adopted.[155] Reference to intentionalism in South Africa was in any event mostly lip service as it was assumed that the legislature encoded its intention within the text of statutes.[156]

The Constitutional Court in *Association of Personal Injury Lawyers v Heath* rejected originalist intentionalism outright.[157] As such, it is important to understand the use of the rule in its historic textual context. Textualism need not be originalist as "[a] textualist might insist on reading the text in accordance with its meaning at the time of interpretation, as opposed to at the time of its enactment".[158] Scalia advocated a textualist originalist view "that judicial interpretation should aim to discern the objective indication of the words as they would have been understood at the time of their enactment".[159] On this view, judges in a democracy may not "tinker with

---

purpose of the statute in question requires that words should be interpreted flexibly to keep pace with the fast pace of technical change so as to avoid the legislature constantly having to update the statute.

152 *Union Government (Minister of Finance) v Mack* 1917 AD 731 739; *Mayfair South Townships Pty Ltd v Jhina* 1980 1 SA 869 (T) 879H; *HMBMP Properties Pty Ltd v King* 1981 1 SA 906 (N) 909A; *Nyembezi v Law Society Natal* 1981 2 SA 752 (A) 757H; *S v Du Plessis* 1981 3 SA 382 (A) 403H and *S v Henckert* 1981 3 SA 445 (A) 451G-H.

153 Du Plessis (n 12) 2C102-2C103.

154 Cowen "The interpretation of statutes and the concept of 'the intention of the legislature'" 1980 *THRHR* 347 391.

155 Such confusion seems to be widespread. Du Plessis (n 12) 32-41 states that "intentionalism and its place in constitutional interpretation remains a live issue in the world's oldest constitutional democracy: in the United States of America, originalists have maintained that the US Constitution must be read and understood as faithfully as possible in accordance with the original intent of its framers. Indeed, it is fair to say that in some form or another, original intent is endorsed by a plurality if not a majority of the US Supreme Court." One of the foremost advocates of originalism, Scalia J, can hardly be said to advocate intentionalism and instead uses textualist arguments to justify originalism.

156 Du Plessis (n 12) 2C-57.

157 2001 1 SA 883 (CC) par 19.

158 Stack "The divergence of constitutional and statutory interpretation" 2004 *University of Colorado LR* 1 10 n 20.

159 Above 10.

statutes" and thus the meaning of a statute cannot change over time.[160] The debate as to the time frame within which statutes are to be construed has been most strong within the field of constitutional interpretation. James Madison, author of the American Constitution, asked: "Can it be of less consequence that the meaning of a constitution should be *fixed or known*, than that the meaning of a law should be so? Can, indeed, a law be fixed in its meaning and operation, unless the constitution be so"?[161]

In South Africa, a number of arguments have been raised against originalist reasoning primarily because they are "reminiscent of intentionalist-speak in statutory interpretation",[162] although the Constitutional Court has regularly asked what the framers of (both the Interim and Final) Constitution had "intended".[163] Although it may be true that originalist reasoning may be inappropriate due to constitutional reasons, the problem that occurs, is that such arguments ignore the textual argument for originalism. For Scalia and Gardner, the real aim of the rule should be to ascertain "original meaning, as opposed to original intention".[164]

Originalism is not a challenge to purposivism. Purposivists start with the text but do not end there.[165] This means that adherence to originalism does not mean that an interpreter will also adhere to intentionalism or literalism. Additionally, purposivists would not have deduced – on Scalia and Gardner's example of Queen Ann's commenting of St Paul's Cathedral that it was awful, artificial, and amusing – that she meant to say that the cathedral was unpleasant, synthetic, and comical. They would have determined that she meant that the cathedral was awe-inspiring, highly artistic, and thought provoking by determining the purpose of the statement. Purposivists achieve this feat by considering the text but also by considering factors such as history, values, context and legal comparative experience.[166]

---

160 Scalia (n 26) 40.

161 Scalia and Gardner (n 149) 80.

162 Du Plessis (n 12) 32-41.

163 *S v Makwanyane* 1995 3 SA 391 (CC) par 392; *S v Mhlungu* 1995 3 SA 867 (CC) par 100, 102 and 105; *Ferreira v Levin NO; Vryenhoek v Powell NO* 1996 1 SA 984 (CC) par 15; *Bernstein v Bester* 1996 4 BCLR 449 (CC) par 53; *Du Plessis v De Klerk* 1996 3 SA 850 (CC) par 45; *Executive Council of the Western Cape v Minister for Provincial Affairs and Constitutional Development of the RSA; Executive Council of KwaZulu-Natal v President of the RSA* 2000 1 SA 661 (CC) par 39–41 and *S v Twala (Human Rights Commission Intervening)* 2000 1 SA 879 (CC) par 9–17.

164 Scalia and Gardner (n 149) 92. According to Scalia (n 26) 17 "it is simply incompatible with democratic government, or indeed even with fair government, to have the meaning of law determined by what the lawgiver meant, rather than what the lawgiver promulgated".

165 *United States v Am. Trucking Ass'ns, Inc.* 310 U.S. 534 1940 543-544. In this case the US Supreme Court held that "[t]here is, of course, no more persuasive evidence of the purpose of a statute than the words by which the legislature undertook to give expression to its wishes. Often these words are sufficient in and of themselves to determine the purpose of the legislation."

166 Du Plessis (n 12) 32-159.

1.4   OTHER CONSTITUTIONAL WAYMARKS

The Constitution contains various explicit and implicit waymarks that are essential for the interpretation of statutes.[167] The Constitution, for example, does not explicitly mention the principles of interpretation in conformity with the Constitution or the separation of powers. These principals impact on the interpretation of statutes and can be deduced from the explicit provisions of the Constitution or the structure thereof.[168] The Constitutional Court has held that implicit provisions of the Constitution are just as much part of the Constitution as express provisions.[169] In what follows, the most important constitutional waymarks are considered.

1.4.1 Application

Woolman summarises the doctrine contained in section 8 of the Constitution:[170]

> All law governing disputes between the state and natural persons or juristic persons is subject to the direct application of the Bill of Rights. All state conduct that gives rise to disputes between the state and natural persons or juristic persons is likewise subject to the direct application of the Bill of Rights. Disputes between natural persons and/or juristic persons *may* be subject to the direct application of the Bill of Rights, if the specific right asserted is deemed to apply. Where direct application of the right asserted occurs in terms of s 8(2), and the court further finds a non-justifiable abridgment of that right, then the court must develop the law in a manner that gives adequate effect to the right infringed.[171]

This section delineates the ambit of the Bill of Rights and determines the impact thereof on existing law, the functions of the legislature, the executive, the judiciary and organs of state, and on natural persons and on juristic persons.[172] As such, these matters have a significant impact on the interpretation of statutes. Although this section is not primarily an interpretive clause in the same way that section 39 of the Constitution is, significant guidance may be sought from the provision to determine, for example, if a law binds the state or a natural or juristic person and to determine how rights should be limited and the common law developed.

---

167   Above 32-116.

168   Above 32-133.

169   *South African Association of Personal Injury Lawyers v Heath* 2001 1 SA 883 par 20.

170   The section reads: "(1) The Bill of Rights applies to all law, and binds the legislature, the executive, the judiciary and all organs of state. (2) A provision of the Bill of Rights binds a natural or a juristic person if, and to the extent that, it is applicable, taking into account the nature of the right and the nature of any duty imposed by the right. (3) When applying a provision of the Bill of Rights to a natural or juristic person in terms of subsection (2), a court (a) in order to give effect to a right in the Bill, must apply, or if necessary develop, the common law to the extent that legislation does not give effect to that right; and (b) may develop rules of the common law to limit the right, provided that the limitation is in accordance with section 36 (1). (4) A juristic person is entitled to the rights in the Bill of Rights to the extent required by the nature of the rights and the nature of that juristic person."

171   Woolman "Application" in Woolman, Roux and Bishop (eds) *Constitutional Law of South Africa* (2014) 31-7.

172   Du Plessis (n 12) 32-126.

1.4.2 Basic (or founding) values

The Constitution is a value-laden document. It encompasses the hopes and aspiration of our society. Section 1 enshrines the values of human dignity, equality, the advancement of human rights and freedoms, non-racialism and non-sexism, supremacy of the Constitution and the rule of law, universal adult suffrage, a national common voter's roll, regular elections and a multi-party system of democratic government, to ensure accountability, responsiveness and openness.[173] These provisions are significant interpretive waymarks. Its status is underscored by the requirement that 75 per cent of the National Assembly, and the six out of the nine provinces in the National Council of Provinces, is needed to amend section 1.[174]

These values can be described as the aims of South African society, which are to be achieved by "political and other means under the Constitutions guidance and control".[175] It "connotes an enterprise of inducing large-scale social change through non-violent political processes grounded in law".[176] The object of the Constitution is to achieve a society that is reflective of these values. The attainment of these values is *sine qua non* for the achievement of a socially just society – which is the central vision of the Constitution.[177]

The Constitution comprises values and rules, as it is the primary source of citizens' rights and obligations. The judiciary has placed values, and not rules, at the centre of its jurisprudence and demonstrated a preference for dealing with values, even when more precise "rules" of the Constitution such as those found in the Bill of Rights are potentially relevant.[178] This is so as the Constitutional Court has established the principle that when legislation gives effect to a right in the Bill of Rights, a claimant cannot rely directly on the Constitution".[179]

This does not mean that the Constitution will play no role in adjudication, as legislative provision in question must be interpreted so as to promote the spirit, purport and objects of the Bill of Rights.[180] Interpretation of statutes on the approach adopted by the Constitutional Court is essentially teleological. This approach distinguishes between the spirit or purport of a statute and its words. The former is allowed to supersede the latter.[181] Teleological interpretation does not require reference to the

---

173 Similarly, s 195 contains values that are important for the interpretation of provisions dealing with public administration, which may be relevant within the context of public sector employment.

174 Du Plessis (n 12) 32-119.

175 Michelman "Expropriation, eviction and that gravity of common law" 2013 *Stellenbosch Law Review* 245.

176 Klare "Legal culture and transformative constitutionalism" 1998 *SAJHR* 146 150.

177 Preamble of the Constitution.

178 Woolman "The amazing, vanishing Bill of Rights" 2007 262 263.

179 *Sali v National Commissioner of the South African Police Service* 2014 9 BLLR 827 (CC) par 4, 72 and n 2. See also *S v Mhlungu* 1995 3 SA 867 (CC) par 59, *MEC for Education: KwaZulu Natal v Pillay* 2008 1 SA 474 (CC) and *South African National Defence Union v Minister of Defence* 2007 5 SA 400 (CC) par 51.

180 s 39(2).

181 Devenish *Interpretation of Statutes* (1992) 39-40.

mere purpose of the statute, but to all other considerations and values that can be applied, such as the values that exist within the legal system as a whole, including constitutional values.[182] The effect of the preference for indirect application of the Constitution over direct application means that the Court has consequently also favoured values over the (arguably more) concrete rules of the Constitution.[183]

Constitutional values are not a catalogue of all possible values in our legal system.[184] Constitutional values interact with common law. In the context of the interpretation of statutes, several foundational values may be found. Canons and presumptions of statutory interpretation are foundational values because they represent the "political and moral concerns and traditions of the community".[185] These principles may also be described as public values.[186] These canons are verbalisations of values vital to the sustenance of a just and effective legal order".[187] These values include equity, reasonableness, equality, legality, legal certainty, public interest and the like. It is therefore possible to rely on these canons when they are consistent with the Constitution and have not been subsumed under the Constitution, or when they have been left unaffected thereby. If these values have been subsumed under the Constitution then the constitutional values will take precedence. Du Plessis has identified the possibility that the presumptions can "augment, enrich and enhance" the Constitution.[188] The author submits that the presumptions could fulfil a number of useful functions:

> First they can supplement, facilitate and mediate resort to constitutional values ... Second, they can advance foundational values consistent with – but not explicitly spelled out in – the Constitution. Third, they can amplify foundational values embodied in the Constitution ... Finally, they can guide constitutional interpretation itself and amplify certain of its procedures.[189]

---

182 Above 45.

183 Refer to Woolman "True in theory, true in practice: why direct application still matters" in Woolman and Bishop (eds) *Constitutional Conversations* (2008) 113.

184 Du Plessis *Re-Interpretation of Statutes* (2002) 151-152.

185 Dworkin *Taking Rights Seriously* (1977) 67 and Du Plessis (n 184) 149.

186 Elhauge *Statutory Default Rules: How to Interpret Unclear Legislation* (2008) 3. The common law has, *inter alia,* presumed that: delegated legislative powers are to be exercised by the *delegatus* itself; legislation applies to general instances as opposed to specific instances; legislation does not alter the existing law more than is necessary; legislation does not bind the state in the event that, if the state were bound, it would hamper the fulfilment of an essential function; legislation does not contain a *casus omissus*; legislation does not contain invalid or purposeless provisions; legislation does not have extraterritorial effect; legislation does not operate retrospectively; legislation does not violate international law; legislation does not interfere with the jurisdiction of the courts; legislation is not unjust, inequitable or unreasonable; legislation is presumed to be constitutional; legislation promotes the public interest; references in legislation to acts and conduct are references to legal acts and conduct; remedial legislation must be construed generously; the existing meaning of words and phrases must be preserved; and words and phrases bear the same meaning throughout a legislative text. Refer to Van Staden "A comparative analysis of common-law presumptions of statutory interpretation" 2015 *Stellenbosch Law Review* 550 for a full discussion of these values.

187 Du Plessis (n 184) 151.

188 Above 152.

189 Above 153.

Du Plessis still utilises an explanation that insists upon a distinction between constitutional values and "foundational" common-law values. This is a logical distinction as common-law values originate from a source different than a justiciable constitution. There are some who hold the view that the origin of the value should not play such a seminal role in describing their status. Michelman writes:

> Is it beyond imagining that you would sometimes think of the animating human rights ideals of your country's constitutional bill of rights as being essentially continuous with a human rights tradition ensconced in your country's historical, common law *corpus juris*? These ideals would belong to the set ... of your country's public values. Thus perceiving the set to encompass both constitutional and common-law values, principles, or ideals, you might sometimes think of testing the constitutionality of a questioned statutory solution to a rights controversy by looking to see how the statute's specific dictates and implicit principles compare with those of the extant and historic common-law solutions.[190]

In fact, the Constitutional Court has already done so.[191] It may be argued that the Constitution, through calling for the development of the common law and its values through the prism of the Constitution, supports such an argument.[192] The point is that the presumptions of statutory interpretation may be important, beyond merely supplementing, facilitating and mediating, they resort to constitutional values, as the values inherent in the common-law presumptions may be viewed as public and thus constitutional values. On such a view, common-law values may in fact in themselves be seminally important, foundational values. Giving effect to extra-constitutional norms can also protect rights.[193]

1.4.3 Interpretation of statutes and the Bill of Rights

Section 39(1)(*a*) of the Constitution reads as follows: "When interpreting the Bill of Rights, a court, tribunal or forum must promote the values that underlie an open and democratic society based on human dignity, equality and freedom". Section 39(2) of the Constitution reads as follows: "When interpreting any legislation, and when developing the common law or customary law, every court, tribunal or forum must promote the spirit, purport and objects of the Bill of Rights."

Because the interpretation of the Bill of Rights and other legislation are dealt with in different subsections of section 39, this may suggest that there is a difference between constitutional and statutory interpretation. Because theories of statutory interpretation are characterised by the factors discussed above (that is the relevance

---

190 Michelman "The Bill of Rights, the common law, and the freedom-friendly state" 2003 *University of Miami Law Review* 401 401.

191 Above 402. The author refers to the early cases of *Bernstein v Bester* 1996 4 BCLR 449 (CC) and *S v Zuma* 1995 4 BCLR 401 (CC).

192 S 39 of the Constitution and *Carmichele v Minister of Safety and Security* 2001 10 BCLR 995 (CC) par 39.

193 Du Plessis (n 12) 32-14.

of the intention of the legislature, the nature and function of language, the role of the judiciary in the interpretation of statutes and the time frame within which statutes operate), it is not possible to hold different theories for different statutes to be interpreted. In the context of the United States, some have drawn a distinction between the approaches to constitutional and "normal" or "ordinary" statutory interpretation.[194] In contemporary scholarship, there is an uncharacteristic agreement between defenders of opposing theories of statutory interpretation that constitutional and statutory interpretation should converge rather than differ.[195]

De Ville has argued that both subsections command a similar interpretive approach because a theory of statutory interpretation indicates the role of the court *vis-à-vis* the legislature.[196] Because an approach is derived from the Constitution, a major difference in the interpretive approach between the Constitution and statutes is therefore not warranted. Similarly, both Scalia[197] and Eskridge[198] (who are theoretically opposed) have invoked separation of powers, democratic and rule of law arguments to justify their respective positions that theories of statutory and constitutional interpretation should converge.

Put differently, an interpreter cannot justify the use of different theories of statutory interpretation when interpreting different documents because the interpreter cannot justifiably have different attitudes in regard to conceptions of the relevance of the intention of the legislature, the nature and function of language, the role of the judiciary in the interpretation of statutes and the time-frame within which statutes operate. This is so as these factors are not (necessarily) influenced by the document that happens to be the subject of interpretation, but rather independently thereof by constitutional theory or "theories of authority".[199] Theories of statutory interpretation depend upon theories of authorities. It would therefore be problematic to reconcile for example a literalist approach to "ordinary" statutory interpretation with a purposive approach to constitutional interpretation.[200] This does not mean to refute the existence of particular differences between constitutional interpretation and the interpretation of other enacted law. It only challenges the idea that the approach to the interpretation of the Constitution and other enacted law is different.[201]

---

194 See Stack "The divergence of constitutional and statutory interpretation" 2004 *University of Colorado LR* 1.

195 Above 3.

196 De Ville *Constitutional and Statutory Interpretation* (2000) 58.

197 Scalia (n 26).

198 Eskridge and Frickey "The Supreme Court, 1993 term-foreword: law as equilibrium" 1994 *Harvard Law Review* 26 77.

199 Raz "On the authority and interpretation of constitutions: some preliminaries" in Alexander (ed) *Constitutionalism: Philosophical Foundations* (1998) 153 157.

200 Botha (n 83) 114.

201 Du Plessis (n 184) 134-135: "(a) The Constitution, as supreme law, is a long-lasting, enacted law-text at the apex of the legal system. (b) The Constitution is justiciable and, therefore, a standard for the assessment of the validity of both 'law' and 'conduct' in every (legislative and executive) echelon of government. (c) The Constitution verbalises, in characteristically broad, inclusive and open-ended

When both subsections are read together, taking into account the argument developed above that there can be no difference between an approach to constitutional interpretation and to normal interpretation, it is clear that the Constitution endorses a teleological model to both modes of interpretation. It may be argued that an interpretation that promotes the values that underlie an open and democratic society based on human dignity, equality and freedom will necessarily promote the spirit, purport and objects of the Bill of Rights (*et vice versa*). In the case of constitutional interpretation, the Constitution therefore requires a teleological mode of statutory interpretation. The purpose of the Constitution is to transform South African society into a society that is reflective of the Constitution's foundational values. The purpose of the Constitution and its values are therefore two sides of the same coin.

The Constitution obliges us to advance constitutional values. If this was not the case then the purpose, object or spirit of the Constitution could not be promoted. Because there can be no difference between (normal) statutory interpretation and constitutional interpretation, ordinary interpretation must also advance the purpose of the statute (in light of constitutional values). It is not possible for purposes of a statutory provision to be at odds with constitutional values. If it is averred by a litigant that the purpose of a statutory provision does not advance constitutional values, it will be incumbent on a court to cure the defect by interpreting the provision in conformity with the Constitution or to a remedy the defect in terms of section 172 of the Constitution.

1.4.4 Interpretation in conformity with the Constitution

Interpretation in conformity with the Constitution is a reading strategy associated with constitutional interpretation.[202] The principle was best described in *Hyundai Motor Distributors*:[203] "judicial officers must prefer interpretations of legislation that fall within constitutional bounds over those that do not, provided that such an interpretation can be reasonably ascribed to the section".[204] In *Van Rooyen v The State*,[205] the Constitutional Court held that "legislation must be construed consistently

language, values and beliefs associated with democracy and the constitutional state (or *Rechtsstaat*)." In *Hunter v Southam Inc* 1984 2 SCR 145 155 the Supreme Court of Canada held: "The task of expounding a constitution is crucially different from that of construing a statute. A statute defines present rights and obligations. It is easily enacted and as easily repealed. A constitution, by contrast, is drafted with an eye to the future. Its function is to provide a continuing framework for the legitimate exercise of governmental power and, when joined by a Bill or a Charter of Rights, for the unremitting protection of individual rights and liberties. Once enacted, its provisions cannot easily be repealed or amended. It must, therefore, be capable of growth and development over time to meet new social, political and historical realities often unimagined by its framers. The judiciary is the guardian of the constitution and must, in interpreting its provisions, bear these considerations in mind. Professor Paul Freund expressed this idea aptly when he admonished the American courts not to read the provisions of the Constitution like a last will and testament lest it become one."

202 Du Plessis (n 12) 32-138.

203 *Investigating Directorate: Serious Economic Offences v Hyundai Motor Distributors (Pty) Ltd In re: Hyundai Motor Distributors (Pty) Ltd v Smit* 2001 1 SA 545 (CC) (hereafter *Hyundai*).

204 par 23.

205 2002 5 SA 246 (CC).

with the Constitution and thus, where possible, interpreted so as to exclude a construction that would be inconsistent with … [the Constitution]".[206] The principle is also described as a presumption of constitutionality.[207] If this is not possible then it is incumbent upon the courts to declare the relevant provision invalid.[208] Similarly, the US Supreme Court has adopted the so-called "constitutional-doubt canon",[209] and has stated that where a statute is susceptible of two constructions, by one of which grave and doubtful constitutional questions arise and by the other of which such questions are avoided, our duty is to adopt the latter.[210] The Court has also confirmed that this principle is "beyond debate".[211] This principle was endorsed by section 35(2) of the 1993 Constitution, which stated that

> [n]o law which limits any of the rights entrenched in this Chapter, shall be constitutionally invalid solely by reason of the fact that the wording used *prima facie* exceeds the limits imposed in this Chapter, provided such a law is reasonably capable of a more restricted interpretation which does not exceed such limits, in which event such law shall be construed as having a meaning in accordance with the said more restricted interpretation.[212]

Although this section is not repeated in the 1996 Constitution, it is accepted that courts are required to read in conformity with the Constitution in terms of section 39(2) of the Constitution.[213] It was stated in *De Lange v Smuts* that the principle is "a sound principle of constitutional interpretation" which is recognised by other

---

206   par 88.

207   Du Plessis (n 12) 32-138.

208   s 172(1)(*a*) of the Constitution.

209   Scalia and Garner (n 149) 247.

210   *United States ex rel. Attorney General v Deleware & Hudson Co* 213 US 366 (1909) 408.

211   *Edward J DeBartolo Corp v Florida Gulf Coast Bldg & Constr Trades Council* 485 US 568 (1988) 575. According to Scalia and Garner (n 149) 251 this principle together with the principle that "if a case can be decided on either of two grounds, one involving a constitutional question, the other a question of statutory construction or general law, the Court will decide only the latter" are known as the "rules of constitutional avoidance". The authors argue that the two principles should not be conflated, as the constitutional-doubt canon is a matter of statutory interpretation while the latter principle is a rule of judicial procedure. There exists a similar principle in South African law. In terms of the principle of subsidiarity "[w]here there is legislation giving effect to a right in the Bill of Rights, a claimant is not permitted to rely directly on the Constitution". Refer to *Sali v National Commissioner of the South African Police Service* 2014 9 BLLR 827 (CC) par 4, 72 and n 2. This does not imply that the Constitution will play no part, as s 39(2) of the Constitution obliges the judiciary to "promote the spirit, purport and objects of the Bill of Rights" in all cases when interpreting any legislation. This is referred to as indirect application.

212   Refer also to s 232(3) of the Constitution of the Republic of South Africa Act 200 of 1993. In *Bernstein v Bester* 1996 2 SA 751 (CC) par 59 n 87 it was observed that "[t]he formulation of this subsection bears a close resemblance to the rule of construction adopted by the United States Supreme Court as formulated by Justice Brandeis in *Ashwander v Tennessee Valley Authority* [1936] USSC 36; 297 US 288 (1936) 346 as the seventh principle enunciated in that case". The court also went on to show how various other jurisdictions also apply this rule. *Verfassungskonforme Auslegung*, as this principle is known in German law, is according to Bakker "Verfassungskonforme Auslegung" in Bakker, Heringa and Stroink *Judicial Control: Comparative Essays on Judicial Review* (1995) 9 9 "an essentially German concept" which can be traced back to the decision of the *Bunderverfassundsgericht* of 7 May 1953 where it was expressed as follows: "*Ein gesetz ist nicht verfassungswidrig, wenn eine Auslegung möchlich ist, die im Einklang mit dem Grundgestz steht, und das Gesetz bei dieser Auslegung sinvoll bleibt.*"

213   Currie and De Waal *The Bill of Rights Handbook* (2013) 65.

democratic societies such as the United States of America, Canada and Germany.[214] In *Ynuico Ltd v Minister of Trade and Industry*, it was explained that the origins of this rule may be found in the common law rule of interpretation of *ut res magis valeat quam pereat* which had its origins in Roman law and had been tested and applied over many centuries.[215]

Because it is believed to be narrower than other possible readings, reading in conformity with the constitution is generally referred to as "reading down".[216] The principle should not be equated to only restrictive interpretation as it might be possible for generous readings to conform to the Constitution and restrictive readings not to.[217] This is generally referred to as "reading up".[218] According to Rautenbach the purpose of the rule is to "avoid indiscriminate invalidation of legislative provisions and to encourage the laundering and refreshing of existing fixed interpretations".[219] In *Wary Holdings Pty Ltd v Stalwo Pty Ltd*, it was found that where two interpretations are possible, the interpretation that better reflects the Constitution should be adopted.[220] The Constitutional Court has found that limits must be placed on the application of this principle so that an interpretation should not be unduly strained.[221]

1.4.5 Limitation of rights

Section 36 of the Constitution is the most openly and frequently relied on interpretive waymark.[222] This is so as the provision embodies the operative provisions that set

---

214 1998 3 SA 785 (CC) par 85. This *dicta* was endorsed in *Hyundai* (n 203) par 23.

215 1995 11 BCLR 1453 (T) 1468G-J. This rule was set out in *Digest* 1.3.19 (*in ambigua voce legis ea potius accipienda est signification, quae vitio caret*) which had been accepted through Roman-Dutch law into our law in *R v Pickering* 1911 TPD 1054 and *R v Correia* 1958 1 SA 533 (A) 542.

216 Du Plessis (n 12) 32-138.

217 *Daniels v Campbell* 2004 5 SA 331 (CC) par 31.

218 Du Plessis (n 12) 32-141.

219 Rautenbach "Introduction to the Bill of Rights" in LexisNexis (eds) *Bill of Rights Compendium* (2011) par 1A18.

220 2009 1 SA 337 (CC) par 46.

221 *Hyundai* (n 203) par 24. Refer also to Rautenbach "The Bill of Rights and statutory interventions with common law delictual remedies in compensation schemes for road accidents and work-related injuries and diseases" 2011 TSAR 527 538-540. Rautenbach (n 219) par 1A18 lists the limits of the principle: The rule can be applied only if a law can reasonably be interpreted in conformity with the Constitution. The rule applies only to the interpretation and not to the interpretation of the Bill of Rights. This means that the judiciary should not interpret the Bill of Rights in such a (limited) way as to validate the statute under consideration. Section 36 of the Constitution must be considered to determine if an interpretation is one which can be said to be in conformity with the Constitution. This point will be considered in the following paragraph. Rights may also be constitutionally limited and the principle does therefore not involve promoting the rights of individuals at all costs. An interpretation that is otherwise consistent with the Constitution is not permissible if it would extend the scope of a crime. An interpretation in conformity with the Constitution must be clear and precise. Interpretation in conformity with the Constitution is a reading strategy as supposed to a constitutional remedy. The principle only applies when the constitutionality of a provision is in issue. The rule does not apply to the provision when only one meaning can be attached to it and there is no alternative reasonable interpretation.

222 Du Plessis (n 12) 32-127. The section reads as follows: (1) "The rights in the Bill of Rights may be limited only in terms of law of general application to the extent that the limitation is reasonable and justifiable

constitutionally acceptable limits to rights. It has not been considered how section 36 affects ordinary statutory interpretation. Arguably, the section affects ordinary statutory interpretation in two distinct ways.

First, when the courts interpret legislation in conformity with the Constitution, section 36 must be considered to determine if an interpretation is one that can be said to be in conformity with the Constitution. The principle of interpretation in conformity with the Constitution comprises distinct steps.[223] At the outset, it must be determined whether two or more meanings can reasonably be inferred from the text. Thereafter, it must be determined whether these interpretations are consistent with the Bill of Rights. To do so, it must be considered if a provision limits a right and, if so, whether the limitation is justifiable in terms of limitation clauses. If for example, two interpretations are possible which both limit constitutional rights, the one will survive which has less serious consequences.[224] Second, the section is particularly value-laden. Consider the phrase "an open and democratic society based on human dignity, equality and freedom".[225] Section 36 is therefore important within the context of a teleological model of statutory interpretation where the primary objective is to give effect to the purpose of a statutory provision in light of constitutional values.

1.4.6 Rights

Section 7 of the Constitution is similar to section 1 and it's founding provisions.[226] It reasserts the Bill of Rights as the cornerstone of democracy, reaffirms the obligation of the state to make good on the promises of the Constitution, and reiterates that rights may only be limited in accordance with section 36 of the Constitution. The ideals embodied in the section would come to naught if not advanced through interpretation. The value statement contained in section 7 is therefore of particular importance within the context of teleological interpretation. Constitutional rights impact upon legislation law in three distinct ways: First, the validity of legislation can be tested against these rights. Second, legislation must be interpreted to give effect to these rights. Third, rights can be used to develop the common law.[227]

---

in an open and democratic society based on human dignity, equality and freedom, taking into account all relevant factors, including (a) the nature of the right; (b) the importance of the purpose of the limitation; (c) the nature and extent of the limitation; (d) the relation between the limitation and its purpose; and (e) less restrictive means to achieve the purpose. (2) Except as provided in subsection (1) or in any other provision of the Constitution, no law may limit any right entrenched in the Bill of Rights".

223 Rautenbach (n 219) par 1A18.

224 s 36(1)(c).

225 s 36(1).

226 The section reads: "(1) This Bill of Rights is a cornerstone of democracy in South Africa. It enshrines the rights of all people in our country and affirms the democratic values of human dignity, equality and freedom. (2) The state must respect, protect, promote and fulfil the rights in the Bill of Rights. (3) The rights in the Bill of Rights are subject to the limitations contained or referred to in section 36, or elsewhere in the Bill."

227 Van Niekerk and Smit (eds) Law@work (2015) 36.

1.4.7 The Preamble to the Constitution

In *S v Mhlungu*,[228] the Constitutional Court stated that the Preamble

> should not be dismissed as a mere aspirational and throat-clearing exercise of little interpretive value. It connects up, reinforces and underlies all of the text that follows. It helps to establish the basic design of the Constitution and indicate its fundamental purposes.[229]

Although the Preamble does not give rise to rights and duties of its own, it is an important interpretive aid.[230] The Constitutional Court has treated the Preamble as a purpose statement.[231] The Preamble, within the context of a teleological approach to the interpretation of statutes, should be understood to imply a purposive approach to interpretation, and to be an important source for determining what those purposes are.[232] The courts have relied on the Preamble to determine interpretive purposes without imposing the literalist qualification that reliance is only acceptable where the language of the Constitution is ambiguous or unclear.[233]

1.5 CONCLUSION

The theory of statutory interpretation that an interpreter prescribes to, strongly influences a particular interpretative outcome. It was also noted that the goal of statutory interpretation is central to the understanding of the theories and methods of statutory interpretation. Literalists, intentionalists and purposivists have distinct understandings as to the goal of statutory interpretation. Literalists hold the view that the goal of statutory interpretation is to discern and give effect to the meaning of the very words in which a statutory provision is couched. Intentionalists hold the view that that the goal of statutory interpretation is to discern and give effect to the

---

228 *S v Mhlungu* 1995 3 SA 867 (CC) par 112. The principle was confirmed in *Van Vuuren v Minister of Correctional Services* 2010 12 BCLR 1233 (CC). The Preamble of the Constitution: "We, the people of South Africa, recognise the injustices of our past; honour those who suffered for justice and freedom in our land; respect those who have worked to build and develop our country; and believe that South Africa belongs to all who live in it, united in our diversity. We therefore, through our freely elected representatives, adopt this Constitution as the supreme law of the Republic so as to heal the divisions of the past and establish a society based on democratic values, social justice and fundamental human rights; lay the foundations for a democratic and open society in which government is based on the will of the people and every citizen is equally protected by law; improve the quality of life of all citizens and free the potential of each person; and build a united and democratic South Africa able to take its rightful place as a sovereign state in the family of nations. May God protect our people. *Nkosi Sikelel' iAfrika. Morena boloka setjhaba sa heso. God seën Suid-Afrika.* God bless South Africa. *Mudzimu fhatutshedza Afurika. Hosi katekisa Afrika.*"

229 par 47.

230 Devenish *The South African Constitution* (2005) 27-29.

231 *Bato Star Fishing (Pty) v Minister of Environmental Affairs* 2004 4 SA 490 (CC) par 72–73; *First National Bank of South Africa Ltd t/a Wesbank v Commissioner, South African Revenue Service; First National Bank of South Africa Ltd t/a Wesbank v Minister of Finance* 2002 4 SA 768 (CC) par 52 and *Islamic Unity Convention v Independent Broadcasting Authority* 2002 4 SA 294 (CC) par 43.

232 Fowkes "Founding provisions" in Woolman, Roux and Bishop (eds) *Constitutional Law of South Africa* (2014) 13-3.

233 Du Plessis (n 12) 32-118.

real or subjective intentions of the legislature, while purposivists view the goal of statutory interpretation discerning meaning by asking what the objective purpose of the law is. History has shown that none of these theories have dominated the approach of statutory interpretation in the Anglo-American legal tradition.

These theoretical positions rest upon the following considerations: the relevance of the intention of the legislature, the nature and function of language, the role of the judiciary in the interpretation of statutes, and the time-frame within which statutes operate. While literalists reject the notion that the intention of the legislature can be relevant (or that such intentions should [exclusively] be discerned from the language employed by the legislature), intentionalists are primarily concerned with the real intentions of the legislature while purposivists are concerned with the intentions of a reasonable or hypothetical legislature.

While literalists assume that there is a grammatical structure inherent in all language that allows for a fixed and stable ordinary effect of language, intentionalists and purposivists hold that meaning is not retrieved from a construable text, but that it is made in dealing with the text (although intentionalists and purposivists disagree as to the sources that may be considered to determine meaning). Theorists also diverge in their views related to vague and precise legal language. This study has displayed that vagueness may be an important legislative instrument and that all statutory language undergoes processes of interpretation.

There is also disagreement amongst those who adhere strictly to the text and those who are willing to determine meaning with reference to extra-textual sources that is rooted in differing views of power distribution and the separation of powers. These views are strongly influenced by the theorist's view of the nature of law. Literalists, for example, reject the idea that interpreters may use extra-textual sources, as they would view this action as amounting to a usurpation of the legislative powers of Parliament. Similarly there can be disagreement as to the time frame within which statutes operate, although such disagreement is not necessarily connected to adherence to any specific theory of statutory interpretation.

Although the Constitution does not profess allegiance to a singularly accepted theory of interpretation, it is clear that significant guidance is given in the Constitution as to the proper approach thereto. The implicit and explicit waymarks in the Constitution should inform our understanding of the teleological model of interpretation. In fact, the Constitution provides much more guidance than just the interpretive clause on interpretive practices.

A HATE-CRIME MODEL FOR THE SOUTH AFRICAN CONTEXT

*Joanna Botha**

2.1   INTRODUCTION

This chapter explores the appropriate legal framework to regulate the phenomenon of hate crimes in South Africa. South Africa is yet to enact a legislative hate-crime offence. Instead, evidence of group-based hatred during the commission of an offence is considered as an aggravating factor only during sentencing.[1] Following years of social activism by numerous nongovernmental organisations and the intervention of international human rights monitoring bodies,[2] the first version of the Prevention and Combating of Hate Crimes and Hate Speech Bill (the Hate Bill)[3] was introduced in 2016. The second version of the Bill was published in March 2018, but unfortunately lapsed in early May 2019. Although revived in October 2019 by the National Assembly, there have been no further legislative developments.[4]

---

1   Terblanche *The Guide to Sentencing in South Africa* (2016) par 6.3.3 and 6.4.4; Mollema and Van der Bijl "Hate crimes: The ultimate anathematic crimes" 2014 35 3 *Obiter* 672; Naidoo "The *raison d'être* of hate-crime laws" 2016 29 *SACJ* 158-160. Also see *S v Zinn* 1969 2 SA 537 (A) confirming that during sentencing the court has a wide discretion and must consider the triad of sentencing principles, namely the circumstances of the crime, the position of the offender and the interests of society; *S v Combrink* 2012 1 SACR 93 (SCA) and *S v Matela* 1994 1 SACR 236 (A) where the respective courts used the hate-crime label and took hatred into account when determining sentence. Additionally, s 28(1) of the Promotion of Equality and Prevention of Unfair Discrimination Act (the Equality Act) 4 of 2000 provides that if unfair discrimination on the grounds of race, gender or disability played a part in the commission of any offence, this must be treated as an aggravating circumstance for sentence. This section, however, has not been promulgated.

2   See Naidoo "The Shaping, Enactment and Interpretation of the First Hate-Crime Law in the United Kingdom – An informative and Illustrative Lesson for South Africa" 2017 *PER* 12-15, who discusses the history of hate crime activism in South Africa.

3   Prevention and Combating of Hate Crimes and Hate Speech Bill B-2016 and B9-2018. All references hereafter are to the 2018 Hate Bill.

4   Sabinet law https://legal.sabinet.co.za/articles/prevention-and-combating-of-hate-speech-bill-to-be-revived/ (2019-07-30). According to the Parliamentary Monitoring Group, the Bill was revived on 29 October 2019, see https://pmg.org.za/bill/779/ (2020-04-20).

*   BA LLB (Rhodes); LLD (NMMU); Associate Professor, Faculty of Law, Nelson Mandela University.

Various possibilities have been advanced for the legislative delay. These include: the awkward coupling of hate crime regulation with the criminalisation of hate speech;[5] the broad definition of the hate speech offence;[6] the extended lists of victim groups for both hate crimes and hate speech;[7] and the suggestion that restorative justice be considered as an alternative to criminalisation.[8] A more fundamental problem, however, is the contested meaning of the "hate-crime" concept, coupled with the model of criminalisation used in the Hate Bill, and the underlying basis for the regulation of such conduct by way of the criminal law.[9]

The impasse presents an opportunity to address the framing of the regulatory model in the Hate Bill and some of the critiques of hate-crime laws. These aspects of hate-crime regulation are unpacked in this chapter in order to provide clarity and spearhead the finalisation of South Africa's legislative process. It is critically important that the hate-crime project be finalised, especially in light of the unacceptably high hate-crime commission rate in South Africa. Examples of recent hate crimes abound and include xenophobic violence, the targeting of people belonging to religious groupings, crimes committed against the LGBTI+ community, and race-based crimes.[10] The harm caused to hate-crime victims, their communities, and the achievement of the constitutional mandate, is profound and cannot be ignored.

The chapter begins by introducing the typical elements of a hate crime, followed by a discussion of the hate-crime offence as framed in the Hate Bill. Thereafter, "hate crime" as a modern conceptual problem is presented, moving to the reasons why hate crimes should be specifically regulated by the criminal law. From here, the chapter explores the various hate-crime legislative models used in other domestic

---

5   The Hate Bill is two-pronged. It criminalises hate speech and introduces hate crimes into our law. The dualist approach has probably delayed the enactment of the Bill unnecessarily, because the criminalisation of hate speech is highly contentious. In its submission to the Department of Justice and Constitutional Development on the first draft of the Hate Bill, the SAHRC recorded that it did not approve this approach. See https://www.sahrc.org.za/home/21/files/SAHRC%20Submission%20to%20DOJCS%20re.%20Hate%20Crimes%20&%20Hate%20Speech%20Bill-31.1.17%20FINAL.pdf (2019-07-21).

6   This issue is a separate problem and is not addressed here.

7   The listed group characteristics for the hate offence number 17, more extensive than any other jurisdiction. See Gerstenfeld *Hate Crimes: Causes, Controls and Controversies* (2017) 57-70; Schweppe "Defining characteristics and politicising victims: A legal perspective" 2012 *Journal of Hate Studies* 173 177-178; Schweppe and Haynes "Protecting commonly targeted groups in the context of 'new politics': the case of Ireland" 2019 *Crime, Law and Social Change* 307 309-310; Mason "The symbolic purpose of hate crime law: Ideal victims and emotion" 2014 *Theoretical Criminology* 75 79 For a South African response see Botha "The selection of victim groups in hate-crime legislation" 2019 *SALJ* 781.

8   See https://www.parliament.gov.za/press-releases/justice-and-correctional-committee-updated-hate-crimes-and-hate-speech-bill (2019-06-15).

9   It is clear that for hate crimes laws to transcend the black-letter law, and form part of the social fabric, clarity is required for the law to be efficient and well-received. This ensures "precision, transparency, legitimacy, and accountability". See Brax "Hate Crime Concepts and their Moral Foundations: A Universal Framework" in Schweppe and Walters (eds) *The Globalization of Hate* (2016) 49 50.

10   For a detailed account of hate-crime incidents in South Africa, see generally The Hate and Bias Crimes Monitoring Form Project http://hcwg.org.za/wp-content/uploads/2018/02/Report-Hate-Bias-Crimes-Monitoring-Form-Project-SCREEN.pdf (2020-04-20); Gordon "Understanding zenophobic hate crime in South Africa" 2020 *Journal of Public Affairs* 2076.

law systems, linking these to the hate-crime rationales. The chapter responds to the current legislative hold-up by proposing recommendations for the regulation of hate crimes for the South Africa context, with specific reference to the hate-crime model (encompassing the question of motive) and the type of sanction to be imposed on perpetrators. The chapter also demonstrates that an effective criminal law response to hate crimes requires clear laws, buttressed by an understanding of the normative basis for hate crime and an appreciation of how these laws work in practice.[11] The legislative framework cannot be addressed in a vacuum and without reference to its effective implementation.

2.2   ELEMENTS OF A HATE CRIME

Hate-crime legislation is emerging worldwide as a means to punish perpetrators who commit crimes where victims are selected because of group "hatred".[12] Although hate-crime laws can take various forms,[13] a hate crime is generally defined as a crime which is motivated by intolerance or bias towards the victim of the crime, because of the victim's group-based identity characteristics.[14] There are two main criteria, namely the underlying criminal act, such as murder, assault or rape (the base offence), and a requirement that the perpetrator select the victim based on group status (the bias or prejudice requirement).[15] Group victimhood is key,[16] with commonly protected characteristics in hate-crime legislation including race, ethnicity, gender, disability and religion.[17] Unlike the victims of parallel crimes, hate-crime victims are not selected because of their individual identity, but rather for what they represent, usually depicted as "the other".[18] This is why hate crimes are often described as "message" or "symbolic" crimes.

The essential characteristic of a hate crime and the type of legal intervention needed are, however, difficult to formulate.[19] Typical challenges include whether motive is

---

11   Brax (n 9) 50.

12   See generally Schweppe and Walters "Introduction: The globalization of hate" in Schweppe and Walters (eds) *The Globalization of Hate* (2016) 1.

13   See the detailed discussion in section 2.6 below.

14   Hall *Hate Crime* (2013) 1-3; Gerstenfeld (n 7) 5-6; Craig "Retaliation, fear, or rage: An investigation of African American and White reactions to racist hate crimes" 1999 *Journal of Interpersonal Violence* 138 139; Goodall "Conceptualising 'Racism' in Criminal Law" 2013 *Legal Studies* 215 222-3; ODIHR *Hate Crime Laws: A Practical Guide 2009* https://www.osce.org/odihr/36426 (2019-02-01) 16-17; Bleich "The Rise of Hate Speech and Hate Crime Laws in Liberal Democracies" 2011 37 6 *Journal of Ethnic and Migration Studies* 917 918. In South African law a biased motive is currently regarded as an aggravating circumstance for sentencing only.

15   ODIHR (n 14) 16-17.

16   Despite a wide discrepancy in victim groups in domestic hate crime legislation, an issue which falls beyond this contribution. See note 7 above.

17   Hall (n 14) 1-3; Gerstenfeld (n 7) 5-6; Craig (n 14) 139; Goodall (n 14) 222-3.

18   Perry "The Sociology of Hate: Theoretical Approaches" in Perry et al (eds) *Hate Crimes* (2009) 55-56.

19   Walters "A general theories of hate crime? Strain, doing difference and self control" 2011 *Critical Criminology* 313; Garland and Funnell "Defining Hate Crime Internationally: Issues and Conundrums" in Schweppe and Walters (eds) *The Globalization of Hate* (2016) 15-27.

an element of the crime; if the offender must actually hate the victim; and the type of legal model to use in the legislative framework. Some sceptics also question whether the criminalisation of hate with an enhanced sanction is an appropriate legal response to criminal acts committed with a biased motive.[20] The hate-crime offence in South Africa's Hate Bill is not immune to these types of conceptual problems.

2.3 THE HATE SPEECH OFFENCE IN THE HATE BILL

Clause 3(1) of the 2018 Hate Bill creates the hate-crime offence, defined as follows:

> [A]n offence recognised under any law, the commission of which by a person is motivated by that person's prejudice or intolerance towards the victim of the crime in question because of one or more of the following characteristics or perceived characteristics of the victim or his or her family member or the victim's association with, or support for, a group of persons who share the said characteristics.

The victim is defined as a person, including a juristic person, or group of persons, against whom a hate crime has been committed. Seventeen protected characteristics are then listed in alphabetical order. These are: age; albinism; birth; colour; culture; disability; ethnic or social origin; gender or gender identity; HIV status; language; nationality, migrant or refugee status; occupation or trade; political affiliation or conviction; race; religion; sex, which includes intersex;[21] or sexual orientation.[22]

Clause 3(2) of the Bill provides that any person who commits a hate crime will be guilty of an offence and liable on conviction to a sentence as contemplated in clause 6(1).[23] Clause 6 of the Bill sets out the penalties which a court may impose. Clause 6(1) provides that, subject to sub-clause (2), any person who is convicted of a hate crime is liable to any of the ordinary forms of sentencing usually available to a court in terms of sections 276 or 297 of the Criminal Procedure Act, such as imprisonment, correctional supervision and/or a fine. Clause 6(2) provides specifically:

> If a person is convicted of an offence referred to in section 3, the court that imposes the sentence must—
>
> (a) if section 51 of the Criminal Law Amendment Act, 1997 (Act No. 105 of 1997), is not applicable; and

---

20   Gerstenfeld (n 7) 45.

21   Defined as a congenital sexual differentiation which is atypical, to whatever degree.

22   The reader will note that the constitutionally protected grounds of marital status, pregnancy, conscience and belief in s 9 of the Constitution have been omitted. The following grounds have been added: albinism; HIV status; nationality, migrant or refugee status; occupation or trade; political affiliation or conviction; intersex; and gender identity.

23   Cl 3(3) contains prosecutorial safeguards. Prosecutions must be authorised by the Director of Public Prosecutions having jurisdiction. Cl 5 of the Bill requires prosecutors to produce a victim impact statement when adducing evidence or addressing the court on sentence. Such a statement is "a sworn statement or affirmation by the victim ... which contains the physical, psychological, social, economic or any other consequences of the offence for the victim and his or her family member or associate".

(b) in the case of—

(i) damage to, the loss of, or the destruction of, property or the loss of money;

(ii) physical, or other injury; or

(iii) loss of income or support,

suffered by the victim as a result of the commission of the offence, regard the fact that the person has been convicted of a hate crime as an aggravating circumstance.

A reading of clauses 3 and 6 together demonstrates that the drafters of the Hate Bill have used the uncommon hybrid hate-crime model to frame the South African hate-crime offence. This model is a combination of the "discriminatory selection" hate-crime model (where victims are selected because of their identity), the penalty enhancement model (where an enhanced sentence is imposed on perpetrators), and the so-called *animus* model (where the perpetrator's prejudice towards the victim becomes an element of the offence).[24] It seems that the drafters intended to give the courts the authority to declare an existing offence committed with a biased motive as aggravated both in law *and* at the sentencing phase.[25] While this approach may enhance the law's symbolic effects, it could impact negatively on the implementation and understanding of the law.

Before analysing the merits of these provisions, a brief overview of the objectives of the Hate Bill follows, focusing specifically on the regulation of hate crimes (as opposed to the criminalisation of hate speech).

2.4 OBJECTIVES OF THE HATE BILL

The preamble to the Hate Bill records the constitutional promise, namely the establishment of a society that is based on the democratic values of social justice, human dignity, equality and the advancement of human rights and freedoms, non-racialism and non-sexism. The preamble proceeds to recognise the relevance of the unfair discrimination measures in section 9 of the Constitution for the enactment of a hate crime offence.[26] It then acknowledges the severity of the harm caused by hate crimes,[27] both to the victim and to his or her group, and states that South Africa's

---

24   The differences between these models are explained in further detail below.

25   Goodall and Walters "Legislating to Address Hate Crimes against the LGBT Community in the Commonwealth" *Report prepared for Equality and Justice Alliance* (2019) https://www.humandignitytrust.org/wp-content/uploads/resources/Legislating-to-Address-Hate-Crimes-against-the-LGBT-Community-in-the-Commonwealth-Final.pdf (2019-08-03); SAHRC Submission (n 5) stating that "The SAHRC notes from section 3(1) that the elements of the crime of 'hate crime' are not easily identifiable from the section and would welcome clarity on the elements which would need to be proved for a crime of 'hate crime', as noted from section 3(2)(a) of the Bill that 'hate crime' is a separate offence in and of itself."

26   The Preamble also acknowledges the constitutional right to dignity (s 10) and the obligations cast on the State in terms of ss 7(2) and 8 of the Constitution.

27   The Bill defines harm to mean: "any emotional, psychological, physical, social or economic harm".

obligations in terms of the International Convention on the Elimination of all Forms of Racial Discrimination ("ICERD")[28] require the criminalisation of acts of violence based on race or ethnic origin.[29]

Clause 2 of the Hate Bill sets out its objectives. With reference to hate crimes specifically, these are to give effect to the Republic's obligations regarding prejudice and intolerance as contemplated in international instruments and to provide for: the prosecution and sentencing of hate offenders; the prevention of hate crimes; effective enforcement measures; coordinated implementation, application and administration of the Act; combating of hate crimes and hate speech in a coordinated manner and the gathering and recording of hate data.[30] The Bill's objectives focus on the practical aspects of hate-crime regulation and show a sound appreciation of the need to link the regulation of hate crimes to their prevention and prosecution and the collection of data and reporting.[31] It is critical, however, that the objectives of the Bill be better aligned with the hate-crime construct and specifically the harm caused to vulnerable groups by hate crimes. A rational connection between the hate-crime framework and the objective of hate-crime regulation is needed, an issue which is addressed below.

2.5   THE HATE-CRIME CONSTRUCT AND THE RATIONALE FOR HATE-CRIME REGULATION

The term "hate crime" was first used in the United States (the "US") in the 1980s when the federal Hate Crime Statistics Act obliged the US Department of Justice to gather and publish data on the nature and prevalence of crimes committed where there was an element of prejudice on the grounds of race, religion, sexual orientation or ethnicity.[32] Since then, most modern democracies have introduced hate-crime

---

28   The ICERD, adopted 21 December 1965, entered into force 4 January 1969, ratified by South Africa 10 December 1998. Art 4 of the ICERD places a positive obligation on States parties to criminalise the forms of racist speech identified therein and acts of violence and incitement thereto on the grounds of race. The preamble to the Bill also mentions South Africa's undertakings in terms of the UN World Conference against Racism, Racial Discrimination, Xenophobia, held in Durban, 2001. It is concerning that the preamble refers only to international instruments and agreements which address the harm caused by racism.

29   It is clear that the Bill extends beyond the grounds of race and ethnic origin.

30   cls 2(c) to (g).

31   Cl 7 provides directives to assist the prosecuting authority in achieving the Act's objects. The Hate Crimes Working Group has criticised this. It suggests that cl 7 be amended to require training for other stakeholders, including SAPS. Cl 8 casts the responsibility for the collection of data and reporting on the Minister of Justice and Correctional Services. While the Minister has an important role to play, cl 8 should also give responsibility to the Minister for Police. In addition, the interplay between the roles of the SAPS and the NPA in the collection and dissemination or relevant data should be addressed in cl 8, specifically the obligation to publish such data. See http://hcwg.org.za/wp-content/uploads/2019/02/HCWG-submission-HCB-2019.02.15_fin.pdf (2019-04-20).

32   Mason "Not Our Kind of Hate Crime" 2001 *Law and Critique* 252 256-7; Mason "The Hate Threshold: Emotion, Causation and Difference in the Construction of Prejudice-motivated Crime" 2014 *Social and Legal Studies* 293 295 referring to the recognition of anti-discriminatory laws and the need to advance identity politics.

laws, either by creating a new self-standing crime, or by enhancing the penalties for existing crimes committed on the basis of a victim identity characteristic.[33]

However, the hate-crime concept remains highly contested worldwide. There is little consensus regarding its key characteristics.[34] The debates concerning what type of conduct counts as a hate crime and how hate crimes should be regulated are well documented and ongoing.[35] The position is further complicated by the reality that the hate-crime field, including law-making, policy development and academic scholarship, is an interdisciplinary one involving *inter alia* criminologists, sociologists, politicians and lawyers. For this reason, and in order to transcend the disciplinary divisions and create an acceptable legislative model, a sound normative framework encompassing hate crime as a social construct is a necessary starting point.

2.5.1 Hate crimes as a conceptual problem

Researchers categorise hate crimes as crimes that are aimed at groups of persons who are not valued by society, and who are considered an "out-group" and marginalised.[36] Barbara Perry's hate crime scholarship has been influential here. She defines a hate crime from a sociological and criminological perspective as "a mechanism of power intended to sustain somewhat precarious hierarchies" through violence and verbal or physical threats of violence directed at groups of persons who are different and "traditionally stigmatized and marginalized".[37] This understanding of hate crimes treats the phenomenon as a social construct and one which is not static, but is "historically and culturally contingent, the experience of which needs to be seen as a dynamic social process involving context, structure and agency".[38] As Perry explains, hate crimes occur in order to remind those targeted, and their broader social groups, of their "proper" position in society and are a means to perpetuate social inequalities.[39] For this reason, Perry's highly influential hate-crime theory has been described as one that contextualises "doing difference".[40] The challenge facing

---

33   Walters "Repairing the harms of hate crime: towards a restorative justice approach?" 2, paper presented Jan 2019 at UNAFEI 171st International Senior Seminar, Tokyo; Hall (n 14) 19; Gerstenfeld (n 7) 271. South Africa is the only commwealth country not to legislate against hate crimes.

34   Garland "Difficulties in defining hate crime victimization" 2011 *International Review of Victimology* 25 26-27.

35   For a recent critique, see Duff and Marshall "Criminalizing hate?" in Brudholm and Johansen (eds) *Hate, Politics, Law: Critical Perspectives on Combating Hate* (2018).

36   Chakraborti "Framing the Boundaries of Hate Crime" in Hall et al (eds) *The Routledge International Handbook on Hate Crime* (2014) 13.

37   Perry *In the Name of Hate: Understanding Hate Crimes* (2001) 3.

38   Chakraborti and Garland *Hate Crime: Impact, Causes and Responses* (2009) 6. Also see Lawrence "The Punishment of Hate: Toward a Normative Theory of Bias-Motivated Crimes" 1994 *Michigan Law Review* 320 343 *et seq* for a detailed account of the impact of hate crimes on the victim, target community and society as a whole.

39   Perry (n 37) 10.

40   Walters (n 19) 318.

the drafters of the Hate Bill is to connect the hate-crime regulatory framework to the objective that the law be able to protect vulnerable groups of persons who are the regular targets of criminal conduct motivated by group hostility. It is also important that the Bill be aligned with the rationales for hate-crime regulation.

2.5.2 Hate-crime rationales

The rationales underlying the need to introduce hate-crime legislation and increased punishment for perpetrators align with Perry's framework of hate crimes.[41] These rationales are categorised into three broad types, namely: retribution, symbolic effects and utilitarian.[42] The specific purpose of this chapter is to analyse the hate-crime model introduced by the Hate Bill, so the theories underlying the rationales for hate crimes regulation are not dissected. Instead, they are introduced to demonstrate that the hate-crime model used in the Hate Bill must align with the hate-crime construct and the need to punish persons who commit criminal acts against vulnerable "outgroups".[43]

The crux of the retributive theory for hate-crime regulation is that hate crimes are more serious than ordinary (or parallel) crimes,[44] justifying a stricter punishment for the perpetrator. Hate crimes are argued to be especially bad, because the perpetrator's biased motive against members of marginalised groups is morally reprehensible, rendering the perpetrator more blameworthy.[45] Additionally, hate crimes cause greater harm (to the victim, his or her group, and society as a whole)[46] and may spark

---

41 Hall (n 14) 164-183; Gerstenfeld (n 7) 12; Naidoo (n 1) 158; Naidoo "Hate crimes: Some theoretical considerations and their possible application to the South African context" 2016 *Acta Criminologica: Southern African Journal of Criminology* 37-52.

42 The rationales are aligned with the usual theories of punishment. See generally Terblanche (n 1) par 9.3–9.6; Terblanche "Sentencing Guidelines for South Africa: Lessons from Elsewhere" 2003 *SALJ* 858.

43 Naidoo (n 1) 160.

44 A parallel crime refers to a crime which is not committed with a bias motive, for example, assault versus assault on the grounds of race or rape versus the sometimes incorrectly named corrective rape. Goodall and Walters (n 25) explain that the term is a misnomer for the targeted rape of lesbian and bisexual women with the purpose of "correcting" the victim's sexual orientation.

45 Hurd and Moore "Punishing hatred and prejudice" 2003 *Stanford Law Review* 1081 1087.

46 Iganski "Hate crimes hurt more" 2001 *American Behavioral Scientist* 626. These are the three levels of harm traditionally identified. Iganski extends these to 5 waves: the victim; the victim's group; the victim's immediate group; other targeted communities; and harm to societal norms. Iganski and Lagou "Hate crimes hurt some more than others: implications for the just sentencing of offenders" 2015 *Journal of Interpersonal Violence* 1696 have conducted extensive empirical research. The authors analysed data from 3 years of the Crime Survey for England and Wales. They found that victims of racially motivated crimes were twice as likely as the victims of ordinary crimes to say that they had been affected "very much" by the incident. Plus, the hate-crime victims (targeted on the basis of race) reported a significant number of aggravated emotional effects after the incident. They concluded that this "demonstrates that as a group, victims of racist crime collectively experience greater emotional and psychological harms compared with victims of parallel crimes". Also see McDevitt, Balboni, Garcia and Gu "Consequences for victims: A comparison of bias and non-bias motivated assaults" 2001 *American Behavioral Scientist* 697 709; Perry and Alvi "'We are all vulnerable' The in terrorem effects of hate crimes" 2012 *International Review of Victimology* 57; Pezzella and Fetzer "The likelihood of injury among bias crimes: An analysis of general and specific bias types" 2017 *Journal of Interpersonal Violence* 703. Pezzler and Fetzer used data from the 2013 US National Crime Victimization Survey (NCVS). They analysed 4,645,961 violent crimes –

intergroup retaliation and conflict.[47] Thus, it is correct that the offender be ordered to pay a higher price to society and receive his or her just punishment. Moreover, enhanced penalties are needed to uphold the system of law and to vindicate the hate-crime victim.[48]

One of the more frequent criticisms of hate-crime laws, however, is that crimes committed on the basis of group bias are no worse than ordinary crimes and that all victims of crime experience similar harmful effects.[49] This critique is often aligned with the assertion that there is insufficient empirical evidence to demonstrate that hate crimes actually cause more harm and that the biased motive of the hate criminal is no more blameworthy than the ordinary criminal.[50] These criticisms notwithstanding, and despite related difficulties with the practical implications of the enactment of hate-crime laws, on balance, criminalisation serves a valuable purpose in democracies which value social cohesion, multiculturalism, the advancement of social justice, and respect for those who are different.[51] Thus, persons who deny hate-crime victims the equal respect they deserve should be more severely punished for their increased culpability. The enactment of hate-crime laws ensures that this culpability is "reflected in law".[52]

The second rationale underlying the introduction of hate-crime laws is that they send a symbolic message that crimes committed on the grounds of group bias are condemned and not tolerated. These laws signify to vulnerable target groups that they will be protected from victimisation by dominant groups and that there is state support for their plight (the "fair protection paradigm").[53] In this manner, hate-crime laws have both a symbolic purpose and a denunciatory effect. They are

---

4,343,475 of which were non-bias motivated and 302,486 of which were bias motivated. They concluded that when an assault was motivated by bias, the likelihood of the victim suffering traumatic feelings was 150% greater than for an assault not motivated by bias. The criticism of this view is acknowledged, some scholars claiming that all victims suffer emotional harm, regardless of the crime. This criticism began in Jacobs and Potter *Hate Crimes: Criminal law and Identity Politics* (1998) 83. Also see Lawrence *Punishing Hate: Bias Crimes under American Law* (1999); Naidoo "Are the perceived greater harms caused by hate crimes a plausible justification for the existence of hate-crime laws?" (2016) *Stell LR* 634.

47 Gerstenfeld (n 7) 18; ODIHR (n 5) 20.

48 Naidoo (n 1) 162, who explains that the argument from retribution is used to symbolise that the perpetrator must pay a price to society either to vindicate law or to avenge the victim. Plus, the offender must pay for his or her wrongdoing. If the wrongdoer were not punished, this would undermine state law and the "laws of a higher moral order". Punishment restores the balance. Also see Snyman *Criminal Law* (2008) 14; Feinberg *The Expressive Function of Punishment* (1965) 76.

49 See generally Gerstenfeld (n 7) 16-17. See, however, the research set out in n 46 above. Another argument is that hate is no worse than other bad motives, such as greed and revenge. See Al-Hakim and Dimock "Hate as an aggravating factor in sentencing" 2012 *New Criminal Law Review* 572 588.

50 Jacobs and Potter (n 46); Blee "Racial violence in the United States" 2005 *Ethnic and Racial Studies* 599 608.

51 The link to the South African constitutional mandate is clear.

52 Goodall and Walters (n 25) 14.

53 Walters (n 33) 3; Blake "Geeks and Monsters: Bias Crimes and Social Identity" 2001 *Law and Philosophy* 121. In this way hate-crime laws act as a public vindication of the values of tolerance, equality and respect for vulnerable groups in society.

symbolic, because the extra punishment imposed on offenders informs victims that they are worthy of the law's protection, with the law designed to be reflective of the injury caused.[54] They are denunciatory, because they align with the moral norms of society and are intended to inculcate those norms in society.[55] So, hate-crime laws serve as a denunciation of acts of violence motivated by group bias.[56] It is worth noting, however, that hate-crime legislation has been criticised for being highly politicised,[57] and for serving as a vehicle of state policy, with punitiveness used as a means to achieve the "remoralisation" agenda.[58] This is why it is critical that South Africa's hate-crime legislative model align with the constitutional paradigm, where human dignity, equality and non-racialism are foundational values,[59] and that the sanction imposed be reflective of the harm suffered by victims and the need to secure marginalised communities.[60]

The utilitarian rationale in support of hate-crime laws is an extension of the consequentialist theory of punishment. It postulates that regulation is needed as a means to eliminate or reduce the harm caused to hate-crime victims, and ultimately to ensure a positive outcome for society.[61] In terms of this theory, enhanced penal legislation is argued to be justifiable on at least five grounds. Firstly, because an increased sanction will deter would-be offenders from committing the crime;[62] secondly, because an enhanced sanction should prevent the offender from harming society again;[63] thirdly, because punishment serves as a means to rehabilitate

---

54   In the UK hate crime penalty enhancement laws "were enacted primarily in order to address the denial of equal respect and dignity to minorities and people who are generally seen as 'other'". See UK Law Commission "Hate Crime: Should the Current Offences be Extended?" Law Commission No 348 (2014) 81-82.

55   The South African Equality Act (n 1) has a similar object, but has been criticised for being idealistic. The reality is that the Equality Act has no chance of achieving its objectives until Chapter 5 of the Act is enacted.

56   See the criticism of Jacobs and Potter (n 46) 27 who argue that the regulation of discrimination does not warrant a criminal law response.

57   Schweppe (n 7) 178-179. This criticism applies specifically to the selection of victim groups.

58   Mason (n 32 (2014)) 294; O'Malley "Volatile and Contradictory Punishment" 1999 *Theoretical Criminology* 175. The Organization for Security and Co-operation in Europe (OSCE) claims that hate crime laws "both express the social value of equality and foster the development of these values". See ODIHR (n 5) 7.

59   Section 1 of the Constitution entrenches the foundational values, which shape the course of South African constitutional and human rights discourse.

60   Mason (n 7) 76; Mason (n 32 (2014)) 295-6 referring to Moran "'Invisible minorities': Challenging community and neighbourhood models of policing" 2007 *Criminology and Criminal Justice* 417, who explains that one of the main factors influencing the introduction of hate crime laws in western democracies was the need to introduce better and more effective laws to protect minority communities from acts of hostility.

61   Naidoo (n 1) 166. The criminalisation of hate offences also plays an important role for the effective implementation of justice interventions to monitor and prevent hate crime. See ss 7-9 of the Hate Bill. Also see the discussion in Walters, Awusa-Bempah and Wiedlitzka "Hate Crime and the 'Justice Gap': The Case for Law Reform" 2018 *Criminal Law Review* 961.

62   Naidoo (n 1) 166.

63   Morris "Paternalistic Theory of Punishment" in Sartorius (ed) *Paternalism* (1983) 238; Von Hirsch and Ashworth *Principled Sentencing* (1998) 54; Cohen "Incapacitation as a strategy for crime control: Possibilities and pitfalls" 1983 *Crime and Justice* 1 2.

the offender;[64] fourthly, because hate crimes have retaliatory effects and must be prevented;[65] and finally because hate-crime laws have an educative deterring effect.[66] It is also worth mentioning that in the recent independent review of hate-crime legislation in Scotland, it was recorded that one of practical benefits of enacting hate-crime legislation is that such laws require the courts to consider and record the aggravation when sentencing offenders. The aggravation then forms part of the offender's criminal record and is considered in the event of repeated offending. Plus, the maintenance of records and collection of data provides statistical information which allows the authorities to monitor the hate-crime problem and put further interventions in place.[67]

There are, however, a number of credible counter-arguments to the utilitarian rationale justifying hate-crime laws. These include the critique that persons who commit a crime on the grounds of identity bias are unlikely to be deterred by an increased punishment. They already have prejudiced views, which are usually intensively experienced.[68] Additionally, if the base crime attracts a sanction, then the pre-existing sanction should serve as the underlying deterring factor. If the base sanction cannot do its work, then why would an enhanced sanction play an additional deterring role?[69] It is also argued to be highly unlikely that a prison term will serve a rehabilitative function and reform hate offenders. Consequently, a number of prominent theorists, including Mark Walters, propose that restorative practices be used to address the harm caused by hate crimes.[70]

Notwithstanding these objections, and even if a restorative approach is introduced, whether on its own or as a supplement to the more usual forms of punishment, there are sound reasons justifying the introduction of a hate-crime law in South Africa to address the harm caused to vulnerable groups.[71] The rationales and critiques discussed also demonstrate that South Africa's proposed hate-crime legislative framework must be closely connected to the normative principles underlying the

---

64   Snyman (n 48) 21.

65   Gerstenfeld (n 7) 18-19. The OSCE reported in 2012 that hate crimes "can escalate rapidly into broader social unrest, are often severely under-reported, and they can be exacerbated by or take place in a context of intolerant discourse".

66   Linking to the symbolic value of the law. See Mason (n 7) 78; Walters (n 33) 3. Mason explains that hate crime laws can achieve their purpose by placing discriminatory violence on the public agenda as a recognisable social problem and inculcating new norms into society.

67   Scottish Government "Independent Review of Hate Crime Legislation in Scotland: Final Report" (May 2018)   https://www.gov.scot/publications/independent-review-hate-crime-legislation-scotland-final-report/pages/3/ (2019-08-06).

68   Gerstenfeld (n 7) 20; Walters (n 33) 4, arguing that it is unlikely that a harsher punishment will make the offender hate the victim less.

69   Gerstenfeld (n 7) 20-21.

70   See Walters *Hate Crime and Restorative Justice: Repairing Harms, Exploring Causes* (2014) for a full account.

71   In particular, the law will serve the important purpose of denouncing criminal behaviour motivated by group bias and also demonstrates that vulnerable groups exposed to such harm are protected. This aligns with the constitutional imperative. See Naidoo (n 2) 18, who expresses a similar view.

hate-crime concept as a socio-legal construct and the underlying basis justifying hate-crime regulation, including blameworthiness and the criminalisation of hate. The challenge is to translate this research into a working legislative model for our context. As demonstrated below, the choice of hate-crime model plays a crucial role in the process as it forces the drafters to engage with the problematic issues of motive, the hate threshold and type of sanction. It is to this analysis that the chapter now turns.

2.6   HATE-CRIME MODELS

There are two main forms of hate-crime legal models, namely the discriminatory selection model and the *animus* model.

In the discriminatory selection model, the victim is chosen by virtue of, or *because of*, a protected identity characteristic.[72] Despite the use of the term "hate", actual hatred or hostility against the victim or his or her group is not needed to found the offence. However, the "because of" requirement makes it necessary to prove a causal link between the accused's conduct and the selection of the victim.[73] Many hate-crime laws in the US make use of this model, the classic example being the Violent Crime Control and Law Enforcement Act of 1994. Here, a hate crime is defined as one "in which the defendant intentionally selects a victim, or in the case of a property crime, the property that is the object of the crime, because of the actual or perceived" identity of the victim.[74]

Hate crimes falling within the ambit of the discriminatory model usually take the form of sentence (penalty) enhancement legislation.[75] These laws increase sentences for crimes where the perpetrator selected the victim based on bias, prejudice or hate. The base crime attracts the initial penalty, but the sentence is supplemented if the

---

72   Goodall (n 14) 222-3; Breen and Nel "South Africa – A home for all? The need for hate crime legislation" 2011 *SA Crime Quarterly* 33 35. The definition of a hate crime in the ODIHR Guide (n 5) is based on the discriminatory selection model.

73   Breen and Nel (n 72) 37; Naidoo and Karels "Hate Crimes against Black Lesbian South Africans: Where Race, Sexual Orientation and Gender Collide (Part 11)" 2012 *Obiter* 600 607. The Australian decision of *R v Aslett* [2006] NSWCCA 49 124 is a good example of victim selection based on expedience. The accused targeted an Asian family for a burglary because Asians are apparently most likely to keep valuables in their homes. There was no evidence of hostility towards Asian people. The family was targeted merely because of an exploitable characteristic. Lawrence, in his seminal work, *Punishing Hate: Bias Crimes under American Law* (1999), provides further examples, such as the purse-snatcher who selects women as his target because it is easier to steal from them compared to men. The criminal has selected his victim on the basis of gender, but does not hate women. There is no gender hatred.

74   Matthew Shepard and James Byrd Jr. Hate Crimes Prevention Act of 2009. Later extended to include disability, gender identity and sexual orientation in terms of the Hate Crimes Prevention Act.

75   Bleich (n 14) 918; Goodall (n 14) 224. A distinction is also drawn between sentence aggravation laws and penalty enhancement laws. Penalty enhancement models usually alter the maximum (and sometimes the minimum) penalty applicable to the offence. Sentencing aggravation models do not increase the maximum penalty for the crime, but identify the hate aspect of the offence as an aggravating factor. They require that the court take this into account when sentencing. See Mason "Legislating against hate" in Hall et al (eds) *The Routledge International Handbook on Hate Crime* (2015) 59-60.

crime is committed with a biased motive.[76] The element of hate or bias only becomes relevant during the sentencing stage after the perpetrator has been convicted. Furthermore, the way in which the sentence is enhanced can either be general or specific. A general penalty enhancement provision applies to a broad range of criminal offences.[77] Specific penalty enhancement provisions are narrower and apply only to named crimes.[78] Further permutations include penalty enhancement laws which specify the degree of increased sentence by imposing a new maximum (or minimum) sentence, whereas other laws leave this to the court's discretion (called sentence aggravation laws, as opposed to sentence enhancement laws).[79]

An example of a penalty enhancement hate-crime law is the US Hate Crime Sentencing Enhancement Act,[80] which provides for enhanced sentencing for federal crimes on the grounds of race, colour, religion, national origin, ethnicity or gender. Many other countries have followed the lead of the US by enacting sentence enhancement legislation for bias crimes.[81]

The other frequently used model for hate-crime laws is the "*animus* model", also known as the "hostility model".[82] The focus is on the moral culpability of the offender.

---

76   Bleich (n 14) 918. The penalty enhancement is therefore derivative of another crime. Lawrence (n 73) 696.

77   ODIHR (n 5) 33-35. Within the OSCE region, 23 countries list some form of bias motive as a factor that can lead to a penalty enhancement for *all* crimes.

78   ODIHR (n 5) 33-35. Within the OSCE region, 25 countries list some form of bias motive as a factor that can lead to a penalty enhancement for *specific* crimes. For example, Belgium doubles the sentence for hate crimes committed with a biased motive for a few specific crimes, including indecent assault, rape, manslaughter, intentional injury, and arson.

79   In Malta arts 222A(2), 251D and 325A of the Criminal Code specify that punishments for selected offences on the grounds of group hatred are to be increased by one to two degrees. See Goodall and Walters (n 25) 29. Also see ODIHR (n 5) 34, explaining that some laws require the court to state explicitly the reasons for applying the penalty enhancement. Also, most jurisdictions require prosecutors to investigate any factor that might increase the sentence and to bring such facts to court. For example, in the UK, the Crown Prosecution Service requires prosecutors to lead admissible evidence of group aggravation. South Africa has also adopted this approach in the Hate Bill.

80   USC 994, enacted into law as Section 280003 of the Violent Crime Control and Law Enforcement Act of 1994. In *Wisconsin v Mitchell* 508 US 476 (1993) the US Supreme Court upheld a hate-crime statute which enhanced maximum penalties where the offender intentionally selected the victim "because of" a listed ground. The court reasoned that the provision was constitutional as it penalised the offender's conduct and not his thought or expression.

81   Although these countries tend to use the *animus* model, requiring that the offender be motivated by bias. Examples include Italy (s 3 Italian Law No 205/1993), the UK (ss 145 and 146 Criminal Justice Act of 2003), France (Law 2003-88 of 3 February 2003, expanded by Law 204 of 9 March 2004), Germany (s 46 *Strafgesetbuch* or German Penal Code), Canada (s 718.2(a)(i) Criminal Code, 1996) and Australia (e.g., s 6A Sentencing Act 1995 of the Northern Territory, Australia). For Australia, see further Mason "The Penal Politics of Hatred" 2009 *The Australian and New Zealand Journal of Criminology* 275. Note that in 2008 the EU adopted a Framework Decision on Racist and Xenophobic Crime and Hate Speech requiring EU States to adopt hate crime laws. The ODIHR has assisted many EU States to draft appropriate hate-crime legislation (although there are numerous variations). See Garland and Chakraborti "Divided by a common concept? Assessing the implications of different conceptualizations of hate crime in the European Union" 2012 *European Journal of Criminology* 38 44. The purpose of the Framework was to ensure the "harmonization" of "clear and comprehensive legislation" across the EU for hate crimes – ODIHR (n 5) 27.

82   Goodall (n 14) 222; Breen and Nel (n 72) 35.

The hatred or prejudice in question becomes an element of the offence and is part of the determination of guilt.[83] So, the prosecution must show that there was an element of hatred or prejudice when the offence was committed. New free-standing crimes are usually created and the offender is sentenced for a named hate-crime offence.[84] It is, however, possible for the *animus* model to be used in combination with penalty enhancement laws.

In the *animus* model, the "hate" threshold in the offence differs between jurisdictions, with some laws requiring that the perpetrator be motivated by hatred or hostility, whereas others ask for mere prejudice or intolerance.[85] As Goodall and Walters point out, hate-crime laws "vary along a spectrum".[86] For this reason, the "hate" in hate crimes is often a misnomer.[87] Another variance is that some laws require that the perpetrator be motivated by *animus* (the subjective *animus* model),[88] whereas other laws are worded to capture the mere *demonstration* of hostility or prejudice (the objective *animus* model). The latter approach is far broader, and has been criticised,[89] as it includes cases where the offender may not have actually intended to commit the offence with a hostile motivation, but nevertheless demonstrated hostility during the commission of the offence.[90] The advantage, however, is that the objective test renders the law more capable of achieving its aim.

A law combining both the subjective and objective *animus* model is the hate crime enacted in terms of the UK's 1998 Crime and Disorder Act. An offence will be regarded as racially or religiously aggravated if the offender commits a pre-existing

---

83   Goodall (n 14) 222; Goodall and Walters (n 25) 35.

84   Lawrence "The Hate Crimes/Hate Speech Paradox" 1993 *Notre Dame Law Review* 673 696. Note, however, that Lawrence explains that the majority of the US bias crimes statutes (which he calls the "because of" model) evade easy classification in terms of either the *animus* or discriminatory models. The ODIHR states (n 5) 32-33 that these types of hate-crime laws are relatively rare. In the OSCE region, for instance, only the Czech Republic and the US have introduced substantive hate crimes. But, compare Goodall and Walters (n 25) stating that most of the commonwealth countries include *animus* in their laws

85   Garland and Chakraborti (n 81) 42; Goodall and Walters (n 25) 35. The ODIHR (n 5) 16 offers a broad conception of hate crimes using the *animus* model. Hate related prejudice is defined as "pre-conceived negative opinions, intolerance or hatred directed at a particular group". Canada uses "motivated by bias, prejudice or hate". New South Wales in Australia uses similar terminology – "motivated by hatred for or prejudice against". However, Chakraborti and Garland point out that a number of other EU States insist on "hatred". Similarly the Council of Europe's Cybercrime Protocol, intended to regulate and restrict racism on the Internet, uses the term "hate" repeatedly.

86   Goodall and Walters (n 25) 35.

87   Brax "Motives, Reasons and Responsibility in Hate/Bias Crime Legislation" 2016 *Criminal Justice Ethics* 230 233.

88   Goodall and Walters (n 25) 34-35.

89   See the discussion below.

90   Walters, Wiedlitzka and Owusu-Bempa "Hate crime and the legal process: options for law reform" *Project Report University of Sussex* (2017). Prosecutions in terms of these laws are much easier as they focus on the expression of hatred or hostility, as opposed to actual motive.

listed offence,[91] and demonstrates, or was motivated by, hostility on the grounds of race or religion during the commission of that offence.[92]

A third hate-crime model sometimes used is the so-called hybrid model, which is a combination of the discriminatory selection and *animus* models. Here, any ordinary crime can be aggravated both in law and at the sentencing stage.[93] Instead of enacting new substantive offences with new enhanced sentences for each offence, the law adds the hate component to the basic offence, using the *animus* model. Thereafter, if the hate crime is proven, the judge must enhance the offender's punishment. This model works similarly to the sentence enhancement laws explained earlier, but with the key distinction that the offence is re-labelled in law upon conviction and must be recorded as a hate crime.[94]

Scotland uses a hybrid approach in its current hate-crime legislation (which comprises a number of separate pieces of legislation).[95] The crux of these laws is that any existing offence can be aggravated by prejudice in respect of a protected characteristic. This approach does not involve the creation of new offences. Instead, a crime will be treated as a hate crime where the offender "evinces malice and ill will towards the victim based on the protected characteristic" or "if the offence is motivated (wholly or partly) by malice and ill will" towards a group member.[96] Where a person is convicted of a hate crime a number of consequences follow. First, the aggravation is recorded and considered during sentencing. Secondly, the crime records must be updated to record the conviction. This allows statistics and trends to be identified and monitored. Thirdly, the aggravation appears on the offender's criminal record. If the offender commits another offence, the earlier aggravated conviction is considered.[97]

As indicated earlier, South Africa's Hate Bill also introduces a hybrid model of hate-crime regulation. This chapter now engages with the merits of this approach. In order to do so, the advantages and disadvantages of the three hate-crime models are considered.

---

91   The listed offences include grievous bodily harm, assault and battery, and harassment.

92   ss 29-32. A higher sentence can then be imposed.

93   Goodall and Walters (n 25) 30.

94   Goodall and Walters (n 25) 31.

95   For a full discussion, see Scotland's Final Review (n 67). Note that the Final Review has recommended that the laws be consolidated. In November 2018 the Scottish government released a consultation paper calling for public comments in respect of the recommendations. See https://www.gov.scot/ publications/one-scotland-hate-home-here-consultation-hate-crime-amending-current-scottish-hate-crime-legislation/pages/2/ (2019-08-01).

96   Scotland's Final Review suggests that the laws should be retained, but that the language used in the hate element should be updated to require that the offender either demonstrates hostility towards the victim or was motivated by hostility (either in whole or in part).

97   Scotland's Final Review (n 67).

2.7   ADVANTAGES AND DISADVANTAGES: HATE-CRIME MODELS COMPARED

Starting with the discriminatory selection model, the first advantage is a practical one. These laws usually make use of penalty enhancement, which is generally regarded as being easier to design and apply, because it can be incorporated alongside existing penal codes.[98] Penalty enhancement can also apply to a broad range of criminal acts and failure to prove bias will not jeopardise a conviction on the base offence.[99]

The second benefit is that the hate element does not form part of the offence. It must only be shown that the offender acted "because of" or "by reason of" the victim's protected characteristic. In this way, emphasis is placed on group victimhood and the impact on the victim is specifically acknowledged.[100] This approach aligns with Perry's theory that hate crimes should be treated as a consequence of systemic inequality in the societal order, which allocates status to groups of people based upon their vulnerabilities.[101]

Thirdly, when using the discriminatory selection model, the controversial hate debate and the problem of motive are side-stepped.[102] The *animus* model, as we have seen, incorporates prejudice and/or hate as an element of the offence. The critics of hate-crime laws use this requirement to support their argument that hate-crime laws punish the motive of the offender and are therefore fatally flawed.[103] The basis for the argument is that motive is not traditionally included amongst the recognised forms of *mens rea*[104] and therefore cannot become an element of an offence.[105] Motive – the reason why an offender commits a crime – is irrelevant because culpability can only be considered as an aggravating factor during the sentencing phase.[106] Thus, the discriminatory selection model is argued to be a better legal framework, because for the offender to be guilty of the crime, evidence of subjective feelings of prejudice towards the victim is not necessary. Only objective evidence that the offender selected the victim by reason of his or her group membership is required.[107]

---

98   Goodall and Walters (n 25) 29; ODIHR (n 5) 35.

99   Goodall and Walters (n 25) 29; ODIHR (n 5) 35. The South African Hate Bill incorporates this feature.

100   Goodall (n 14) 228.

101   Perry (n 38) 10; Perry (n 9) 60-61. Conversely, it is also argued that by not recognising the group-hate element, these laws undermine the symbolic value of the law. See Ashworth *Principles of Criminal Law* (2009) 76, dealing with the importance of fair labelling and Chalmers and Leverick "Fair Labelling in Criminal Law" 2008 *Modern Law Review* 217.

102   Mason (n 32 (2014)) 298.

103   For a sound South African perspective on this issue, see Naidoo "Reconsidering motive's irrelevance and secondary role in hate crime legislation" 2017 *TSAR* 337.

104   In South African criminal law, *mens rea* is defined as "the will to commit an act or cause the prohibited result which is contained in the definition of a crime while possessing the knowledge that such conduct is unlawful". See Snyman (n 48) 176; Naidoo (n 103) 342.

105   Brax (n 87) 234-235. The classic statement is that "*mens rea* should not be confused with motive" – *R v Moloney* 1985 AC 905 (HL). Another oft-cited quote is that "hardly any part of penal law is more definitely stated than that motive is irrelevant", quoted by Brax (n 87) 231.

106   Motive is defined simply as the reason why a person commits an act. See Hessik "Motive's role in criminal punishment" 2006 *Southern California Law Review* 89 95.

107   Mason (n 32 (2014)) 299; Naidoo (n 103) 337.

The reality, however, as Kamban Naidoo has convincingly argued, is that the subordinate role that motive plays in the criminal law is over-stated.[108] He explains that numerous crimes include motive as an element of the offence, such as those which criminalise possession for an unlawful purpose or those which require evidence of dishonesty or those which insist on "specific intent".[109] Additionally, many criminal law defences take motive into account.[110] From a philosophical perspective, one of the justifications for excluding motive from the elements of a crime is that its inclusion moves the law into a theory of punishment which focuses on thoughts and character, as opposed to one that punishes acts. So, hate-crime regulation is objectional from a moral perspective, because these laws pass a moral judgment on the offender's values.[111] This argument is linked to the principle of legality and the claim that the criminal law should not be used to impose liability on the basis of indiviudal ethics.[112] In relation to hate crimes, the answer to these critiques is simple. One of the purposes of the law is to shape public morals. Hate-crime laws demonstrate that all persons are worthy of protection regardless of their status and, from the South African perspective, respond to the need to promote the values underlying the constitutional democracy. Accordingly, there should be no objection to using motive as an element of the offence in terms of the *animus* model for hate-crime legislation.

In any event, as explained, many of the hate-crime laws framed in the mould of the *animus* model do not require subjective intention, but use terminology such as "demonstrates hostility or prejudice".[113] This is an objective form of intention, where evidence is not needed of subjectively-felt identity bias, but merely that the offender's conduct at the time of commission of the offence reveals that he or she demonstrated bias towards the victim's protected group characteristic.[114] The result is that there is a fine line between laws using the discriminatory selection model and laws using the *animus* model, which explains the considerable confusion worldwide around the issue of which model is actually implemented.[115]

The discussion so far has demonstrated that although there are advantages to using the discriminatory selection model,[116] there is a negligible benefit to excluding the

---

108 Naidoo (n 103) 348.

109 Naidoo refers to crimes such as treason, intimidation and abduction.

110 For example, self-defence requires an examination of the accused's reason for defending himslef or herself.

111 Brax (n 87) 232.

112 Naidoo (n 103) 346; Burchell *Principles of Criminal Law* (2016) 354.

113 Scotland and the UK's Crime and Disorder Act 1998 use this approach. Research shows that these laws have a better successful prosecution rate. See Goodall and Walters (n 25) and Scotland's Final review (n 67) for a full analysis.

114 Walters, Wiedlitzka and Owusu-Bempa (n 90). Prosecutions in terms of these laws are much easier as they focus on the expression of hatred or hostility, as opposed to actual motive.

115 Goodall (n 14) 225, 229.

116 The ODIHR Guide (n 5) 48-49 prefers this approach. It states that these laws "may do a better job of addressing the kind of harm that hate crime laws are intended to prevent".

prejudiced motive from the definition. For the sake of completeness, it is important to highlight the disadvantages of the discriminatory selection laws. Firstly, some scholars claim that the model is inappropriate because it regulates cases where the perpetrator does not consciously hate the victim.[117] As Goodall explains, "what matters is whether someone has chosen to target a person from a protected vulnerable group, not why they did so."[118] This undermines the essence of what the hate-crime law aims to achieve. Secondly, the model is also criticised because when hate laws are framed in a way that does not give explicit recognition to the bias motive, the hate-crime law loses its symbolism (a core aspect of the need to criminalise). This argument is an obvious advantage of the *animus* model. Thirdly, and given that discriminatory selection hate-crime laws usually take the form of penalty enhancement, it is a problem that many of these laws do not specifically require the collection of hate-crime data. To overcome this problem, the legal framework should insist that the penalty enhancement be recorded, so that an accused's criminal history is determined at the sentencing stage and so that reliable data is gathered.[119] So, while discriminatory selection laws may be easier to implement, their drawback is that they do not fulfil the expressive function of hate-crime laws, which specifically condemn criminal acts committed on the basis of group prejudice.

Moving now to the *animus* model, the most important advantage is that when hate crimes are elevated to substantive offences, the symbolic value of the crime is enhanced. The crime is specifically labelled and the prohibited bias motive, a key aspect, is condemned.[120] The crime also becomes more prominent, linking to the denunciatory function of law.[121] Similarly, the *animus* model does well because it reflects the essence of hate crimes as expressions of prejudice or identity-based hostility against marginalised groups. The use of words such as hate, prejudice, bias, or hostility ensures that the state is clear about the exact "social mischief" it aims to regulate.[122] A related benefit is that a substantive offence enables the policing and prosecution of the crime because the criminal justice personnel are more aware of

---

117 Yet, this model ensures that crimes targeting victims because they are perceived to be innately vulnerable or an "easy target" may fall within the ambit of hate-crime laws. Proponents believe that it is important to include such victims because even though not "hated" by the offender, the perpetrator still treats them as being less worthy. The offender's decision to target the victim helps to sustain their marginalisation: i.e., selecting some victims by reason of their identity is both discriminatory and a form of prejudice.

118 Goodall (n 5) 233.

119 In states such as Germany, the reasons for enhancement cannot be recorded publicly – see ODIHR (n 5) 36.

120 Lawrence (n 73) 73; Jenness and Grattet *Making Hate a Crime: From Social Movement to Law Enforcement* (2001) 18; Perry and Perry-Kessaris "Participatory and Designerly Strategies for Sociolegal Research Impact: Lessons from Research Aimed at Making Hate Crime Visible" (2019) https://papers.ssrn.com/sol3/papers.cfm?abstract_id=3387479 (2019-08-06).

121 Goodall (n 14) 230; Mason (n 7) 78.

122 Goodall (n 14) 237-238; Duff and Marshall "Criminalizing Hate?" 2015 Research Paper No. 15-34 *Legal Studies Research Paper Series* 17.

the crime's existence and its specific elements.[123] The crime is therefore more likely to be used by prosecutors.

However, this model has its limits. The first is that can be extremely difficult to prove hate or prejudice. The position is worse where the offender is actually "motivated" by prejudice, but does not reveal hostility when committing the offence.[124] This makes it more difficult to secure a conviction and prosecutors may be reluctant to proceed with tough cases.[125] The "demonstrates hostility or prejudice" requirement is often added to hate-crime laws to overcome the problem. Although criticised for introducing an objective intent requirement,[126] the reality is that most successful prosecutions for hate crimes occur when there is evidence that the crime was accompanied by "hateful" conduct or words (the outward manifestations) during the commission of the crime.[127]

The second disadvantage is that the wide variety of language used for the hate threshold in the various formulations of the offence is argued to undermine the hate-crime construct and to create vagueness.[128] A counter-critique is that the inclusion of terms such as "hostility", "prejudice" and "bias" highlights that hate crimes are not caused by hate *per se*,[129] but as a consequence of structural hierarchies of inequality and prejudice (linking to Perry's hate-crime construct).[130] Thus, the broader hate threshold is valuable because it acknowledges that hate-crime victims are regularly targeted, not because they are hated, but because they are regarded as being vulnerable or "different" with "outsider status".[131] In fact, research shows that there is little evidence of actual hate in most recorded hate crimes.[132] So, a definition that insists upon "hate" excludes a high percentage of offences motivated by bias or prejudice. Thus, the term "bias crime", rather than "hate crime", has become common.

---

123 Goodall and Walters (n 25) 34. This can increase the likelihood of these offences being used in practice. Hate crime data is also easier to collect.

124 It is clear that expressing prejudice or hatred during the course of an offence is not "incidental". This is an integral aspect of the offence and aggravates the harm. For this reason, the "demonstrates hostility" requirement is practically very attractive.

125 ODIHR (n 5) 35-36.

126 Malik "'Racist crime': Racially aggravated offences in the Crime and Disorder Act 1998 Part II" 1999 *Modern Law Review* 409-424.

127 Goodall and Walters (n 25) set this out in their comprehensive report of hate crime laws in the Commonwealth. An analysis of the cases involved falls beyond the scope of this chapter.

128 See generally Mason (n 32 (2014)) 299.

129 In *R v Keegstra* 1990 3 SCR 697 777, the Supreme Court of Canada famously defined hate (in the context of hate speech) as an "emotion of an intense and extreme nature", which implies that members of the specified group are to be "despised, scorned, denied respect and made subject to ill treatment". This definition has become trite in both international and domestic law.

130 Mason (n 32 (2014)) 304-305.

131 Garland (n 34) 27; Brax (n 87) 233-234.

132 McDevitt et al (n 46).

Finally, it is necessary to consider the merits of the hybrid model. Given that this type of law encompasses aspects of the various hate-crime models, only the distinguishing factors are mentioned. Goodall and Walters argue that the hybrid model seems to offer an effective working solution for the regulation of hate crimes.[133] Positives include the elimination of a dual system of sentence enhancement laws and specific substantive offences, as occurs in countries such as the UK. This approach is easier to manage, for police and prosecutors, and is less complex. Moreover, because the hate element is specifically recorded, statistics and data can be collected and monitored. A negative is that because "no new substantive offences are specifically created it is less likely that higher sentencing maxima can be set. This means that although the courts are expected to enhance the sentence, they can only sentence up to the maximum which is set for the basic offence".[134] The result is that the law's symbolic effect could be minimised. However, when coupled with the more fundamental criticisms discussed above, this critique is not significant.

2.8   APPLIED TO THE HATE OFFENCE IN THE HATE BILL

As indicated earlier, South Africa's Hate Bill uses the hybrid model for hate crimes.[135] Clause 3 of the Bill defines a hate crime as *any* existing offence where the offender is motivated by prejudice or intolerance towards the victim of the crime on a protected ground. It is clear that the drafters have favoured the *animus* model encompassing prejudice, as opposed to the higher hatred-threshold. There are three main benefits to this approach. Firstly, the *animus* model emphasises blameworthiness and enhances the symbolic value of the law. Secondly, the focus on prejudice and intolerance, instead of hate, reflects the reality that victims are often targeted because of bias and structural prejudices. Thirdly, the creation of a substantive hate offence, in a specifically named law (albeit as a general offence), indicates to victims and perpetrators that the state regards criminal conduct committed on the grounds of group-based prejudice as a serious matter deserving of the law's intervention.[136]

A challenge, however, is that the drafters have relied upon the subjective *animus* test, which is likely to impact upon successful prosecutions. It is recommended that the objective "demonstrates prejudice" test be considered. As explained earlier, and despite some misgivings, this approach has many benefits. For example, in Scotland, which also uses a hybrid model and where the government has conducted an extensive review of the existing hate-crime laws, the recommendation is that the offences should be reworded to include "the demonstration of hostility" requirement.

---

133   Goodall and Walters (n 25) 31.

134   Goodall and Walters (n 25) 31.

135   The SAHRC (n 5) has criticised the drafters for not making their intention concerning a new substantive offence clear. However, upon detailed analysis, this critique appears misplaced.

136   The advantage, however, is undermined by the coupling of hate crimes and hate speech in one piece of legislation.

The reasoning is that this approach works in practice and also "highlights the context of that offending behaviour".[137]

Another problem is that the Hate Bill drafters have not made use of the phrase "in whole or in part" which may cause difficulties when there is evidence of a number of motivating factors for the crime.

Turning to sentence, the drafters have stipulated that for (i) damage to property; or (ii) physical, or other injury; or (iii) loss of income or support, suffered by the victim as a result of the offence, the court must "regard the fact that the person has been convicted of a hate crime as an aggravating circumstance". It is clear that sentence enhancement is contemplated. The broad conception of harm to the victim, including economic harm, is welcomed. The wording of the provision, however, is complicated and difficult for the layman to understand.[138] This is exacerbated by the fact that clause 3(1) of the Bill provides that a hate crime is an offence under "any law", yet the Schedule to the Bill refers specifically only to the crimes of murder, rape, robbery and housebreaking which are subject to the minimum sentencing provisions of the 1997 Criminal Procedure Amendment Act. The question is whether only these crimes are capable of becoming hate crimes, as opposed to a crime under "any law". It appears, however, that the drafters intended that any offence committed on the basis of group prejudice can be aggravated and that the Schedule only relates to amendments of current legislation.[139]

Finally, a positive aspect of the Hate Bill is the recognition that the mere enactment of legislative offence will not overcome the hate-crime problem in South Africa. To this end, although refinements are necessary,[140] the drafters are commended for inserting provisions requiring that hate-crime data be recorded and collected and that educative measures be implemented. The result is that the creation of the hate offence is coupled with the implementation of justice interventions to monitor and prevent hate crime.

2.9   CONCLUSION

The successful implementation and reception of South Africa's proposed hate-crime legislative framework requires that the law be aligned with the normative principles underlying hate crimes as a socio-legal construct and the rationales justifying hate-crime regulation, specifically the retributive and symbolic functions

---

137   See Scotland's Final Review (n 67).

138   See HCWG Comment (n 31).

139   Reference is made to cl 11: "The laws referred to in the second column of the Schedule are hereby amended to the extent indicated in the third column of the Schedule." It seems that this means that "without taking away from the general provisions in the Act, the Schedule adds further amendments to existing legislation, where that was considered necessary". The author is indebted to Professors Naidoo and Terblanche of UNISA who provided emailed clarity on this point.

140   HCWG Comment (n 31).

of hate-crime laws. The reality is that the mere enactment of hate-crime legislation will not eradicate criminal behaviour motivated by prejudice. People also need to understand the meaning of the hate-crime concept and a principled criminal justice response must be implemented. Clear and precise hate-crime legislation is needed to enhance the law's effectiveness, increase awareness of hate crime, and to give victims the assurance that the law will protect them.

The Hate Bill makes use of the broader hate threshold (incorporating prejudice) in conjunction with the *animus* hate-crime model and couples this with sentence enhancement for offenders. Instead of enacting additional substantive offences with new enhanced sentences, the Bill provides that any ordinary crime can be aggravated by hate both in law and during sentencing. In this way, the Bill utilises the benefits of the penalty enhancement model, creating a less complex system and one which is easier to understand and implement, but with the important refinement that the offence be recorded as a hate crime.

Moreover, on the whole, the wording of the offence in clause 3 of the Bill is sound. The inevitable criticism that the use of the *animus* model permits the inclusion of motive as an element of the offence has been shown to be an unsubstantiated and clichéd argument. To the contrary, the advantage of incorporating *animus* as an element of the offence ensures that the prohibited bias motive, a key aspect of the essence of hate crimes, is specifically labelled and condemned. In so doing, the Bill serves as a denunciation of criminal conduct motivated by group bias, with the law reflecting the need to protect vulnerable victim groups in society. Going forward, the drafters are advised nonetheless to consider extending the *animus* required to include the objective "demonstrates prejudice" requirement. The drafters are also urged to legislate hate crimes and the criminalisation of hate speech separately, because the definition of a hate speech offence is an extremely complicated matter, and one which is likely to cause unnecessary legislative delays.

Finally, government is urged to finalise the hate-crime project, which is long overdue, and to ensure that adequate state resources are employed to ensure the effective implementation of the legislative framework. Government must accept that hate crimes cause considerable harm to the victims and undermine the constitutional mandate. Indeed, as Walters and Kay Goodall have recently commented, the failure of many countries to regulate hate crimes constitutes "one of the key human rights issues of our time".[141]

---

141 See (n 25).

3

HEADS OF STATE IN VIOLATION OF THE LAW

A Typology of the Responsibility Framework and
its Effectiveness from a Domestic, Regional
and International Perspective

*Roxan Venter**
*Martha M Bradley*****

3.1 INTRODUCTION

The head of state in most democratic systems wields considerable power. The abuse of power has dire consequences for the state, its economy, the population at large and for the future of democracy. In most democracies, the domestic law has extensive mechanisms in order to keep the heads of the national executive authority of states responsible and accountable to those who elect them. These mechanisms ought to ensure that abuses do not occur or should provide effective procedures that can be implemented against a head of state who has acted in contravention of his or her duties. The effectiveness of the enforcement of these measures, however, is sometimes questionable, especially in developing countries where political unrest, intimidation and even state capture are influences on the implementation and effectiveness of these measures. In addition, contravention of the law by heads of state could have international repercussions and infringe on international norms and customs and violate human rights. From an international law perspective, it is necessary that heads of state be held accountable by the international community through various state responsibility mechanisms. These measures could be implemented either on a regional or an international basis through various international tribunals and international courts. Implementing and enforcing international mechanisms can be just as problematic as is the case with domestic mechanisms.

* Senior Lecturer in Constitutional law and Human Rights Law, University of Johannesburg.
** LLB, LLM (International Air, Space and Telecommunication Law), LLD (UP); LLM (Shipping Law) (UCT); Research Associate, South African Research Chair in International Law, University of Johannesburg, and Lecturer, Department of Public Law, Faculty of Law, University of Pretoria.

In this chapter, the authors discuss the responsibility framework with regard to heads of state and the various mechanisms on domestic, regional and international levels which can be implemented in order to keep heads of state responsible and accountable. Firstly, from a domestic perspective we consider mainly accountability measures in terms of South African law, but include a number of examples from other African countries, and examine the effectiveness of these measures. In relation to international law, we consider the application and effectiveness of various international criminal law responsibility-mechanisms against heads of state at both international and regional levels. Finally, the chapter expresses some observations about the ineffectiveness of these measures and makes some suggestions as to what could be implemented in order to address these deficiencies and thereby ensure that states and their citizens are protected against heads of state who flout their constitutional and international duties.

3.2 DOMESTIC MECHANISMS***

There are several examples of domestic accountability mechanisms relating to heads of state and members of the national executive authority that may be used in keeping them responsible and accountable. In this section, the authors discuss some of the most prominent South African mechanisms and their effectiveness, as well as examples from other African countries. For the sake of completeness, it should be mentioned that there exist within parliaments various less conspicuous accountability measures which are directed at the head of state and the national executive. However, these mechanisms do not necessarily apply in instances where the president acts unlawfully and therefore these measures will not be discussed in this chapter. Question time in parliament, parliamentary committees, the tabling of subordinate legislation and approval of the national budget are examples of these measures.[1]

The structure of this part of the chapter briefly is as follows: first, independent institutions such as ombudspersons are discussed in the context of South Africa, Namibia, Zimbabwe and Zambia. Second, the chapter focuses on motions of no-confidence and impeachment proceedings in South Africa, Nigeria, Cameroon and Gabon. Third, the mechanism of criminal prosecution (and the issue of domestic immunity of heads of state) in South Africa, Lesotho, Namibia, Botswana and Nigeria is given attention. Fourth, the chapter discusses the appointment of commissions of inquiry in South Africa, Zimbabwe and Malawi. Finally, judicial control as an accountability mechanism in South Africa, Botswana and Cameroon is discussed.

---

[1]   For a discussion of these measures in the South African context, see Rautenbach *Rautenbach-Malherbe Constitutional Law* (2012) 158-159.

*** Section 3.2 of the chapter is partially based on a paper delivered by Venter at the World Congress for Constitutional Law on "Violent Conflicts, Peace-Building And Constitutional Law" of the International Association for Constitutional Law, held in Seoul, South Korea, 18-22 June 2018, with a paper titled, "The courts as the gate-keepers of struggling democracies: a South African perspective".

3.2.1 Ombudspersons

Ombudspersons act as independent authorities that keep a check on organs of state. In states which employ such a mechanism, the institution of an ombudsperson performs a valuable role in conducting investigations into corruption, misappropriation of funds and malfeasance.

3.2.1.1 South Africa

In South Africa, the Public Protector is an ombudsperson-like institution that (mainly) is responsible for investigating maladministration and corruption in government. The Public Protector can launch an investigation into the activities of the head of state, the executive and other organs of state. The Public Protector is regarded as a completely independent entity in terms of chapter 9 of the South African Constitution and reports directly to parliament.[2]

Until recently, great confusion surrounded the enforceability of the decisions of the Public Protector. The South African executive and other organs of state ignored the Public Protector's remedial action in various instances, until the binding effect of the Public Protector's decisions and determinations were confirmed in a number of groundbreaking judgments. In *South African Broadcasting Corporation Soc Ltd v Democratic Alliance;*[3] *Economic Freedom Fighters v Speaker of the National Assembly;* and *Democratic Alliance v Speaker of the National Assembly,*[4] the Supreme Court of Appeal and the Constitutional Court respectively confirmed the important status and binding effect of the decisions of the South African Public Protector.[5] In both instances, the executive and legislative organs involved had not only disregarded their constitutional duties but also the remedial action determined upon by the Public Protector.

In the case of *South African Broadcasting Corporation*, the Public Protector's report on maladministration at the South African Broadcasting Corporation (South Africa's national broadcasting authority) was ignored by the broadcaster as well as by parliament.[6] In the case of the *Economic Freedom Fighters v Speaker of the National Assembly*, the Public Protector's report on the mismanagement of funds in the upgrading of the private residence of the former South African President, Mr Jacob Zuma, was at issue.[7] In *President of the Republic of South Africa v Office*

---

2   See ss 181-183 of the Constitution. Although there are several ch 9 institutions listed in the Constitution, this chapter will only be focusing on the Public Protector.

3   *South African Broadcasting Corporation Soc Ltd and Others v Democratic Alliance and Others* 2016 2 SA 522 (SCA).

4   *Economic Freedom Fighters v Speaker of the National Assembly; Democratic Alliance v Speaker of the National Assembly* 2016 3 SA 580 (CC) (hereinafter *Economic Freedom Fighters* (I) case).

5   For a discussion of these cases see Venter 2017 "The executive, the public protector and the legislature: 'The lion, the witch and the wardrobe'?" *TSAR* 176-189.

6   Venter (n 5) 178-181.

7   Venter (n 5) 181-184.

of the Public Protector,[8] the president challenged the Public Protector's prescribed remedial action following her investigation into the so-called "state capture" of the South African government. In this case the court concluded that the president's objections to the Public Protector's decisions (to have a commission of inquiry appointed to investigate the matter further, to let the Chief Justice appoint the judge that would lead the investigation and to direct the manner in which the investigation should be conducted) should be rejected and the remedial action suggested by the Public Protector should be implemented.[9] After these cases, it is clear that the Public Protector's decisions can be questioned only by taking them on review, otherwise the decisions and proposed remedial action must be followed.

As a mechanism that keeps the head of state responsible and accountable, the office of the South African Public Protector definitely gained prominence and effectiveness following the aforementioned judgments. Unfortunately, after the appointment of a new Public Protector in 2016, the office lost credibility following certain judgments involving ABSA Bank Ltd and the South African Reserve Bank.[10] In these cases, it was found that the Public Protector acted not only contrary to her mandate and the Constitution but also dishonestly and with bias against the Reserve Bank.[11] This is a most unfortunate development and it is hoped that the situation is soon remedied. Therefore, there is uncertainty as to whether investigations by the Public Protector in the future will remain an effective mechanism in keeping the South African president and the executive authority responsible and accountable.

3.2.1.2 Namibia

The Constitution of the Republic of Namibia of 1990 and the Ombudsman Act 7 of 1990 make provision for the office of the Namibian Ombudsman. The Namibian Ombudsman seems to have a much broader mandate than the counterpart in South Africa. In terms of article 91 of the Namibian Constitution and section 3 of the Ombudsman Act, the Ombudsman has the authority to investigate fundamental rights violations, corruption and maladministration and administrative practices as well as offences with regard to the environment.[12] With regard to the enforcement of the decisions and findings of the Namibian Ombudsman there seems to be quite a difference between the positions of the Namibian Ombudsman and the South African Public Protector. According to Ruppel-Schlichting the decisions of the Namibian Ombudsman are enforced chiefly by means of alternative dispute resolution (mediation and arbitration) mechanisms and apparently the Ombudsman does not

---

8   *President of the Republic of South Africa v Office of the Public Protector* 2018 2 SA 100 (GP).

9   *President of the Republic of South Africa v Office of the Public Protector* case (n 8) par 150 152–154.

10 *South African Reserve Bank v Public Protector* 2017 6 SA 198 (GP); *Absa Bank Limited and Others v Public Protector* [2018] 2 All SA 1 (GP).

11 *Absa Bank Limited and Others v Public Protector* [2018] 2 All SA 1 (GP) par 123.

12 See Venter (n 5) 187; see Horn "The process of human rights protection in Namibia" 2009 *Journal of Namibian Studies* 99; see also Mubangizi 2006 "The constitutional protection of socio-economic rights in selected African countries: a comparative evaluation" *African Journal of Legal Studies* 1.

possess "coercive powers".[13] Disputes between organs of state and the Ombudsman therefore are resolved by means of "negotiations and compromise" and the decisions are not subject to judicial review, mainly because the decisions are not binding in the first place.[14] Although this approach means that an amicable resolution can be reached and that good relations are maintained between the various organs of state and the Ombudsman, it is uncertain how effective this mechanism truly is when political roleplayers are unwilling or unable to negotiate or reach a compromise. It is wholly different from the South African approach that has now been confirmed by the courts that the decisions of the Public Protector are binding and are subject only to judicial review.

3.2.1.3   Zimbabwe

In the Republic of Zimbabwe, the office of the Zimbabwean Public Protector was removed in terms of the 2017 amendment to the Constitution of the Republic of Zimbabwe of 2013. In future, all cases that would have been investigated by the Public Protector now should be investigated by the Zimbabwean Human Rights Commission. This is perhaps not the best approach since the investigation of maladministration and corruption in government does not necessarily fall within the expertise of a Human Rights Commission. Therefore, it is uncertain how effective the investigation of maladministration in government will be in future.

3.2.1.4   Zambia

In terms of article 243 of the Constitution of the Republic of Zambia of 1991 (as amended in 2016), an office of the Zambian Public Protector is established, which will be decentralised to the provincial governments and "progressively to the districts" of the country. The Public Protector Act 15 of 2016 gives effect to these constitutional provisions and further provides for the powers and functioning of the office of the Public Protector. In terms of section 19(3) of the Zambian Public Protector Act, the Public Protector may take steps to give effect to its own recommendations if the relevant government organ, after having received a report by the Public Protector following an investigation, has taken no steps within 30 days after receipt of such a report. This provision clearly empowers the Public Protector to make sure that there is enforcement and compliance with its decisions and recommendations and has the added benefit of statutory confirmation of the enforceability of its powers. This new office replaces the previous office of Investigator General and the status of the enforcement of its powers has also been improved considerably.[15] These changes should go a long way towards making effective investigations into maladministration committed by the head of state and the government.

---

13   Ruppel-Schlichting "The independence of the ombudsman in Namibia" in Horn and Bösl *The Indepen-dence of the Judiciary in Namibia* (2008) 284; see Venter (n 5) 188.

14   Venter (n 5) 188.

15   See Mwittah "Up close with Zambia's Public Protector" *Zambia Daily Mail* 20 Nov 2017 https://www.daily-mail.co.zm/up-close-with-zambias-public-protector/ (2018-08-11).

3.2.2 Motions of no-confidence and impeachment proceedings

Motions of no-confidence and impeachment proceedings are further examples of accountability measures that the legislative authority can utilise in order to provide a check on the actions of the president and the national executive organs or even to remove those organs if the motions are successful.[16]

3.2.2.1 South Africa

In the South African context, these accountability measures have not been successful. In spite of a number of no-confidence motions as well as a motion of impeachment tabled against the former South African President, Mr Jacob Zuma, none of these motions were adopted.[17] In one instance, the entire parliamentary procedure for the adoption of these motions was put into question before the South African Constitutional Court because parliament failed to fulfil its constitutional duty to create parliamentary rules that give effect to motions of no-confidence. In other words, there was no effective procedure to table a motion of no-confidence, even though this accountability measure is prescribed by the Constitution.[18] In effect, this omission left the executive unchecked. However, even after the amendment of the Rules of the National Assembly, there has been no successful motion of no-confidence.

The Constitutional Court was approached to make a similar ruling with regard to motions of impeachment since it was argued parliamentary rules similarly do not give effect to impeachment procedures.[19] In another judgment, the Constitutional Court was approached to decide whether a motion of no-confidence could be conducted via secret ballot – a procedure for which no provision had been made either in the Constitution or in the Rules of the National Assembly.[20] The Court argued that because general elections in South Africa were conducted using secret voting (section 19(3)(a) of the Constitution) and the fact that the president is elected by the National Assembly using a secret ballot procedure (Part A, Schedule 3 of the Constitution) this supports the contention that it should also be possible to conduct the removal of the president via secret ballot in the correct circumstances.[21] Even

---

16 Ss 102 and 89 of the Constitution give effect to motions of no-confidence and motions of impeachment respectively.

17 For general information on the dates and results of the motions that were adopted in the period of former President, Jacob Zuma, see https://africacheck.org/factsheets/factsheet-many-motions-no-confidence-sa-president-zuma-faced/ (2018-08-04).

18 *Mazibuko v Sisulu* 2013 6 SA 249 (CC). For a discussion of this case see Venter 2014 "Motions of no confidence: parliament's executive check and checkmate" *TSAR* 407 and for a discussion of the parliamentary rules that were created following this judgment see Venter 2015 "The new parliamentary rule on motions of no confidence: an exercise in legislative incompetence or judicial mockery?" *TSAR* 395-404.

19 *Economic Freedom Fighters v Speaker of the National Assembly* 2018 2 SA 571 (CC) (hereinafter *Economic Freedom Fighters* (II) case).

20 *United Democratic Movement v Speaker of the National Assembly* 2017 5 SA 300 (CC).

21 *United Democratic Movement* (n 20) par 51, 56.

after the Speaker decided to have the motion of no-confidence voted on by means of a secret ballot procedure the motion, nevertheless, was unsuccessful.

At the very least, motions of no-confidence or of impeachment should be effective mechanisms indicating to the president and the executive authority that there are perceived deficiencies in their approach to governing the state and that serious consideration should be given to addressing those deficiencies. At best, the motions should serve to remove an incompetent government from office. In the South African experience, however, neither of these outcomes has been gained from these types of motions. A reason for this failure is the strong level of representation that the ANC enjoys in parliament. It is difficult to reach a two-thirds majority or even an absolute majority (the majorities needed to succeed with impeachment or a motion of no-confidence respectively) when the ANC holds more than half the seats in parliament. This fact begs the question as to whether the requirements for these mechanisms need to be revised in order to address the political reality of the composition of the South African Parliament.

3.2.2.2   Nigeria

In the Federal Republic of Nigeria, impeachment procedures are frequently used (or rather abused) for the purposes of political retribution rather than for the real purpose of acting as a measure to keep the head of state responsible and accountable.[22] Section 143 of the Constitution of the Federal Republic of Nigeria of 1999 makes provision for the removal of the Nigerian president by means of impeachment. As Nigeria has a presidential system, there is no provision for motions of no-confidence. Unfortunately, the Nigerian Constitution has a specific provision that prohibits judicial interference in impeachment proceedings against the chief executives at national and state level.[23] The Nigerian courts, however, have determined that this so-called "ouster clause" applies only to adjudication by the courts if the legislative bodies seeking the impeachment have followed all the prescribed constitutional procedures.[24] Therefore, if any of the procedural guidelines have been breached, this is sufficient grounds for judicial scrutiny.[25] Most impeachments in Nigeria, however, are the result of "bitterness, sentiments and political vendetta[s]" and therefore are not used for their intended purpose of removing the heads of the executive authority at national and state levels when those officials contravene the law.[26] This misuse seriously affects the effectiveness of impeachment proceedings in Nigeria in keeping the executive accountable and the circumstances are exacerbated by the fact that it is the only method to remove and criminally charge a sitting Nigerian president since

---

22   Fagbadebo and Francis "Impeachment as an accountability measure in a presidential system? Views from Nigeria's Fourth Republic" 2014 *African Journal of Governance and Development* 16 26-28.

23   s 188(10) of the Nigerian Constitution.

24   See *Inakoju v Adeleke* [2007] 2 FWLR (pt 366) 2403; *Dapianlong v Dariye* (2007) 27 WRN 1.

25   For a detailed discussion of the issue see Taiwo "Judicial review of the impeachment procedure in Nigeria" 2009 *Malawi Law Journal* 236-272.

26   Taiwo (n 25) 272.

the president enjoys domestic criminal immunity for the period of his or her office according to section 308 of the Nigerian Constitution. The political elite in Nigeria, therefore, is protected from removal from office and prosecution as a result of the protection of their political cronies, corruption and ineffective legal measures.[27] Fagbadebo and Francis submit that "with systemic corruption, governing measures to induce good governance would be an exercise in futility [in Nigeria]... [a]nd [that] impeachment will remain an instrument of political harassment and vendetta".[28]

3.2.2.3 Cameroon and Gabon

In many other African states, especially those influenced by the French legal system, impeachment proceedings can be instituted against a head of state only in cases of high treason, for example in Cameroon and Gabon.[29] In Cameroon, article 53 of the Constitution of the Republic of Cameroon of 1972 provides that the president may be impeached only for high treason by a court of impeachment and may be indicted only by both houses of parliament with a four-fifths majority of the members by means of an open ballot. Article 78 of the Constitution of the Republic of Gabon of 1991 provides that the president may be impeached only for a contravention of the oath of office or the offence of high treason and may be indicted by a two-thirds majority of the members of parliament in a public ballot.

Even in African countries with more elaborate impeachment provisions and the inclusion of more impeachable offences, the impeachment mechanism does not seem to be an effective check on most African heads of state.[30] Fombad and Nwauche rightly submit that in most struggling African democracies impeachment proceedings have become "dead letters", on the one hand because their effectiveness depends on parliamentary majorities and the prevalence of entrenched dominant parties makes this almost impossible to achieve, and on the other hand simply because "an old imperial president is replaced by a new one with the help of the powerful and deeply entrenched dominant parties".[31] Until African states find ways to make their impeachment proceedings more effective, it seems that these mechanisms will continue to be abused by parliamentary majorities rather than being used for their intended purpose.

3.2.3 Domestic criminal prosecution and immunity

Arguably, criminal prosecution is the most serious domestic accountability mechanism that can be implemented against a sitting president for contravention of the law. Some states provide civil immunity to heads of state, and in some cases both civil and criminal immunity, but civil immunity is not the main focus of this chapter.

---

27   Fagbadebo and Francis (n 22) 31.

28   Fagbadebo and Francis (n 22) 31.

29   Fombad and Nwauche "Africa's imperial presidents: immunity, impunity and accountability" 2012 *African Journal of Legal Studies* 91 106.

30   Fombad and Nwauche (n 29) 108.

31   Fombad and Nwauche (n 29) 107-108.

Unfortunately, the constitutions of many African states under the influence of their erstwhile colonial rulers provide criminal (and civil) immunity to heads of state while in office or even after leaving office.[32]

3.2.3.1   South Africa

South Africa may be seen as a fortunate exception. The South African Constitution does not afford any criminal or civil immunity to the South African president. In 2016, criminal charges pertaining to the 1990s so-called "Arms Deal" were reinstated against the then sitting South African President, Mr Jacob Zuma.[33] Following the reinstatement of the charges a court battle ensued wherein Mr Zuma attempted to get the charges dropped again. In October 2017, the Supreme Court of Appeal, however, dismissed the application for a review of the High Court ruling which reinstated the criminal charges.[34] The matter of the prosecution of Mr Zuma gave rise to yet another dispute regarding the appointment and dismissal of the head of the National Prosecuting Authority.[35] In the *Corruption Watch* case, a civil rights organisation took the president to court for the alleged unlawful removal of the previous National Director of Public Prosecutions, Mr Nxasana, and in order to have him vacate his position, providing him with an alleged unlawful settlement to the amount of R17.3 million, and the alleged unlawful appointment of a new Director, Advocate Abrahams.[36] The complication was that President Zuma was soon to face criminal charges of corruption and therefore was not competent to make a decision on the appointment or dismissal of the Director of Public Prosecutions. The High Court decided that the president indeed was "unable" to make a decision in this instance because of the conflict of interest. Section 90(1) of the Constitution states that in the event of the president being "unable" to act the deputy president must perform the presidential duties, therefore the Court concluded that the actions of the president were to be set aside and that the deputy president should make the appointment.[37] It is trite that the president should not benefit from the appointment of a new, perhaps more sympathetic, Director of Public Prosecutions if the president faces imminent prosecution. The drafters of the National Prosecuting Authority Act 32 of 1998 obviously did not envision the possibility that the president might be the subject of a prosecution when the provisions relating to the appointment of the director were drafted. The criminal prosecution of a sitting president in South Africa therefore is not without its challenges.

---

32   See Fombad and Nwauche (n 29) 95.

33   In *Democratic Alliance v Acting National Director of Public Prosecutions* [2016] 3 All SA 78 (GP) the court found that the original decision to drop the charges against Mr Zuma was "irrational" (par 94).

34   *Zuma v Democratic Alliance; Acting National Director of Public Prosecutions v Democratic Alliance* [2017] 4 All SA 726 (SCA); 2018 1 SA 200 (SCA).

35   *Corruption Watch (RF) NPC v President of the Republic of South Africa; Council for the Advancement of the South African Constitution v President of the Republic of South Africa* [2018] 1 All SA 471 (GP) (hereinafter the *Corruption Watch* case).

36   *Corruption Watch* (n 35) par 1–3.

37   *Corruption Watch* (n 35) par 112–114.

It is interesting to note that even after the criminal charges against the South African president were reinstated the National Assembly failed to remove the president by means either of a motion of no-confidence or impeachment. It is a strange state of affairs when a head of state has been charged criminally but remains in office and cannot be removed *and* is unwilling to step down himself. It also sets a dangerous precedent for the future. Criminal prosecution is a viable option as an accountability mechanism, but it presupposes that other procedures are in place in order to preclude a president from abusing his position in the prosecution process, such as with regard to the appointment of the Director of Public Prosecutions or by unduly frustrating the prosecution process through delay tactics and launching successive reviews and appeals.

Fombad and Nwauche submit that many African states protect their heads of state against both domestic criminal prosecution and civil liability.[38] The reason behind these immunities, amongst others, is that heads of state are conferred with extensive powers and authority and should be able to exercise these powers without fear of court proceedings being instituted against them which may "distract his attention or embarrass and hamper him from concentrating on his responsibilities".[39] The same reasoning applies to the exercise of the head of state's extensive discretionary powers; these need to be exercised fearlessly and vigorously in order to be effective. As well, immunity protects the so-called dignity of the office.[40] Fombad and Nwauche rightly point out that absolute immunity cannot easily be justified in a modern democracy.[41] Presidents do not need to be protected in order for them to perform their duties effectively; the opposite is probably more accurate. If presidents know they will be held accountable, they will be more meticulous when it comes to the exercise of their powers and functions. In addition, the dignity of the office of the president is an outdated remnant arising out of the dignity accorded the monarch in the various legal systems that have influenced the constitutional systems of many African countries. There is no place for such "dignity" in relation to the office of president in a modern constitutional democracy where the head of state possesses real executive powers and is not merely the holder of a ceremonial office.

3.2.3.2   Lesotho

Immunities for heads of state take various forms. Absolute immunity entails that a head of state is shielded from both civil and criminal liability. In terms of section 50 of the Constitution of the Kingdom of Lesotho of 1993, the king (who is a constitutional monarch) enjoys civil and criminal immunity for anything done (or not done) in both his personal and official capacity. Perhaps this is not surprising

---

38   Fombad and Nwauche (n 29) 101-102.

39   Fombad and Nwauche (n 29) 101.

40   Fombad and Nwauche (n 29) 101.

41   Fombad and Nwauche (n 29) 101.

as the king is a constitutional monarch and is "not likely to engage in any activities that incur liability".[42] These types of immunities are common in states headed by a monarch where the monarch occupies a ceremonial office.

3.2.3.3 Botswana

Qualified immunity, for instance, can relate only to criminal (but not civil) liability. In terms of section 41(1) of the Constitution of the Republic of Botswana of 1966, the president may not be held criminally accountable for any act or omission performed in his or her personal or official capacity while in office. Additionally, no civil proceedings may be instituted against the president regarding any act or omission performed during his or her term, but only in his or her private capacity. The Constitution of Botswana therefore provides a qualified civil immunity. These immunities expire when the president vacates the office.

3.2.3.4 Namibia

Some forms of immunity do not fall squarely within the absolute or the qualified categories. The President of the Republic of Namibia is protected from civil and criminal liability while in office in terms of article 31 of the Constitution of the Republic of Namibia of 1990. However, this civil protection extends further than the president's term if the act or omission was done in the president's official capacity according to article 31(3)(a) of the Namibian Constitution. If the president's actions occurred in his or her personal capacity, but during the president's term of office, then a court with civil or criminal jurisdiction may have jurisdiction in proceedings against the president after his or her term has ended if

> Parliament by resolution has removed the President on the grounds specified in this Constitution and if a resolution is adopted by Parliament resolving that any such proceedings are justified in the public interest notwithstanding any damage such proceedings might cause to the dignity of the office of President.[43]

In terms of the Namibian Constitution, therefore, there is a correlation between impeachment proceedings and instituting criminal proceedings.

3.2.3.5 Zambia

In terms of the Constitution of the Republic of Zambia of 1991 (revised in 2016), article 98(4) makes provision for the president's immunity from criminal liability to continue even after the president ceases to hold that office. However, immunity may be waived by the National Assembly.[44] In July 2002, the immunity of Zambia's former President, Frederick Chiluba, was removed by parliament after allegations of

---

42   Fombad and Nwauche (n 29) 102.

43   a 31(3)(b) of the Namibian Constitution.

44   a 98(5) of the Zambian Constitution.

misappropriation of funds were made against the former head of state.[45] Although Chiluba was later acquitted of any wrong-doing, at least there was a (seemingly) credible investigation, trial and a verdict.[46] It remains questionable, however, for such an immunity to be afforded to a head of state which can be waived only by parliamentary majority as parliamentary majorities have proven troublesome with regard to effective action in many African countries with dominant majority party governments.

3.2.3.6   Nigeria

Section 308 of the Constitution of the Federal Republic of Nigeria, 1999 has provision for the criminal immunity of the president. The Nigerian Supreme Court, however, held that this provision may be interpreted to mean that criminal investigations concerning the president and other officials may proceed while these officials are still in office although the officials concerned may not be charged or questioned until they have left office.[47] Fombad and Nwauche rightly remark that the usefulness of this approach at best is questionable even if it means that an investigation can get underway and it is not necessary to wait until the officials have all left office.[48]

3.2.4   Commissions of inquiry

The power to appoint commissions of inquiry usually vests in the head of state. However, if the head of state is the subject of such an investigation, this could complicate matters. The question it raises relates to whether the president is the only official authorised to call for such an investigation or if another organ can perform this function if the president is involved. A further problem refers to the appointment of the person leading the investigation since it is usually the head of state who makes this appointment.

3.2.4.1   South Africa

These problems are clearly illustrated in South African examples. In terms of section 84(2)(f) of the South African Constitution, the South African president has the power to appoint a commission of inquiry into any matter that requires investigation. The reports of these commissions, in turn, are considered by parliament. As in the case of the appointment of the Director of Public Prosecutions, the fact that the president alone can appoint the commission of inquiry is a major drawback to the effectiveness of this accountability measure; clearly, the drafters of the Constitution did not foresee that the president could be the subject of such a commission of

---

45   See News24 Archives "Chiluba loses immunity, his ex-FM kills himself" 16 July 2002 https://www.news24.com/xArchive/Archive/Chiluba-loses-immunity-his-ex-FM-kills-himself-20020716 (2018-08-12).

46   See Berger "Zambia's ex-president Frederick Chiluba cleared of theft" *The Telegraph* 17 Aug 2009 https://www.telegraph.co.uk/news/worldnews/africaandindianocean/zambia/6044417/Zambias-ex-president-Frederick-Chiluba-cleared-of-theft.html (2018-08-12).

47   *Fawehinmi v Inspector General of Police* [2002] FWLR (Pt. 108) 1355.

48   Fombad and Nwauche (n 29) 104.

inquiry. In *President of the Republic of South Africa v Office of the Public Protector,* the Public Protector prescribed that a commission of inquiry be appointed to investigate the issue of "state capture" and the president's alleged involvement in this matter.[49] In order to avoid the apprehension of bias and to promote an open and transparent investigation, the Public Protector suggested that the Chief Justice and not the president appoint the judge responsible for heading the commission of inquiry.[50] The High Court agreed and ordered that the Public Protector's recommendations be implemented as set out in her report. The Court remarked that the president obviously has an interest in the outcome of the investigation and therefore cannot be involved in the appointment of the commission.[51]

3.2.4.2 Zimbabwe

In the Republic of Zimbabwe, the president is not afforded the authority to constitute commissions of inquiry in terms of section 110 of the Constitution of the Republic of Zimbabwe, 2013 (revised in 2017), which makes provision for all the executive functions of the president. The president, however, is afforded this authority in terms of the Commissions of Inquiry Act (Chapter 10:07). The President of the Republic of Malawi has the power to appoint commissions of inquiry in terms of section 89 of the Constitution of the Republic of Malawi, 1994 (revised in 2017) and the Commissions of Inquiry Act (Chapter 18:01). As in the case of South Africa, these Acts do not contain any provisions or guidelines that address the scenario of the president being the one under investigation. This oversight is also a serious defect in the Zimbabwean and Malawian provisions.

A commission of inquiry, at least in theory, can serve as an effective accountability measure only if the president's involvement in the appointment process is removed when he or she has a vested interest in the outcome of the investigation.

3.2.5 Judicial control

For many new democracies, the inclusion of judicial control in their new constitutional order meant the end of parliamentary sovereignty and the beginning of democracy and constitutionalism. Fombad and Nwauche argue that prior to the 1990s the judicial authorities in many African countries were mere "handmaidens" of the executive authority in those states and were "incapable of operating effectively" or protecting fundamental human rights.[52] What is true for many African democracies was also the case in South Africa. The independence of the judicial authority is crucial to its control function. The relationship between the judicial, executive and legislative organs in these states determine the extent and effectiveness of the judicial authority's influence on the laws and actions of the

---

49 *President of the Republic of South Africa v Office of the Public Protector* 2018 2 SA 100 (GP).

50 *President of the Republic of South Africa v Office of the Public Protector* (n 49) par 58.

51 *President of the Republic of South Africa v Office of the Public Protector* (n 49) par 143.

52 Fombad and Nwauche (n 29) 96.

other organs of state. When national executives (and also legislatures) continue to wield considerable influence over the judicial authority, it seriously undermines the judicial authority's independence and, in turn, its power to keep a check on the other organs of state. Fombad and Nwauche rightly point out that judicial independence is often "overshadowed by the powerful presence of the president" and his or her intervention in the appointment process of judicial officers in many African countries.

3.2.5.1 South Africa

In terms of sections 2 and 172 of the South African Constitution, all obligations imposed by the Constitution must be fulfilled and the courts have the authority to scrutinise every government action and set aside any law or action that is inconsistent with the Constitution. The courts therefore play an integral part in keeping a check on the executive. Courts, however, should be mindful of the separation of powers and may not encroach on the terrain of the executive authority. Courts therefore may not make pronouncements on the desirability, for instance, of an executive or administrative action if it falls within the constitutionally permissible range of options available to the executive.[53]

When a court is called upon to decide a matter regarding an executive action by the president or the executive authority, there are a number of ways to approach the matter. For example, in terms of the Promotion of Administrative Justice Act 3 of 2000 (PAJA), a common-law review (for instances that do not fall within the scope of PAJA), a statutory right to appeal in terms of the empowering legislation or the Constitution itself can serve to review and declare an administrative or executive action unconstitutional.[54]

In a South African context, judicial control over the actions of the president and the executive authority reflects one of the more effective accountability mechanisms. In many of the cases discussed, the courts played a central role not only by keeping the president accountable but also making sure that the *other* accountability mechanisms are effectively implemented and enforced. In the *Mazibuko* case, for example, the court played an important role in ensuring that parliament established new rules giving effect to motions of no-confidence, thereby making this accountability mechanism more effective. The court played a similar role in relation to the parliamentary rules on motions of impeachment in the *Economic Freedom Fighters II* case. In *President of the Republic of South Africa v Office of the Public Protector*, the Court found that the objections of the president to the remedial action ordered by the Public Protector were unfounded and held that the president must adhere to the remedial action as prescribed. The Court upheld the Public Protector's decision and, again, ensured the effectiveness of this accountability measure.

---

53   Rautenbach (n 1) 159.

54   Rautenbach (n 1) 160-161.

With regard to the appointment of judicial officers in the South African system the presidency exercises a degree of power in this regard but less than its African counterparts. Section 174 of the South African Constitution provides that the Chief Justice and Deputy Chief Justice of the Constitutional Court are appointed after consultation with the Judicial Service Commission and the leaders of the parties represented in the National Assembly. The President and Deputy President of the Supreme Court of Appeal are also appointed after consultation with the Judicial Service Commission. Different procedures apply in the case of the appointment of judges to the Constitutional Court and other courts, but the Judicial Service Commission plays a more important role in these procedures than it does in respect of the appointment of the chief justices of the Constitutional Court and Supreme Court of Appeal. In South Africa, there is less interference by the executive authority in terms of the appointment of the judiciary. This factor is a major advantage and strengthens South Africa's judicial control mechanism considerably. In the South African context, judicial control is an essential and sometimes the ultimate mechanism which ensures executive accountability.

3.2.5.2   Botswana

In the Republic of Botswana, section 96 of the Constitution of the Republic of Botswana, 1966 (revised in 2005) provides that the president appoints the Chief Justice of Botswana, and other judges are appointed by the president on the advice of the Judicial Service Commission. Fombad and Nwauche rightly point out that the Commission consists mostly of persons appointed by the president.[55] The power in the hands of the president in making judicial appointments could have a very negative impact on judicial independence in Botswana.

3.2.5.3   Cameroon

Some states enjoy only symbolic judicial independence. The Constitution of the Republic of Cameroon, 1972 (revised in 2008) is a prime example. Although article 37(2) of the Constitution of Cameroon provides that the judicial authority is independent of the executive and legislative authority, section 37(3) provides that the president ensures the independence of the judicial authority and appoints all "members of the bench and of the legal department". Section 37(3) mentions that the president is assisted by the Higher Judicial Council in the exercise of this authority, but the Council is authorised to give only their opinion on judicial appointments and dismissals. The president is not obliged to follow their advice and has almost absolute influence over the judicial branch. In Cameroon, it is doubtful that the courts will be able to act as an effective control mechanism, keeping a check on the other branches of government.

In the opinion of the authors, these examples demonstrate that judicial control potentially serves as a counterbalance to the power of the other branches of

---

55   Fombad and Nwauche (n 29) 97.

government, and in relation to the head of state and the executive especially, but only if the judicial branch is secure in its independence and insulated from outside interference.

3.3 INTERNATIONAL LAW MECHANISMS

3.3.1 Introduction

In the second substantive part of this chapter, the central question relates to providing an overview of the avenues which exist under international criminal law that hold heads of states individually responsible for the commission of international crimes. As a head of state, the enjoyment of the privilege of immunity is woven into this question. This part of the chapter explores to what extent heads of state enjoy immunity under international law. Specifically, it examines the content of the concept "head of state immunity" under which a head of state cannot incur individual criminal responsibility for the commission of international crimes. It considers if and when the International Criminal Court, a treaty-based body established under the Rome Statute,[56] might resolve the dilemma in providing a counter to the impunity of a head of state to prosecution and be in a position to exercise jurisdiction over heads of states in its role as a permanent international criminal tribunal. From a regional perspective, however, that function could be the responsibility of the African Court of Justice and Human Rights as created by the Malabo Protocol.[57]

The authors submit that the political dimension makes head of state immunity a sensitive topic. While cognisant of the political debate, the focus of this chapter is on a doctrinal analysis of the applicable legal framework, relying on the accepted sources of international law as listed in article 38(1) of the Statute of the International Criminal Court.[58] As African regional discussions of the topic under discussion tend to focus on political arguments, there is a dire need for a positivist approach and legal argument based on doctrinal law. In a different context, another methodology might be more appropriate.

The structure is as follows: First, the doctrine of head of state immunity is explored in light of its customary international law status and by affording a historic overview of cases where immunity has been waived and a head of state consequently has been prosecuted for the commission of international crimes. Next, the complex relationship between articles 27 and 98 of the Rome Statute is examined in order to establish when a head of state may be summoned before the International Criminal Court. The possibility of holding a head of state individually criminally responsible

---

56   Rome Statute of the International Criminal Court (adopted 17 July 1998, entered into force on 1 July 2002) 2187 UNTS 90 (ICC Statute).

57   Protocol on Amendments to The Protocol on The Statute of The African Court of Justice and Human Rights (Malabo Protocol) of 27 June 2014.

58   Statute of the International Court of Justice (adopted 26 June 1945, entered into force 24 October 1945) TS No 993 (ICJ Statute).

under the African Regional Framework in terms of the Malabo Protocol (which is yet to enter into force) and further the possible bar under article 46A*Bis* of this treaty will be discussed.

3.3.2   Criminal prosecution and head of state immunity

Head of state immunity is a manifestation of sovereign immunity.[59] Immunity under international law is generally invoked by state officials, for instance heads of state, to bar the jurisdiction of foreign national tribunals.[60] In this context, the term "foreign tribunals" refers to the courts of states other than the state to which the state official belongs.[61] In brief, the purpose of head of state immunity is to provide the incumbent with immunity from prosecution. Two categories of immunity exist under public international law: *ratione materiae* or functional immunity;[62] and *ratione personae* or personal immunity.[63]

Functional immunity shields public officials from incurring responsibility for actions performed in respect of their official function and in their official capacity on behalf of a state or its organs.[64] This type of immunity is rooted in the idea that the official activities of state organs are performed on behalf of the state and in accordance with

---

59   See also *Southern Africa Litigation Centre v Minister of Justice and Constitutional Development & Others* 2015 5 SA 1 (GP) and *The Minister of Justice and Constitutional Development v The Southern African Litigation Centre* (867/15) [2016] ZASCA 17 (15 March 2016) at par 66 citing James Crawford as follows to explain this relationship and the purpose of such immunity: Professor Crawford describes the basic principles of the international law of immunity in the following terms: "State immunity is a rule of international law that facilitates the performance of public functions of the state and its representatives by preventing them from being sued or prosecuted in foreign Courts. Essentially, it precludes the Courts of the forum state from exercising adjudicative and enforcement jurisdiction in certain classes of case in which a foreign state is a party. It is a procedural bar (not a substantive defence) based on the status and functions of the state or official in question. Previously described as a privilege conferred at the behest of the executive, the grant of immunity is now understood as an obligation under customary international law ... [T]he existence of this obligation is supported by ample authority ... Immunity exists as a rule of international law, but its application depends substantially on the law and procedural rules of the forum."

60   Cassese et al (eds) *International Criminal Law: Cases and Commentary* (2011) 76; For a general discussion on nature Akande "International Law Immunities and the International Criminal Court" 2004 98 *The American Journal of International Law* 409-419; Gaeta "Does President Al-Bashir Enjoy Immunity from Arrest?" 2009 7 *Journal of International Criminal Justice* 320-322; Knuchel "State Immunity and the Promise of *Jus Cogens*" 2011 9 2 *Northwestern Journal of International Human Rights* 149-183; Tladi "Immunity in the Era of 'Criminalisation': The African Union, The ICC, and International Law" 2015 58 *Japanese Yearbook of International Law* 25-30; Zappalá "Do Heads of State in Office Enjoy Immunity from Jurisdiction for International Crimes? The Gaddafi Case Before the French Cour de Cessation" 2001 12 3 *European Journal of International Law* 595-612; Caplan "State Immunity, Human Rights, and *Jus Cogens*: A Critique of the Normative Hierarchy Theory" 2003 97 *The American Journal of International Law* 741-781; Mallory "Resolving the Confusion over Head of State Immunity: The Defined Rights of Kings" 1986 86 *Columbia Law Review* 169-197; Kiyani "Al-Bashir & the ICC: The Problem of Head of State Immunity" 2013 *Chinese Journal of International Law* 486-489; Buzzini "Lights and shadows of immunity and inviolability of state officials in international law: some comments on the *Djibouti v France* case" 2009 22 3 *Leiden Journal of International Law* 455-483.

61   Cassese et al (eds) (n 60) 76.

62   Cassese et al (eds) (n 60) 76.

63   Cassese et al (eds) (n 60) 76.

64   Cassese et al (eds) (n 60) 76-77.

the principles of state sovereignty.[65] A state official with functional immunity enjoys such immunity for the duration of his tenure in office[66] and cannot be prosecuted for official acts conducted during that period.[67] This form of immunity is limited to acts committed in a person's official capacity, and acts which fall outside the scope of an official act can therefore be prosecuted either before the official takes office or after the official no longer occupies the office.[68] An example of such an act falling outside the scope of functional immunity would be if a state official murders a family member.

Personal immunity also derives from customary international law,[69] but is attached exclusively to individuals holding a particular office, for instance heads of state or diplomats.[70] Personal immunity has been described as absolute immunity in that it bars every act of the official, private or otherwise, from prosecution in a foreign jurisdiction.[71] Personal immunities include the inviolability of the person, which means such a person cannot be arrested or detained and has complete immunity from criminal jurisdiction.[72] Personal immunity extends to civil jurisdiction in a foreign court, albeit with some limited exceptions.[73] This type of immunity benefits the recipient during the period that the person remains in the office to which the immunity attaches.[74] Diplomats, for instance, have absolute immunity against prosecution in a foreign court, in a combination of both *ratio personae* and *ratio materiae* while they hold their office, as a means of allowing them to perform their official functions. Heads of state enjoy a similar type of immunity.

The content and the exact nature of the doctrine of head of state immunity are, however, a matter of dispute.[75] Head of state immunity is not codified in treaty law, thus differing from diplomatic immunity which was codified in the Vienna Convention on Diplomatic Relations,[76] as well as consular immunity where the rules regulating consular immunity are codified in the Vienna Convention on Consular Relations.[77] It is generally accepted that heads of state have absolute immunity,

---

65   Cassese et al (eds) (n 60) 76-77.

66   Cassese et al (eds) (n 60) 76-77.

67   Cassese et al (eds) (n 60) 76-77.

68   Cassese et al (eds) (n 60) 76-77.

69   Cassese et al (eds) (n 60) 88.

70   Cassese et al (eds) (n 60) 88.

71   Cassese et al (eds) (n 60) 88.

72   Cassese et al (eds) (n 60) 88.

73   Cassese et al (eds) (n 60) 88.

74   Cassese et al (eds) (n 60) 88.

75   O'Neill "A New Customary Law of Head of State Immunity?: Hirohito and Pinochet" 2002 38 *Stanford Journal of International Law* 289-317.

76   Vienna Convention on Diplomatic Relations, April 18, 1961, 23 U.S.T. 3227, T.I.A.S. No. 7502, 500 UNTS 95.

77   Vienna Convention on Consular Relations, April 24, 1963, 21 U.S.T. 77, T.I.A.S. No. 6820, 596 UNTS 261.

which bars a head of state from being prosecuted in a foreign court.[78] However, this position begs the question as to whether "head of state immunity" is absolute where an international crime has been committed, and specifically crimes which are *ius cogens*.[79] Furthermore, can a head of state be prosecuted once out of office, and, if so, is it only for acts committed in their personal capacity?[80] Does "head of state immunity" under customary international law bar heads of state from being prosecuted for the alleged commission of international crimes before an international criminal tribunal[81] or is immunity limited to prosecution by a foreign court?[82]

3.3.3 Prosecution and head of state immunity in foreign courts

It is generally accepted that a sitting head of state enjoys absolute immunity from prosecution in a foreign jurisdiction.[83] This means that a head of state cannot be prosecuted in the court of another sovereign state.[84] Such immunity derives from the concept of sovereign immunity and allows a state official to carry out his office in a manner similar to diplomatic immunity[85] – which, incidentally, is similar to the domestic immunity that many heads of state enjoy against criminal prosecution as discussed above. Customary international law provides full immunity to a person during their tenure as a head of state. It is uncertain, however, whether at the end of their term of office such a person may then be prosecuted for international crimes committed during that period.[86] Although full immunity covers both official and personal functions when an official commits an international crime, the question is whether the prosecution of the commission of an international crime by a head of state after his tenure in office is an exception. This situation is problematic, since crimes obviously never form part of the duties of a head of state.[87] Unfortunately, there are limited examples of former head of state immunity being questioned by foreign

---

78   Compare Hood and Cormier "Prosecuting International Crimes in Australia: The Case of the Sri Lankan President' 2012 13 *Melbourne Journal of International Law* 236-264 and Fox "The Resolution of the Institute of International Law on the immunities of heads of state and government" 2002 51 1 *International and Comparative Law Quarterly* 119-125; Kiyani (n 60) 486-489.

79   See Akande and Shah "Immunities of state officials, international crimes, and foreign domestic courts" 2010 21 4 *European Journal of International Law* 815-852. For a contrary opinion see Orakshelashvili "Immunities of state officials, international crimes, and foreign domestic courts: a reply to Dapo Akande and Sangeeta Shah" 2011 22 3 *European Journal of International Law* 849-855 and Kiyani (n 60) 486-489.

80   These questions are also considered in Akande and Shah (n 79) 815-852. For a contrary opinion see Orakshelashvili (n 79) 849-855 and Kiyani (n 60) 486-489.

81   Akande and Shah (n 79) 815-852. For a contrary opinion see Orakshelashvili (n 79) 849-855 and Kiyani (n 60) 486-489.

82   Akande and Shah (n 79) 815-852. For a contrary opinion see Orakshelashvili (n 79) 849-855 and Kiyani (n 60) 486-489.

83   See Hood and Cormier (n 78) 236-264; Fox (n 78) 119-125; Kiyani (n 60) 486-489.

84   See Hood and Cormier (n 78) 236-264; Fox (n 78) 119-125; Kiyani (n 60) 486-489.

85   See Hood and Cormier (n 78) 236-264; Fox (n 78) 119-125; Kiyani (n 60) 486-489.

86   See Hood and Cormier (n 78) 236-264; Fox (n 78) 119-125; Kiyani (n 60) 486-489.

87   See Hood and Cormier (n 78) 236-264; Fox (n 78) 119-125; Kiyani (n 60) 486-489.

courts.[88] The available examples are mostly limited to violations of international criminal law.[89] One such an example is the case of ex-President Pinochet of Chile.[90]

---

88   *R v Bow Street Stipendiary Magistrate (Bartle) ex parte Pinochet Ugarte* (No.3), House of Lords, Judgment of 24 March 1999.

89   *R v Bow Street Stipendiary Magistrate (Bartle) ex parte Pinochet Ugarte* (No.3) (n 88).

90   Another exceptional case in which a head of state was tried is the trial of President Saddam Hussain. This case differs from the Pinochet case in that Saddam Hussain was arrested while he was still in office, even though at the time of the case an interim regime was in power. The nature of the tribunal is complex as the trial was held in Iraq under the auspices of the Iraqi transitional government. It is unclear how much control or to what extent the USA intervened in establishing this tribunal. Saddam Hussain, *inter alia*, was accused of committing crimes against humanity for which he was found guilty and received the death penalty. President Hussain's legal team appealed the guilty verdict and death penalty on various grounds, including that owing to the concept of head of state immunity he was immune from prosecution. The appeals decision issued on 12 December 2006 by the Cessation Chamber of the Iraqi High Court, considered the appeal and ruled as follows concerning the status of President Hussain's immunity: "As to the objection based on the immunity of officials we say the immunity is the practical immunity which comes for the purpose of the position; it is not possible for any person to claim that he committed crimes and that his actions are outside the reach of the law; the immunity is limited to the time in the position and does not continue thereafter, and it is tied in its existence and non-existence to the position, and it is not given to the benefit of a person who clings to the position, but it is given for the benefit of society. The immunity does not violate part two of the international criminal law and the constitution; *no state has the right to give its officials immunity from prosecution for crimes against humanity and genocide, and if immunity constitutes a means to avoid prosecution this principle has disappeared after World War II and immunity has no more effect.* The establishment of criminal courts is nothing but a sign of the end of the immunity principle. Since the law of the tribunal permits the trying of any person accused of committing a crime irrespective of his official position because his position does not protect him from punishment or constitute a mitigating circumstance (even if the person were president or member of the government or its council) *and whereas the law of the tribunal contains penalty provisions, therefore the claim of immunity of head of state or that the act was committed by the accused in his official capacity does not constitute an acceptable defense or a reason to reduce the sentence*, and therefore the immunity does not prevent the tribunal from using its jurisdiction to try those persons for the crimes they committed and over which it has jurisdiction. Therefore the immunity must be a cause to increase the sentence and not to reduce it, because whoever enjoys immunity normally has the power to influence a great number of people which increases the seriousness of the losses and damages resulting from the crimes.

The head of state is responsible internationally for the crimes he commits against the international community because it is not logical or just to punish the subordinates who carry out illegal orders issued by the president and his assistants and spare the president who ordered and planned the commission of these crimes. The president is therefore considered a 'gang chief' and not a head of state who respects the law. As such, the supreme president is to be considered responsible for the crimes committed by his subordinates not only on the basis of his knowledge of those crimes but for his negligence in not obtaining such knowledge. The non-action is considered equal to a positive action in light of article (13/1) of the Third Geneva Convention of 1949 which provides that any illegal action or abstention on the part of the authority which causes death or exposes the safety of prisoners of war to danger is prohibited and constitutes a serious violation of this convention." The appeals chamber held that head of state immunity ceased in the event that a head of state committed international crimes such as crimes against humanity. It further argued that the constitutive act of the tribunal itself waived immunity for a head of state and senior officials and thus the tribunal could exercise jurisdiction over the accused. President Hussain lost his appeal and the death penalty was confirmed. He was later executed. However, the value and legacy of the Saddam Hussain prosecution is tainted as the international community did not deem this tribunal to be upholding the values of a fair trial and there are allegations of procedural inconsistencies. The tribunal was accused of displaying victor's justice. Nevertheless, the ruling by the Iraqi Tribunal is in alignment with developments in international criminal law that international criminal tribunals may prosecute heads of states for the commission of international crimes and that in such cases immunity does not apply. However, owing to its composition the Iraqi High Tribunal is neither a foreign court nor a true international criminal tribunal; the court was composed of Iraqi judges and the trial took place in Iraq itself under Iraqi law. For these reasons it represents a problematic example.

Spain issued an arrest warrant against President Pinochet in response to the alleged commission of torture and torture-related crimes committed before and during his tenure in office.[91] President Pinochet was arrested in the United Kingdom in response to an extradition request by Spain to the United Kingdom while he was in England for medical reasons.[92] President Pinochet was tried in a domestic court of the United Kingdom.[93] The decision to try President Pinochet is therefore unique in that it contradicts the customary international law rule that prohibits the exercise of jurisdiction over a foreign head of state.[94] The question of the nature of President Pinochet's jurisdiction (whether absolute or functional) was indeed raised during the appeal case.[95] The House of Lords observed that international criminal law is evolving to the extent that certain categories of international crimes cannot be absolved from foreign prosecution.[96] The House of Lords, by a vote of six to one, concluded that President Pinochet did not enjoy immunity from extradition for some of the crimes in question, specifically torture.[97] The prohibition of torture is a norm of *ius cogens*.[98] The House of Lords reasoned that personal immunity did not extend to crimes which are in contravention of *ius cogens* norms and they are an exception to the general rule of customary international law that heads of state enjoy absolute immunity in a foreign jurisdiction.[99] This case, however, is an exception and evidence of subsequent practice by foreign courts relating to the prosecution of heads of state in foreign jurisdictions after their tenure in office is scarce or non-existent.[100]

For a translation of the Appellate Decision affirming the death sentence against Saddam Hussain see Saliba "Appellate Decision" https://www.loc.gov/law/help/hussein/appellate.php (2018-08-14); for a discussion of the case as it relates to the concept of sovereign immunity of President Hussain see Lee "Sovereign Immunity for Saddam? Not likely" (18 October 2005) https://www.jurist.org/commentary/2005/10/sovereign-immunity-for-saddam-not/ (2018-08-14); Semple "Saddam Hussein is Sentenced to Death" (5 November 2006) https://www.nytimes.com/2006/11/05/world/middleeast/05cnd-saddam.html (2018-08-16). For a summary of the trial see also "Saddam Hussain" (8 November 2016) https://trialinternational.org/latest-post/saddam-hussain/ (2018-08-16); and "Iraq, The Trial of Saddam Hussain" adapted from House of Commons Library, Research Paper 03/51 (3 June 2003) https://casebook.icrc.org/case-study/iraq-trial-saddam-hussein (2018-08-16).

91   Cassese et al (eds) (n 60) 79-88.

92   Cassese et al (eds) (n 60) 79-88.

93   *R v Bow Street Stipendiary Magistrate (Bartle) ex parte Pinochet Ugarte* (No.3) (n 88). For a summary of this case see Cassese et al (eds) (n 60) 79-88; of the Appellate Decision affirming the death Sentence against Sadam Hussain see Saliba (n 90); For another discussion, see Penrose "The Emperor's Clothes: Evaluating Head of State Immunity Under International Law" 2010 7 *Santa Clara Journal of International Law* 85-143.

94   Cassese et al (eds) (n 60) 79-88.

95   Cassese et al (eds) (n 60) 79-88.

96   Cassese et al (eds) (n 60) 79-88.

97   Cassese et al (eds) (n 60) 79-88.

98   See a 53 Vienna Convention on the Law of Treaties. Ultimately, however, President Pinochet was not extradited owing to medical reasons. See Cassese et al (eds) (n 60) 79-88.

99   Penrose (n 93) 85-143.

100 Compare *R v Bow Street Stipendiary Magistrate (Bartle) ex parte Pinochet Ugarte* (No.3) (n 88); for the Appellate Decision affirming the death sentence against Sadam Hussain see Saliba (n 90).

3.3.4 Prosecution and head of state immunity in international criminal tribunals

3.3.4.1 Head of state immunity and international customary law

The argument has been made that developments in international customary law are sufficient to establish an exception to the head of state immunity rule, in that a head of state is not protected if they have acted in violation of international criminal law and can thus be tried before an international court or tribunal.[101] This argument has been disputed[102] and will be tested in the form of a brief overview of the content of customary international law.[103] Article 38(1)(*b*) of the Statute of the International Court of Justice cites customary international law as a primary source of public international law[104] and refers to international custom as being "evidence of a general practice accepted as law".[105] The wording of this provision is significant as it encompasses the two requirements needed for a rule to attain customary international law status. First, "evidence of general practice" refers to what is termed the *usus* requirement[106] and, second, "accepted as law" refers to what is known as the *opinio juris* requirement.[107]

The *usus* requirement refers to the actual practice of states which is consistent with a rule of international law.[108] The *North Sea Continental Shelf* cases considered state practice as it relates to a relevant international law rule, including the practice of especially affected states, to be "extensive" and "virtually uniform".[109] In the *North Sea Continental Shelf* cases, the International Court of Justice summarised the *usus* requirement as the practice of a rule by a state that "should moreover have occurred in such a way as to show general recognition that a rule of law or obligation is involved".[110] During its sixty-fourth session, the International Law Commission

---

101 For a discussion of this development see Akande and Shah (n 79) 815-852; Orakshelashvili (n 79) 849-855.

102 Kiyani (n 60) 486-489.

103 For a more in-depth analysis of customary international law, see Cassese *International Law* (2005) 153-69; Goldsmith and Posner *The Limits of International Law* (2005) 21-82; Brownlie *Principles of Public International Law* (2008) 6-12; Shaw *International Law* (2008) 72-93; Damrosch, Henkin, Murphy and Smit *International Law: Cases and Materials* (2009) 59-121.

104 Statute of the International Court of Justice (ICJ Statute) (n 58).

105 Statute of the International Court of Justice (n 58).

106 Statute of the International Court of Justice (n 58), art 38(1)(*b*); see also Wood *First Report on Formation and Evidence of Customary International Law* International Law Commission, 65th session, Geneva, 6 May–7 June and 8 July–9 August 2013, A/CN.4/663, par 55.

107 Statute of the International Court of Justice (n 58), art 38(1)(*b*); Wood (n 106) par 55; Wood *Second Report on Identification of Customary International Law* 66th session, Geneva, 5 May–6 June and 7 July–8 August 2014, A/CN.4/672, par 14 fn 61.

108 Statute of the International Court of Justice (n 58), art 38(1)(*b*); Wood (n 106) par 55; Wood (n 107) par 14 fn 61.

109 *North Sea Continental Shelf Cases (Federal Republic of Germany v Denmark; Federal Republic of Germany v Netherlands)*, (Judgment) of 20 February 1969, [1969] ICJ Rep.3, par 74, 77, as cited in Wood (n 106) par 54.

110 *North Sea Continental Shelf Cases* (n 109) as cited in Wood (n 106) par 54.

considered the topic "Formation and evidence of customary international law".[111] Subsequently, the International Law Commission released four reports on the "formation and evidence of customary international law" under the guidance of Sir Michael Wood, the Special Rapporteur tasked with this mandate.[112] His reports provide insight into the formation of customary international law generally, and discuss the two requirements necessary to establish custom specifically, as well as giving evidence of the existence of these requirements.[113]

The Second ILC report on the identification of customary international law comments that *usus* (or a general practice) "[i]s the conduct of states which is of primary importance for the formation and identification of customary international law, and the material element of customary international law thus is commonly referred to as 'state practice', that is, conduct which is attributable to states".[114] Draft Conclusion 6 echoes this determination and regards state practice as conduct attributable to the state, irrespective of whether such practice is exercised by its executive, legislative, judicial or other function.[115] Draft Conclusion 9 determines that in order to be sufficient to establish a rule of customary international law, state practice must be "general" but need not be "universal", and it must be "generally consistent".[116] Draft conclusion 9 also determines that if the practice is sufficiently general and consistent, no particular duration is required for such a practice to be considered as *usus*.[117]

The second requirement, *opinio juris*, provides the psychological element of customary international law.[118] This requirement refers to the "subjective attitude" of a state: the fact that a state acts in compliance with a rule on the basis that it is of the opinion that it is legally obliged to do so, means that such a rule is then a rule of customary international law.[119] The International Court of Justice distinguishes customary international law from mere ceremonial acts or protocol where the intent is to adhere to a rule, not because of a belief that the state is under any legal obligation to do so but because such an action is motivated by considerations of courtesy or

---

111 Wood (n 106) par 1.

112 Wood (n 106) par 55. Wood (n 107); Wood *Third Report on Identification of Customary International Law*, International Law Commission, 67th session, Geneva, 4 May–5 June and 6 July–7 August 2015, A/CN.4/882; Wood *Fourth Report on Identification of Customary International Law*, International Law Commission, 68th session, Geneva, 2 May–10 June and 4 July–12 August 2016, A/CN.4/695 21.

113 Wood (n 106) par 55.

114 Wood (n 107) par 33.

115 Wood (n 107) par 37–47.

116 Wood (n 107) par 59.

117 Wood (n 107) par 59.

118 Wood (n 106), Wood (n 107) par 60.

119 Wood (n 106) par 69; *Military and Paramilitary Activities in and Against Nicaragua (Nicaragua v United States)*, Merits, (Judgment) of 27 June 1986 [1986] ICJ Rep 14, 103 par 207 as cited in Wood (n 106) par 58.

tradition.[120] In the *North Sea Continental Shelf* case, the International Court of Justice articulated the relationship between the *usus* and *opinio juris* requirements of international customary law as follows:

> Not only must the acts concerned amount to a settled practice ... but they must also be such or be carried out in such a way as to be evidence of a belief that this practice is rendered obligatory by the existence of a rule of law requiring it. The need for such a belief, i.e., the existence of a subjective element, is implicit in the very notion of the *opinio juris sive necessitatis*. The states concerned must therefore feel that they are conforming to what amounts to a legal obligation.[121]

In the *Nicaragua* case, the International Court of Justice articulated the *opinio juris* requirement as evidence of a belief that state practice is binding owing to the existence of an obligatory rule of law.[122] The International Court of Justice confirmed that it is the very need that requires such a belief which not only serves as evidence of the subjective requirement, but also that such a need is inherent in the very notion of *opinio juris sive necessitatis*.[123] In the more recent case of *Germany v Italy*, the Court formulated the test which determines whether the *opinio juris* requirement is satisfied as being the obligation imposed upon states by international law to abide with the rule in question.[124] The Second Report on the identification of customary international law eloquently phrases the *opinio juris* requirement as feeling "legally compelled to ... [perform the relevant act] by reason of a rule of customary law obliging them to do so".[125]

The analysis above provides insight into the requirements of *usus* and *opinio juris*, and demonstrates the symbiotic nature of these requirements:[126] both requirements are necessary to establish a rule of customary international law.[127] It is not in every case in which a court is faced with asserting the existence of a rule of customary international law that it endeavours to give a comprehensive analysis of both *usus* and *opinio juris*.[128] The case of *Germany v Italy* serves as an example where the

---

120 Wood (n 106) par 57, citing *North Sea Continental Shelf Cases* (n 109) par 74 77.

121 Wood (n 106) par 57, citing *North Sea Continental Shelf Cases* (n 109) par 74 77.

122 Wood (n 106) par 58, citing *Military and Paramilitary Activities in and Against Nicaragua (Nicaragua v United States)* (n 119) par 207.

123 Wood (n 106) par 58, citing *Military and Paramilitary Activities in and Against Nicaragua (Nicaragua v United States)* (n 119) par 207.

124 Jurisdictional Immunities of the State (*Germany v Italy*, (Judgment) of 3 February 2012 [2012] ICJ Rep 434, par 55).

125 Wood (n 107) par 60, 69. Draft Conclusion 10 of this report captures the purpose of *opinion juris*: "Role of acceptance as law: 1 The requirement, as an element of customary international law, that the general practice be accepted as law means that the practice in question must be accompanied by a sense of legal obligation. 2 Acceptance as law is what distinguishes a rule of customary international law from mere habit or usage."

126 Wood (n 107) par 3. The report describes these requirements as being "closely entangled".

127 Wood (n 107) par 31, page 14; Jurisdictional Immunities of the State (*Germany v Italy*) (n 124) par 55.

128 Wood (n 106) par 64 fn 122.

court analysed both *usus* and *opinio juris* in order to establish whether immunity was a rule of customary international law and, if immunity has indeed achieved customary international law status, what the extent of this rule would be.[129] There are other instances where the international court or tribunal merely acknowledged or announced the status of the rule without an explanation.[130] Some courts reason that a straightforward approach is used primarily if it is obvious or undisputed that a rule of law can indeed be categorised as a rule of customary international law.[131] This was the approach the International Court of Justice followed in the *Nicaragua* case when the Court proclaimed that Common Article 3 of the Geneva Conventions had attained customary international law status.[132]

3.3.4.2   The Nuremburg and Tokyo tribunals

There is some evidence in practice that immunity has been waived in regard to sitting heads of state, and former heads of states have been brought before an international tribunal as a result of the commission of the most serious international crimes. The first international criminal tribunal was the Nuremberg Tribunal, which was established to prosecute and punish those persons who acted in the interests of European Axis countries, for example Germany, and committed crimes against peace, war crimes and crimes against humanity during World War II.[133] Article 7 of the Nuremberg Charter explicitly waives head of state immunity in its words: "The official position of defendants, whether as heads of State, or responsible officials in Government departments, shall not be considered as freeing them from responsibility, or mitigating punishment."[134]

Arguably, this declaration in the Nuremberg Charter paved the way for future international tribunals to follow suit. In response to the arguments by the defence in the Nuremberg trials that the actions by the defendants were those of a sovereign state and protected by the doctrine of state sovereignty, the Nuremberg court confirmed that immunity was not a defence in the commission of international crimes. The court argued that individuals indeed could be punished for the violation of international law: "Crimes against international law are committed by men, not by abstract entities, and only by punishing individuals who commit such crimes

---

129   Jurisdictional Immunities of the State (*Germany v Italy*) (n 124) par 55; see also Wood (n 106) par 62.

130   Wood (n 106) par 64.

131   Wood (n 106) par 62, 64.

132   *Military and Paramilitary Activities in and Against Nicaragua (Nicaragua v United States)* (n 119) par 207, 218. Common Article 3 to the Geneva Conventions is a provision common to all four of the Geneva Conventions and provides obligations on both parties to a non-international armed conflict.

133   See The Charter and Judgment of the Nürnberg Tribunal – History and Analysis: Memorandum submitted by the Secretary-General, Topic: Formulation of the Nürnberg Principles http://www.cininas.lt/wp-content/uploads/2015/06/1949_UN_ILC_N_statuto_koment.pdf (2018-08-14), at 4 and also at 6 of the Nürnberg Charter (UN General Assembly, Formulation of the principles recognized in the Charter of the Nürnberg Tribunal and in the judgment of the Tribunal, 21 November 1947, A/RES/177).

134   UN General Assembly, Formulation of the principles recognized in the Charter of the Nürnberg Tribunal and in the judgment of the Tribunal (n 133).

can the provisions of international law be enforced."[135] The court further asserted: "The principle of international law, which under certain circumstances protects the representatives of a State, cannot be applied to acts which are condemned as criminal by international law. The authors of these acts cannot shelter themselves behind their official position in order to be freed from punishment in appropriate proceedings."[136] In addition to this argument, the court then referenced article 7 of its constitutive Charter.[137]

Similarly, the International Military Tribunal for the Far East (the Tokyo Tribunal), which was established by special proclamation of the Supreme Commander for the Allied Powers at Tokyo on January 1946, determined in article 6 of the Proclamation (Charter) that state officials could not rely on immunity to exempt them from the jurisdiction of the Tribunal.[138] Article 6 determined in respect of the responsibility of the accused:

> *Neither the official position*, at any time, of an accused, *nor the fact that an accused acted pursuant to order of his government or of a superior shall*, of itself, *be sufficient to free such accused from responsibility for any crime with which he is charged*, but such circumstances may be considered in mitigation of punishment if the Tribunal determines that justice so requires.[139]

3.3.4.3 *The special tribunals and courts*

Article 7(2) of The Statute of the International Tribunal for the Former Yugoslavia and article 6(2) of the Statute of the International Tribunal for Rwanda mimic the proclamations which abolish immunity before these tribunals: "The official position of any accused person, whether as Head of State or Government or as a responsible Government official, shall not relieve such person of criminal responsibility nor mitigate punishment."[140] The Statute of the Special Court for Sierra Leone explicitly states that an accused person cannot rely on immunity that attaches to his or her position or former position.[141] Article 6(2) of the Statute of the Special Court for

---

135 The Charter and Judgment of the Nürnberg Tribunal – History and Analysis: Memorandum (n 133) at page 42 citing UN General Assembly, Formulation of the principles recognized in the Charter of the Nürnberg Tribunal and in the judgment of the Tribunal (n 133) par 53.

136 The Charter and Judgment of the Nürnberg Tribunal – History and Analysis: Memorandum (n 133) at page 43 citing UN General Assembly, Formulation of the principles recognized in the Charter of the Nürnberg Tribunal and in the judgment of the Tribunal (n 133) par 53–54.

137 The Charter and Judgment of the Nürnberg Tribunal – History and Analysis: Memorandum (n 133) at page 43 citing UN General Assembly, Formulation of the principles recognized in the Charter of the Nürnberg Tribunal and in the judgment of the Tribunal (n 133) par 53–54.

138 The Special Proclamation for the Establishment of An International Military Tribunal For the Far East http://www.un.org/en/genocideprevention/documents/atrocity-crimes/Doc.3_1946%20Tokyo%20Charter.pdf (2018-08-14).

139 a 6 of The Special Proclamation for the Establishment of An International Military Tribunal For the Far East (n 138).

140 Statute of the International Criminal Tribunal for the former Yugoslavia (adopted 25 May 1993) UN Doc S/25704; Statute of the International Criminal Tribunal for Rwanda (adopted 8 November 1994) UN Doc SC/5974.

141 Statute of the Special Court for Sierra Leone (16 January 2002) 2178 UNTS 138.

Sierra Leone determines: "The official position of any accused persons, whether as Head of State or Government or as a responsible government official, shall not relieve such person of criminal responsibility nor mitigate punishment."

These examples of international criminal tribunals are not, *per se*, reflective of state practice. As has been explained, it is only the practice of states that is taken into account in the formation of customary international law. Therefore, if a tribunal is the creation of an international organisation, then the constitutive document does not serve as an example of state practice unless the constitutive document determines that the state itself is fully responsible for the tribunal.

A further question arises with regard to the definition of what constitutes an international criminal tribunal. The Special Court for Sierra Leone, for instance, was established by an Agreement between the United Nations and the Government of Sierra Leone pursuant to Security Council Resolution 1315 (2000) of 14 August 2000, on the basis of which the Security Council mandated the existence of this tribunal. However, the domestic law of Sierra Leone was ultimately applied, and the Sierra Leonean government agreed to establish the court. Consequently, it could be argued that the Agreement of Sierra Leone is a form of state practice, but that does not resolve the problem that this Special Tribunal is the product of a Security Council Resolution. It is difficult to establish which of these statutes, if any, may be considered state practice.

The International Tribunal for the Former Yugoslavia arguably is a truly international criminal tribunal and thus article 7(2) cannot be viewed as a manifestation of state practice, as the International Tribunal for the Former Yugoslavia was established by the Security Council acting under its Chapter VII powers afforded to it by the Charter of the United Nations.[142] On the other hand, the International Tribunal for Rwanda was established by the Security Council under Chapter VII of the United Nations, but in response to a request by the government of Rwanda.[143] The request

---

142 See preamble to the Statute of the International Tribunal for the Former Yugoslavia adopted 25 May 1993 by Resolution 827. "Having been established by the Security Council acting under Chapter VII of the Charter of the United Nations, the International Tribunal for the Prosecution of Persons Responsible for Serious Violations of International Humanitarian Law Committed in the Territory of the Former Yugoslavia since 1991 (hereinafter referred to as 'the International Tribunal') shall function in accordance with the provisions of the present Statute."; Charter of the United Nations (adopted 26 June 1945, entered into force 24 October 1945) ATS 1 (UN Charter).

143 Statute of the Special Court for Sierra Leone (16 January 2002) 2178 UNTS 138: "*Acting under Chapter VII of the Charter of the United Nations*, 1.Decides hereby, having *received the request of the Government of Rwanda (S/1994/1115), to establish an international tribunal* for the sole purpose of prosecuting persons responsible for genocide and other serious violations of international humanitarian law committed in the territory of Rwanda and Rwandan citizens responsible for genocide and other such violations committed in the territory of neighbouring states, between 1 January 1994 and 31 December 1994 and to this end to adopt the Statute of the International Criminal Tribunal for Rwanda annexed hereto." And preamble to Statute: "Having been established by the Security Council acting under Chapter VII of the Charter of the United Nations, the International Criminal Tribunal for the Prosecution of Persons Responsible for Genocide and Other Serious Violations of International Humanitarian Law Committed in the Territory of Rwanda and Rwandan Citizens responsible for genocide and other such violations committed in the territory of neighbouring States, between 1 January 1994 and 31 December 1994 (hereinafter referred

determined that an international tribunal should be established. It is uncertain whether the consent of the state in establishing the tribunal supports the argument that article 6(2) of the Statue of the International Criminal Tribunal for Rwanda is a manifestation of state practice. The Nuremberg and Tokyo Tribunals are international in nature; the Tokyo Tribunal, moreover, was established not by the United Nations Security Council but by General Douglas MacArthur, General of the army of the United States in his capacity as the Supreme Commander for the Allied Powers. He held this authority under the Terms of Surrender agreed upon between Japan and the governments of the United States, Great Britain and Russia.[144]

In *The Minister of Justice and Constitutional Development v The Southern African Litigation Centre*,[145] also known as the Al-Bashir Appeals Judgment, the Supreme Court of Appeal of South Africa considered whether a customary international law rule existed that determined that state officials do not have immunity before an international criminal tribunal in the commission of international crimes.[146] After a thorough analysis of available jurisprudence, the Supreme Court of Appeal of South Africa came to the conclusion that there is no such rule. The judgment emphasised that state practice should be taken into account and not the practice of international criminal tribunals. This ruling is evidence that in the state practice of the Republic of South Africa there is no rule of customary international law of this nature.[147] The Supreme Court of Appeal held:

> But the content of customary international law is not for me to determine and, like Dr Weatherall, I must conclude with regret that it would go too far to say that there is no longer any sovereign immunity for jus cogens (immutable norm) violations. Consideration of the cases and the literature goes no further than showing that Professor Dugard is correct when he says that 'customary international law is in a state of flux in respect of immunity, both criminal and civil, for acts of violation of norms of jus cogens'. In those circumstances I am unable to hold that at this stage of the development of

---

to as 'The International Tribunal for Rwanda') shall function in accordance with the provisions of the present Statute."

144 Special proclamation by the Supreme Commander tor the Allied Powers at Tokyo, 19 January 1946; charter dated 19 January 1946; amended charter dated 26 April 1946: "Article 1. There shall be established an International Military Tribunal for the Far East for the trial of those persons charged individually, or as members of organizations, or in both capacities, with offenses which include crimes against peace."

145 2016 3 SA 317 (SCA).

146 *Minister of Justice and Constitutional Development v The Southern African Litigation Centre* (n 145) at par 68–84. Citing par 68: "Dating back to the instrument that established the Nuremberg Trials, it has been a feature of international instruments dealing with the prosecution of international crimes before specially constituted international tribunals, that those tribunals are constituted on the basis of specific provisions excluding claims of immunity as a defence or mitigating circumstance before those tribunals. The ICJ considered these as well (par 58) and found that they likewise did not enable it to conclude that any such exception existed in customary international law in regard to national Courts. But it was urged upon us that customary international law has moved on and at least when it was concerned with international crimes and international tribunals such as the ICC these principles were subject to an exception."

147 Compare Wood (n 106).

customary international law there is an international crimes exception to the immunity and inviolability that heads of state enjoy when visiting foreign countries and before foreign national Courts.[148]

Contrary to this discussion, and against the ruling in *The Minister of Justice and Constitutional Development v The Southern African Litigation Centre*, some authors opine that a rule exists under customary international law that head of state immunity cannot be relied upon as a bar to the jurisdiction of an international criminal tribunal in the event that an official is charged with the commission of international crimes.[149] Other authors agree that there is simply not enough practice which supports the existence of a rule in relation to the immunity of heads of state in front of an international criminal tribunal.[150] The authors of this chapter share the view that, at present, customary international law neither clearly supports the view that immunity precludes the prosecution of heads of state by an international criminal tribunal for the commission of international crimes, nor does it support the prosecution of heads by waiving head of state immunity.[151] There is simply not sufficient state practice to support either theory.[152]

In order to establish a way to hold heads of state responsible for the violation of international crimes (especially if the state is not a party to the Rome Statute), it is helpful, for purposes of this chapter, that the United Nations Security Council under Chapter VII can act as it did in the case of the International Criminal Tribunal for the Former Yugoslavia. In that instance, the United Nations established an international criminal tribunal which could prosecute those who are responsible for the commission of crimes within a territory, including high-ranking officials such as a head of state.[153] Equally, the United Nations Security Council can act at the request of a state under Chapter VII, as occurred following the Rwandan genocide where it established the International Criminal Tribunal for Rwanda.

3.3.5 Prosecution and head of state immunity in the International Criminal Court

The Rome Statute of the International Criminal Court is a treaty which establishes the International Criminal Court,[154] the purpose of which is to exercise jurisdiction

---

148 *Minister of Justice and Constitutional Development v The Southern African Litigation Centre* (n 145) par 84.

149 *Minister of Justice and Constitutional Development v The Southern African Litigation Centre* (n 145); Kiyani (n 60) 486-489.

150 Kiyani (n 60) 486-489; Tladi "Separating the (Doctrinal) Wheat from the (Normative) Chaff" 2015 13 *Journal of International Criminal Justice* 3-17.

151 Compare Tladi (n 150) 3-17; *Minister of Justice and Constitutional Development v The Southern African Litigation Centre* (n 145).

152 Charter of the United Nations (n 142) at chapter VII and article 103.

153 Charter of the United Nations (n 142) at chapter VII and article 103; De Wet *The Chapter VII Powers of the United Nations Security Council* (2004).

154 Rome Statute of the International Criminal Court (n 56) a 1.

over the most serious international crimes as listed in article 5 of its Statute. The crimes within the jurisdiction of the Court are genocide,[155] crimes against humanity,[156] war crimes[157] and the crime of aggression.[158] The Rome Statute specifically determines that persons cannot rely on any form of immunity conferred upon them either by national or international law if the state of which such a person is a national is a signatory to the Rome Statute.[159] Simply put, article 27 determines that signatories to the Rome Statute consent that head of state immunity, and the immunity of other members of government, are waived in terms of the Rome Statute. The International Criminal Court is thus a forum in which a head of state may be brought to justice for the commission of international crimes if the jurisdictional requirements as set out in the Rome Statute have been satisfied.[160] This section explores article 27 in detail and considers the possibility that heads of non-member states can also be prosecuted by this court.

3.3.5.1 *Article 27 of the Rome Statute*

To avoid any dispute arising in terms of customary international law, the drafters of the Rome Statute explicitly waived all forms of immunity in declaring all persons equal before the International Criminal Court, so that no one can claim immunity in respect of official capacity in order to escape prosecution if the court has jurisdiction over the accused's case.[161] Customary international law may be altered by state parties if they agree to a higher legal standard, in that heads of state do not enjoy immunity before international criminal tribunals for the commission of international crimes, or to incur greater legal obligations owing to acceptance of a stricter rule under treaty law. The nature or content of head of state immunity under customary international law, for purposes of the application of the Rome Statute to member states, is irrelevant as article 27 regulates immunity. Article 27 of the Rome Statute reads as follows:

> Irrelevance of Official Capacity
>
> 1. This Statute shall apply equally to all persons without any discrimination based on official capacity. In particular, *official capacity as a Head of State or Government*, a member of a Government or parliament, an elected representative or a government official *shall in no case exempt a person from criminal responsibility under this Statute*, nor shall it, in and of itself, constitute a ground for reduction of sentence.

---

155 Rome Statute of the International Criminal Court (n 56) a 6.

156 Rome Statute of the International Criminal Court (n 56) a 7.

157 Rome Statute of the International Criminal Court (n 56) a 8.

158 Rome Statute of the International Criminal Court (n 56) a 8*bis*.

159 Rome Statute of the International Criminal Court (n 56) a 27.

160 Rome Statute of the International Criminal Court (n 56) aa 11, 12, 13, 14.

161 Rome Statute of the International Criminal Court (n 56) a 27.

2. Immunities or special procedural rules which may attach to the official capacity of a person, *whether under national or international law*, shall not bar the Court from exercising its jurisdiction over such a person.[162]

Furthermore, the Rome Statute of the International Criminal Court does not allow for any reservations,[163] and therefore member states are bound by the entire treaty.[164] All member states, upon signature or ratification of this instrument, depending on whether the state is monist or dualist, waive head of state and other forms of immunity.[165] The meaning and purpose of article 27(1) clearly supports the view that states consenting to the jurisdiction of the Rome Statute cannot raise immunity in order to protect a head of state from the jurisdiction of this court.[166] Article 27(2) of the Rome Statute confirms that any immunities or special procedural rules which attach to a person owing to their official capacity, for instance the capacity of head of state under national or international law, will not apply in this court. Thus, both sitting and former heads of state have absolutely no special privileges or immunities acting as a bar to the jurisdiction of the International Criminal Court. At present, there are 123 member states to the Rome Statute, 33 of which are on the African continent. The heads of these states do not have immunity before the International Criminal Court.[167]

Article 27 is crucial to eliminating impunity in the commission of international crimes.[168] The core international crimes included in article 5 of the Rome Statute are of such a nature that governmental authorities often play a role in the commission of these crimes, for instance systematic crimes such as genocide and war crimes. It is the purpose of the International Criminal Court to punish those individuals who should be held most responsible for serious crimes of international concern. It is not the purpose of the International Criminal Court to prosecute low-ranking officials; high-ranking officials such as military leaders, heads of state or the most senior officials of organised armed groups or opposition groups are those that should be prosecuted under the Rome Statute. This objective is achievable only because of article 27.

---

162 Emphasis added.

163 Rome Statute of the International Criminal Court (n 56) a 120.

164 For the rules pertaining to reservations see Vienna Convention on the Law of Treaties (adopted 23 May 1969, entered into force 27 January 1980) 1155 UNTS 331 (Vienna Convention) a 19.

165 A 27 read together with a 120, Rome Statute of the International Criminal Court, 1998 2187 UNTS 90.

166 Triffterer and Ambos *Rome Statute of the International Criminal Court: A Commentary* (2016) 1037-1055. See a 31 of the United Nations, Vienna Convention on the Law of Treaties (n 164). For a discussion on the general rules of treaty interpretation see Sorel and Bore "Article 21: Convention of 1969" in Corten and Klein *The Vienna Convention on the Law of Treaties: A commentary, Volume I* (2011) 804-837.

167 For an up-to-date list of the ICC member states see https://asp.icc-cpi.int/en_menus/asp/states%20parties/ Pages/the%20states%20parties%20to%20the%20rome%20statute.aspx (2018-08-14).

168 Rome Statute of the International Criminal Court (n 56).

3.3.5.2   *Article 98 of the Rome Statute*

In order for the International Criminal Court to operate effectively, the cooperation of member states, as well as judicial assistance, is required.[169] Member states of the Rome Statute are obliged to cooperate with the International Criminal Court in relation to the investigations conducted by the court as well as in the prosecution of crimes which fall within the jurisdiction of the court.[170] In order to carry out its task, the International Criminal Court may use diplomatic channels to request cooperation from member states. Such cooperation includes a request for the arrest and surrender of a person on the territory of a member state. However, a request for cooperation may not be made if such a request infringes upon the international obligations of the requesting state in relation to the waiver of immunity. Article 98 determines that

1. The Court may not proceed with a request for surrender or assistance which would require the requested State to act inconsistently with its obligations under international law with respect to the State or diplomatic immunity of a person or property of *a third state*, unless the Court *can first obtain the cooperation of that third State for the waiver of the immunity*.

2. The Court *may not proceed with a request for surrender* which would require the requested State to act inconsistently with its obligations under international agreements pursuant to which the consent of a sending State is required to surrender a person of that State to the Court, unless the Court can first obtain the cooperation of the sending State for the giving of consent for the surrender...[171]

Article 98 confirms the applicability of the third-party rule, which is a rule of customary international treaty law codified in article 34 of the Vienna Convention on the Law of Treaties. Article 34 determines that a "treaty does not create either obligations or rights for a third State without its consent". A unique relationship exists between article 27 and article 98 of the Rome Statute in respect of the waiver of immunity. Only states which consent (for example by becoming member states of the Rome Statute) waive official immunity, including head of state immunity. Non-state parties cannot incur such an obligation as it would automatically be invalid in terms of the third-party rule.

Article 98 reiterates this rule, but determines that a state may exercise jurisdiction over an official, for instance the head of a non-member state, if that third state (the non-member state) consents to waive immunity. Therefore, in this manner such a third state, through agreement, does not incur obligations to which it did not consent.

---

169   Part 9L International Cooperation and Judicial Assistance articles 86–98 Rome Statute of the International Criminal Court (n 56).

170   See Rome Statute of the International Criminal Court (n 56) a 86.

171   Emphasis added.

The International Criminal Court cannot expect member states to cooperate in the investigation, arrest or prosecution of officials of third states (for instance, the head of state of a non-member (third) state) as to do so would cause the member state to violate its obligations under general international law. Similarly, a member state to the Rome Statute cannot be asked to surrender for instance the head of state of a third state if the International Criminal Court did not first secure the consent of the sending state to the surrender. A non-member state, however, in response to a request from the International Criminal Court can consent to the court's jurisdiction under article 12(3)[172] of the Rome Statute and specifically waive the immunity of the official in question. As a result of the consent theory, such an individual loses his immunity and the court is enabled to investigate the case and arrest and prosecute an accused. This is possible as the third state's consent to waive immunity (including for example head of state immunity) would bar the infraction of the third-party rule and obviate the cooperating member state from violating international law. The referral of the situation in Sudan (a state which is not a party to the Rome Statute), by the Security Council of the United Nations to the International Criminal Court on 31 March 2005 as a consequence of events in Darfur which continued as of 1 July 2002, highlights that the value of article 98 arguably is more contentious than a plain reading of the text.[173] Alternative interpretations have been offered in response to South Africa's failure to arrest President Al-Bashir when he visited South Africa in June 2015.[174]

The non-arrest of Al-Bashir opened what amounts to a 'Pandora's box' in terms of legal arguments in relation to what is often referred to as the strained relationship between articles 27 and 98 of the Rome Statute and to the content and nature of article 98.[175] A central legal issue that was raised in relation to the content of

---

172 Rome Statute of the International Criminal Court (n 56) a 12(3): "If the acceptance of a State which is not a Party to this Statute is required under paragraph 2, that State may, by declaration lodged with the Registrar, accept the exercise of jurisdiction by the Court with respect to the crime in question. The accepting State shall cooperate with the Court without any delay or exception in accordance with Part 9."

173 See Resolution UNSC 1593 (2005) "Acting under Chapter VII of the Charter of the United Nations, 1. Decides to refer the situation in Darfur since 1 July 2002 to the Prosecutor of the International Criminal Court...". For a discussion on the legal nature of Security Council referrals to the ICC see Akande "The Legal Nature of Security Council Referrals to the ICC and its Impact on Al-Bashir's Immunities" 2009 7 *Journal of International Criminal Justice* 333-352 and De Wet "Referrals to the International Criminal Court under Chapter VII of the United Nations Charter and the Immunity of Foreign State Officials" 2018 112 *AJIL Unbound* 33-37.

174 See *Southern Africa Litigation Centre v Minister of Justice and Constitutional Development & Others* 2015 5 SA 1 (GP) and *The Minister of Justice and Constitutional Development v The Southern African Litigation Centre* (n 145); see also Tladi "Interpretation and International law in South African courts: The Supreme Court of Appeal and the Al-Bashir saga" 2016 *African Human Rights Law Journal* 310-338; Akande "The Bashir Case: Has the South African Supreme Court Abolished Immunity for all Heads of State?" (29 March 2016) www.ejiltalk.org/the-bashir-case-has-the-south-african-supreme-court-abolished-immunity-for-all-heads-of-states/ (2018-07-20).

175 The following scholarly articles offer several arguments concerning the interpretation of article 98 as well as the relationship between article 27 and 98 in context of the Al-Bashir saga: Kiyani (n 60) 467-508; Gaeta (n 60) 315-332; Tladi "Cooperation, Immunities, and Article 98 of the Rome Statute: The ICC, Interpretation, and Conflicting Norms" 2012 106 *Am. Soc'y Int'l L. Proc* 307-308; Tladi (n 60) 17-44; Triffterer and Ambos (n 166) 2119-2146.

article 98 of the Rome Statute, following the failure of a member state (in this case South Africa, to arrest President Al-Bashir) concerns whether or not article 98 of the Rome Statute can be interpreted as obliging a member state to arrest the head of state of a non-member state which did not consent to the jurisdiction of the International Criminal Court, but in a situation in which there is a Security Council referral and an arrest warrant subsequently issued.[176] As the Al-Bashir case and the interpretation of article 98 have been discussed in great depth, this topic is not given further attention. At this juncture, it should be mentioned that the exact meaning of article 98 is yet to be settled.[177]

3.3.6 Prosecution and head of state immunity in the African Court of Justice and Human Rights

The Protocol on Amendments to the Protocol (the Malabo Protocol) was adopted by the African Union (AU) to amend the Protocol on the Statute of the African Court of Justice and Human Rights.[178] In terms of this Protocol, a separate criminal chamber is constituted which extends the jurisdiction of the yet-to-be-established African Court of Justice and Human Rights (ACJHR) to a closed list of international and

---

176 Compare *Southern Africa Litigation Centre v Minister of Justice and Constitutional Development* (n 174) and *The Minister of Justice and Constitutional Development v The Southern African Litigation Centre* (n 145).

177 See also Akande "An International Court of Justice Advisory Opinion on the ICC Head of State Immunity Issue" (31 March 2016) www.ejiltalk.org/an-international-court-of-justice-advisory-opinion-on-the-icc-head-of-state-immunity-issue/ (2018-07-15); De Hoogh and Knottnerus "ICC Issues New Decision on Al-Bashir's Immunities – But Gets the Law Wrong ... Again" (18 April 2014) www.ejiltalk.org/icc-iccues-new-decision-on-al-bashirs-immunities-but-gets-the-law-wrong-again/ (2018-07-15); Akande (n 60) 407-433; see also *In The Case of The Prosecutor v Omar Hassan Ahmad Al-Bashir* "Request by Prof. Flavia Lattanzi for leave to submit observations on the merits of the legal questions presented in The Hashemite Kingdom of Jordan's appeal against the 'Decision under article 87(7) of the Rome Statute on the non-compliance by Jordan with the request by the Court for the arrest and surrender [of] Omar Al-Bashir'" of 12 March 2018 Appeals Chamber, case no ICC-02/05-01/09 OA2 (30 April 2018), Dapo Akande, *The Bashir Appeal at the ICC* (10 September 2018) https://www.ejiltalk.org/the-bashir-appeal-at-the-icc/#more-16466 (2018-11-19), Talita de Souza Dias *The 'Security Council Route' to the Derogation from Personal Head of State Immunity in the Al-Bashir Case: How Explicit must Security Council Resolutions be?* (19 September 2018) https://www.ejiltalk.org/the-discussion-of-the-security-council-roots-to-the-derogation-from-personal-immunities-in-the-al-bashir-case-how-explicit-must-security-council-resolutions-be/#more-16485 (2018-11-28), Alexandre Skander Galand *Looking for Middle Ground on the Immunity of Al-Bashir? Take the Third 'Security Council Route'* (23 October 2018) https://www.ejiltalk.org/looking-for-middle-ground-on-the-immunity-of-al-bashir-take-the-third-security-council-route/#more-16572 (2018-11-19). Dapo Akande and Talita de Souza Dias *Does the ICC Statute Remove Immunities of State Officials in National Proceedings? Some Observations from the Drafting History of Article 27(2) of the Rome Statute* (12 November 2018) https://www.ejiltalk.org/does-the-icc-statute-remove-immunities-of-state-officials-in-national-proceedings-some-observations-from-the-drafting-history-of-article-272-of-the-rome-statute/#more-16638 (2018-11-19).

178 Protocol on Amendments to the Protocol on the statute of the African Court of Justice and Human Rights. For a general discussion on the Malabo protocol as well as the immunity provision (art 46A*Bis*) see Tladi "Chapter 12: Immunities (Article 46A*Bis*)" in Werle and Vormbaum (eds) *The African Criminal Court: A commentary on the Malabo Protocol* (2017) 203-217; Van Schaack "Immunity Before the African Court of Justice & Human & Peoples rights – The Potential Outlier" (10 July 2010) www.justsecurity.org/12732/immunity-african-court-justice-human-peoples-rights-the-potential-outlier/ (2018-07-13); Abebe "The African Court with a criminal jurisdiction and the ICC: a case for overlapping jurisdiction?" 2017 25 3 *African Journal of International and Comparative Law* 418-429.

transnational crimes.[179] The original purpose of the ACJHR was to establish a court with two sections, one for general affairs and one focusing on human rights.[180] The Malabo Protocol introduces a third chamber or section to the existing structure of the Court. The jurisdiction of this third section, the criminal division of the ACJHR, is restricted to the crimes listed in article 28 of the Malabo Protocol,[181] as well as being limited to member states of the AU that have signed or ratified the Malabo Protocol.[182] To date, only five states have ratified this treaty and 15 ratifications are needed for the court to be established. Only when the requirement of 15 ratifications has been met will ACJHR serve as an African Regional Criminal Court.

It has been suggested that the strained relationship between the ICC and the AU prompted the adoption of the Malabo Protocol. However, there is evidence that an African criminal court delivering justice in an African manner had been discussed at an earlier stage.[183] There are core differences in the make-up of the two instruments, including a regional-specific scope for the ACJHR, the extended list of crimes in the Malabo Protocol and, significantly, the restatement of immunity for sitting heads of state under the Malabo Protocol.[184] There may be overlapping jurisdiction with the Rome Statute, but a discussion on that falls outside the scope of the current contribution.[185]

3.3.6.1 Article 46Bis

"*No charges* shall be commenced or continued before the Court *against any serving AU Head of State or Government*, or anybody acting or entitled to act in such capacity, or other senior state officials *based on their functions, during their tenure of* office."[186] Article 46A*Bis* of the Malabo Protocol, or the so-called immunity clause, is considered the most controversial provision in this treaty[187] as it confers immunity upon sitting heads of state.[188] The ACJHR is unable to prosecute sitting heads of member states to this treaty for the alleged commission of crimes listed under article 28 of the Malabo Protocol. The African Union holds the opinion that

---

179 For a discussion of the Malabo Protocol see the detailed report by Amnesty International, *Malabo Protocol: Legal and Institutional Implications of the Merged and Expanded African Court* Amnesty International 2016.

180 Protocol on The Statute of the African Court of Justice and Human Rights; *Malabo Protocol: Legal and Institutional Implications of the Merged and Expanded African Court* Amnesty International 2016 5.

181 See also *Malabo Protocol* (n 180) 5.

182 The *Malabo Protocol* has been signed by 30 states but ratified by only 5 states.

183 *Malabo Protocol* (n 180) 6 22.

184 *Malabo Protocol* (n 180) 5.

185 *Malabo Protocol* (n 180) 22.

186 *Malabo Protocol*, Article 46A*Bis* (emphasis added).

187 *Malabo Protocol* (n 180) 26.

188 *No charges* shall be commenced or continued before the Court *against any serving AU Head of State or Government*, or anybody acting or entitled to act in such capacity, or other senior state officials *based on their functions, during their tenure of office*.

this provision is merely a manifestation of existing customary international law.[189] The adoption of this provision however is contrary to contemporary trends in international criminal tribunals, for instance the Special Court of Sierra Leone,[190] the International Criminal Tribunal for the Former Yugoslavia[191] and the International Criminal Tribunal for Rwanda,[192] in which immunity for heads of state was not a measure included in these tribunals' constitutive treaties.[193] It is argued that the provision of this measure would have strengthened the hand of those fighting to eliminate impunity in respect of international crimes on the African Continent.[194]

On an initial reading, article 46ABis offers not only functional but absolute immunity to heads of state.[195] The wording "[n]o charges shall be commenced or continued" conforms to the general approach that during their tenure heads of state enjoy absolute immunity.[196] Some authors have suggested that this provision is poorly drafted and that a more restricted form of immunity is envisaged based on the latter part of the provision.[197] The structure of the sentence may be ambiguous. Nevertheless, the wording *"based on their functions, during their tenure of office"* logically refers to the immunity which attaches to "other" state officials, that is, state officials other than heads of state.[198] A textual interpretation of the wording "[n]o charges shall be commenced or continued" in conjunction with article 31(1) of the Vienna Convention on the Law of Treaties is of assistance. The key is the word "no". "No" is negative, the rejection of an idea,[199] and can be replaced by "'not any'[200] charges shall be commenced or continued before the Court against any serving AU Head of State or Government". As the wording forbids any charges, it can be construed that immunity is not limited to covering the official acts of a head of state but is absolute in its application.[201]

---

189 Some members of the drafting committee disputed this assertion. See The Report, the Draft Legal Instruments and Recommendations of the Specialized Technical Committee on Justice and Legal Affairs, Malabo, Equatorial Guinea, 20-24 June 2014, Ex.Cl/846 (XXV), par 25. See also *Malabo Protocol* (n 180) 26.

190 Statute of the Special Court for Sierra Leone (16 January 2002) 2178 UNTS 138.

191 Statute of the International Criminal Tribunal for the former Yugoslavia (adopted 25 May 1993) UN Doc S/25704.

192 Statute of the International Criminal Tribunal for Rwanda (adopted 8 November 1994) UN Doc SC/5974.

193 For a discussion see *Malabo Protocol* (n 180) 27.

194 *Malabo Protocol* (n 180) 27.

195 *No charges* shall be commenced or continued before the Court *against any serving AU Head of State or Government,* or anybody acting or entitled to act in such capacity, or other senior state officials *based on their functions, during their tenure of office.*

196 Protocol on Amendments to the Protocol on the statute of the African Court of Justice and Human Rights, at a 46ABis.

197 Protocol on Amendments to the Protocol on the statute of the African Court of Justice and Human Rights.

198 Protocol on Amendments to the Protocol on the statute of the African Court of Justice and Human Rights, at a 46ABis.

199 O'Niell and Summers (eds) *Collins English Thesaurus* (2015) 573.

200 O'Niell and Summers (eds) (n 199) 531.

201 Protocol on Amendments to the Protocol on the statute of the African Court of Justice and Human Rights, at a 46ABis.

This interpretation of the text is in alignment with the context of this provision which is directed towards buttressing the immunity of heads of state before the African Court of Justice and Human Rights.[202] Furthermore, it is unlikely that the African Union will prosecute a sitting head of state as it supports the principle of sovereignty and has condemned the actions of the International Criminal Court in issuing arrest warrants against sitting heads of states. A reason offered for the general condemnation is that the ICC breached the absolute immunity a head of state enjoys in terms of the African Union's interpretation of immunity.[203] The established interpretation of article 46A*Bis* read together with article 28 of the Malabo Protocol is that sitting heads of state enjoy absolute immunity before the ACJHR, irrespective of whether the alleged crime committed is one of the core crimes (aggression, genocide, torture, crimes against humanity and war crimes).

Article 46A*Bis* confers immunity upon sitting heads of state and protects them from prosecution by the ACJHR. It is unclear if article 46A*Bis* is a regional solution, holding ex-heads of state of states signatory to the Malabo Protocol responsible for the commission of crimes codified in the Malabo Protocol once this instrument has been ratified by a sufficient number of states. An ordinary reading of article 46*Bis* as provided for by article 31(1) of the Vienna Convention on the Law of Treaties suggests that former or retired heads of state may be brought before the African Court of Justice and Human Rights.

In the context of article 46A*Bis*, the term "serving" means "to be of service" or to "perform an official duty or duties".[204] Thus, a serving head of state refers to a person (a head of state) who performs the duties of head of state in an official capacity.[205] The verb in the provision is in the present tense, therefore, arguably, the immunity offered is restricted to serving heads of states and cannot be used by retired, incapacitated or former heads of state. The favoured reading may be that as the reference is purely to the functional immunity attached to the office, the meaning remains open to interpretation. The interpretation of the wording depends on whether the provision is read as entailing absolute immunity for heads of state while in office, or if heads of states enjoy merely functional immunity. It depends on article 46*Bis* being seen as having either one or two parts. Also, this provision may afford sitting heads of states absolute immunity for any alleged crimes codified in article 28 of the Malabo

---

202 See Vienna Convention on the Law of Treaties (n 164) at a 31(1) concerning the primary rules of treaty interpretation. For a discussion on treaty interpretation see in general Linderfalk *On the Interpretation of Treaties: The Modern International Law as Expressed in the 1969 Vienna Convention of the Law of Treaties* (2001); Linderfalk *On the Interpretation of Treaties: The Modern International Law as Expressed in the 1969 Vienna Convention on the Law of Treaties* (2007); Sorel and Bore "Article 31: Convention of 1969" in Corten and Klein (eds) (n 166).

203 It is so that the disdain between the AU and ICC is far more complex and this is but one of the reasons offered by the AU.

204 O'Niell and Summers (eds) (n 199) 728. Compare article 46*Bis* (emphasis added): *No charges* shall be commenced or continued before the Court *against any serving AU Head of State or Government*, or anybody acting or entitled to act in such capacity, or other senior state officials *based on their functions, during their tenure of office.*

205 See also O'Niell and Summers (eds) (n 199) 773.

Protocol, whereas other state officials are limited to having functional immunity. This is a possible reading where the second part of the sentence is viewed as a separate idea split by the comma "or other senior state officials (shall not incur immunity) *based on their functions, during their tenure of office*".[206]

It further remains unanswered if the type of crimes listed under article 28 of the Malabo Protocol ever can be reconciled with the exercise of the normal functions of a head of state. Certain crimes simply are not part of the functions of a head of state. For instance, the illicit exploitation of natural resources or money laundering may be covered by functional immunity if these offences are performed during the office of a president, whereas crimes which contravene norms of *ius cogens*, for instance torture or genocide, may not be covered by functional immunity.[207] These issues fall beyond the scope of this chapter, but they nevertheless require clarification.

As the ordinary meaning of the terms has not clarified what is meant by the content of this provision, which is still obscure, the drafting history can be consulted as a subsidiary means of interpretation.[208] Unfortunately, the drafting history of article 46A*Bis* fails to be of assistance since the drafters have expressed opposing views of the content of the customary rule of head of state immunity before an international criminal tribunal.[209] If such a court ever becomes a reality, the task will fall on it to clarify the extent of the immunity offered to former heads of state.[210] It seems possible under article 46A*Bis* that former heads of state may be prosecuted, at least for the core international crimes. Even this possibility is diminished by the fact that on the African continent some leaders have been in power for so many years that prosecution may not be possible and may not provide victims of international crimes relief in their lifetime knowing that justice has been served.

3.4   CONCLUSION

In the first part of this chapter, the authors explored the domestic accountability mechanisms that states may employ to keep heads of state responsible and accountable in South Africa and other African countries. In the course of this discussion, it became evident that most of these accountability mechanisms in the countries under discussion lack the effectiveness that is necessary to keep a proper check on their heads of state. The measure of having an ombudsperson, for example,

---

206 *No charges shall be commenced or continued before the Court against* any serving AU Head of State or Government, or anybody acting or entitled to act in such capacity, *or other senior state officials based on their functions, during their tenure of office*. Wording added to Protocol on Amendments to the Protocol on the statute of the African Court of Justice and Human Rights, at a 46A*Bis*.

207 Compare Knuchel (n 60) 149-183; Caplan (n 60) 741-781.

208 See Vienna Convention on the Law of Treaties (n 164) at art 32. For guidance on the operation of article 32 see Le Bouthillier "Article 32: Convention of 1969" in Corten and Klein (eds) (n 166).

209 See The Report, the Draft Legal Instruments and Recommendations of the Specialized Technical Committee on Justice and Legal Affairs, Malabo, Equatorial Guinea, 20-24 June 2014, Ex.Cl/846 (XXV).

210 For a discussion on the relationship between *ius cogens* crimes and the doctrine of head of state immunity see Knuchel (n 60) 149-183; Caplan (n 60) 741-781.

is not effective in many African countries because the decisions of these institutions often are not binding. In the South African context, the courts have resolved the uncertainty with regard to the binding nature of the decisions and remedial action prescribed by the Public Protector. This means, at least in the South African context, a head of state could be held accountable by the Public Protector and is obliged to comply with remedial action recommended by the Public Protector. The Zambian Public Protector is another example of a more effective ombudsperson-like institution, since it also has the authority to enforce its remedial action. In contrast, in the Namibian context the Namibian Ombudsman's decisions are not binding, but an alternative dispute resolution procedure is followed. The effectiveness of this measure is questionable since the executive organs involved might be unwilling to negotiate – leaving the Ombudsman without any recourse. In Zimbabwe, the office of Zimbabwean Public Protector has been replaced by a Human Rights Commission, which also is not necessarily the best route to follow for the investigation of governmental maladministration. It is therefore submitted that heads of state and members of the executive authority that contravene the law will be kept responsible and accountable only by ombudsperson-institutions if their decisions are made binding and enforceable by means of appropriate legislative measures.

With regard to motions of no-confidence and impeachment proceedings against heads of state it is submitted that these important mechanisms often are not effectively implemented in many African countries and therefore cannot be used to counterbalance abuse of executive power. There are various reasons why these mechanisms are not effective which are common to various African countries. In many countries, South Africa and Nigeria being good examples, strong majority party governments make it virtually impossible to get the parliamentary majorities required for the adoption either of a motion of no-confidence or of an impeachment against a head of state. Furthermore, as is the case in Nigeria, these processes can be abused in order to serve the agenda of other political parties or as a measure of retribution against an unpopular president rather than to be used for its intended purpose of keeping a check on executive authority in genuine examples of a loss of confidence in a president or in the commission of unlawful acts. As seen in the case of South Africa, voting on these motions by secret ballot has not necessarily resulted in the resolution of the problems either, because of the level of representation of the majority party in parliament. It is submitted that in order to overcome the problem of parliamentary majorities in African countries the requirement in relation to the majority needed for the adoption of such motions needs to be lowered, or these matter may be referred to a court (perhaps a constitutional court) or to a committee consisting of members of all the represented political parties in order to establish whether there are sufficient grounds for the motion to proceed.

The grounds for impeachment in some countries, for example Gabon and Cameroon, are so restrictive that only the most serious crimes, such as high treason, are punishable and less serious crimes are overlooked. This approach is flawed since "less serious" crimes, such as corruption, continue over many years and lead to moral and economic ruin. It is submitted that the grounds for impeachment of a head of state should relate to every contravention of the law and of the constitution, especially actions that pertain to maladministration and corruption. It is important that these unlawful actions are properly defined and are included in the constitution or in other legislation so as to eliminate confusion or misinterpretations. As the discussion of the South African situation demonstrates these measures cannot simply be stated in the constitution unless there is parliamentary provision for the corresponding procedural rules in order effectively to move, vote on and adopt these motions. The constitutional authority which has the measure to check the executive is powerless without a corresponding procedure effectively to implement such a check. The legal systems of countries should ensure that the constitutional authority to introduce motions of no- confidence or impeachment proceedings against heads of state are enforceable by means of corresponding procedural rules.

This chapter considered the domestic criminal prosecution of sitting heads of state as well. As in the case of criminal prosecution in international law, the effectiveness of this domestic mechanism is influenced by the issue of immunity. South Africa is an example of a country that is in the fortunate position of not affording criminal (or civil) immunity to the president, but it does not mean that successful criminal prosecution in South Africa is without challenges. As is evident from the discussion above, the South African president has faced criminal charges while in office but, in effect, it has been impossible to remove him. The president's sole authority to appoint the National Director of Public Prosecutions is an aspect that also proved problematic. It is submitted, even if in terms of the Constitution the South African president does not enjoy criminal immunity, nevertheless the legislature requires a provision that in exceptional circumstances in which a conflict of interests prevents the president from having an unbiased opinion with regard to the appointment of the Director of Public Prosecutions that authority is suspended.

Many African countries protect the head of state by providing them with both civil and criminal immunity and, in some instances, these forms of immunity continue even after the head of state leaves office. This is an untenable situation in which heads of state are never held accountable for crimes committed while in office. Although immunity may be waived by parliament after the president has vacated the office, for instance in Namibia and Zambia, a parliamentary majority party supporting an overwhelming majority government is an unresolved problem. It is recommended in order to hold a head of state accountable, head of state immunity either should be removed completely or at least limited substantially, and not extend after the head of state has left office. Furthermore, it is recommended that there should be other precautionary measures such as an alternative arrangement for the appointment to head the prosecuting authority if there is a conflict of interest on the part of the head of state in the outcome of the appointment. It is to ensure that heads of state do not protect themselves from prosecution by the appointment of a pliant head of the prosecuting authority.

In terms of commissions of inquiry, most African countries that have made provision for such mechanisms nominate the head of state to appoint commissions of inquiry. In the case of the head of state being the subject of such an investigation, either he would not make an appointment at all or would appoint a commission certain to absolve him or her from all wrong-doing. Many African countries, as seen in the examples of South Africa, Zimbabwe and Malawi, have not provided for circumstances in which the head of state is investigated and therefore should not be involved in the appointment of a commission of inquiry. It is recommended that current legislation should be amended in order to cater for the exception in which the head of state is complicit in a pending investigation, if this mechanism is to be used as a viable accountability measure.

Finally, the first part of the chapter considered judicial control as a measure to keep heads of state and members of the executive authority responsible and accountable. Judicial control is a powerful tool that democratic states can utilise to check executive action in terms of supreme constitutions, a measure which is the backbone of constitutionalism. Due to a lack of independence in the judicial branch of government, many African states struggle to use this mechanism effectively. In the cases of Botswana and Cameroon, it was seen that involvement by the head of state in the appointment of judicial officers and the requirement to ensure "the independence of the judiciary" creates a dangerous situation with regard to the separation of powers, and makes the judicial branch vulnerable to interference and manipulation. In the case of South Africa, there is less interference by the executive, yet judgments can be made ineffective through the non-compliance of the executive authority with court orders.

In the South African context, despite the emphasis placed on judicial control, other accountability mechanisms are either underutilised or the courts have to be approached to implement these mechanisms, which are supposed to function effectively on their own, for example, in the case of the enforcement of the decision of the Public Protector and also with regard to the procedural rules regarding motions of no-confidence and impeachment proceedings. This necessarily involves the courts in cases of a political or quasi-political nature and leads to questions in relation to the separation of powers. Political issues should be resolved amongst political roleplayers at a political level and not by recourse to the courts, but sometimes this means that issues will not be resolved unless the courts intervene. Political roleplayers and executive organs do not always show willingness to reach political solutions, which makes the intervention of the courts essential if the democratic nature of the state, its economy and its people are to be protected. It is recommended that there should be measures, which ensure the independence of the judicial branch by removing the power of heads of state to interfere in the appointment of judicial officers and influence the functioning of the courts. Furthermore, there is a need to enforce government compliance with court orders and, at the same time, the courts are to be able to maintain a balance between holding the executive and the head of state accountable and upholding the separation of powers.

The second part of this chapter explored the existing international law avenues in terms of which heads of state can be held accountable and prosecuted for the commission of international crimes. The question of holding heads of state responsible for the commission of international crimes or the violation of international law is complex, as the rules have not been codified and the content of custom either is developing or is disputed. The uncertainty surrounding the content of the doctrine of head of state immunity in respect of the prosecution of international crimes before international criminal tribunals brings the efficiency of the international criminal law provisions to the fore in prosecuting and eliminating the impunity of heads of state of member states who have not ratified the Rome Statute and who commit international crimes. The chapter revealed that head of state immunity shields them from prosecution under customary international law, at least before foreign courts.

What is questioned is whether a similar rule exists under customary international law which prevents international criminal tribunals from prosecuting heads of state for the commission of war crimes as a consequence of the absolute immunity attached to the office. A survey of international law reveals that there is not enough state practice either to suggest that under immunity, jurisdiction is barred, or that immunity is waived in relation to international criminal tribunals. The jurisdiction of the specific international criminal tribunal therefore has to be determined by its constitutive treaty. The doctrine in customary international law, under which heads of state are protected by immunity, applies only to foreign courts and not to international courts.

The current confusion surrounding the relationship between articles 27 and 98 of the Rome Statute, as well as the implicit bar on prosecuting sitting heads of state under article 46A*Bis* of the Malabo Protocol, places strain on the existing legal framework and is a burden to those who seek justice for the violation of international law by heads of state. It was found that article 27 of the Rome Statute explicitly determines that a head of state, or those holding a similar position, cannot rely on any form of immunity which might attach to the office they hold. Member states upon signature of the Rome Statute agree that the head of state will not be able to rely on an immunity defence. Legal certainty is the only means to resolve this untenable situation. The international legal framework is ineffective in ensuring heads of state are held responsible, but important questions have been raised as to the nature of head of state immunity, and the debate is evolving in a manner which should receive urgent attention by academics, policy- and law-makers. States should be supported in developing public state practice in respect of policies pertaining to head of state immunity, not only with regard to its provision for foreign immunity, but also in relation to the immunity of the head of state before an international criminal tribunal.

Less clear is the duty of member states to the International Criminal Court if the court requires member states to cooperate in the arrest or investigation of a head of state of a non-member state party to the International Criminal Court. A first reading of article 98 seems to align it with the third-party rule under the Vienna Convention on the Law of Treaties, but the content of this provision is under scrutiny following the non-arrest of President Al-Bashir by the South African government. Nonetheless, the International Criminal Court can exercise jurisdiction over heads of states which consent by ratifying the Rome Statute or by special consent. Security Council referrals may also trigger the jurisdiction of this Court.

Finally, this chapter explored whether the African Court of Justice and Human Rights has jurisdiction in the prosecution of heads of state for the commission of international crimes. The yet-to-be-established African Court of Justice and Human Rights may exercise jurisdiction over an extensive list of international and transnational crimes. The reach of this Court and its effectiveness in resolving the thorny problem of impunity, which is only too prevalent on the African Continent, however, are limited by article 46A*Bis* of the immunity clause introduced in the Malabo Protocol. Under the Malabo Protocol, sitting heads of states enjoy absolute immunity, which from an African perspective is a serious problem, as some heads of states have occupied that position for a long time.

The position in relation to a former head of state is unclear, but at least it seems possible that former heads of state might be prosecuted for personal acts or international crimes which are of such a nature that they cannot be ascribed to the office of a head of state, such as the act of genocide. The chapter demonstrates that the status of head of state immunity under customary international law, as well as the disputed interpretation of article 98 of the Rome Statute, is the chief source of frustration in establishing the effective prosecution of heads of state for international crimes.

In conclusion, the authors submit, although many African countries have accomplished a great deal since attaining independence in establishing new democracies in the last fifty years, much still needs to be done to make these systems of government effective and to keep them responsible and to hold them accountable domestically, regionally and as part of the international community. Too often they have been plagued by ineffective governments, power-hungry heads of state and governmental corruption and maladministration, all of which have serious consequences for the domestic and regional well-being of those states and the continent at large.

At a domestic level, African countries need to undertake a reconsideration of the various accountability measures that act as a check on the head of state and executive authority and take steps to make these measures as effective as possible. At regional and international levels, an organisation such as the African Union and its member states should radically act to eliminate corruption in government through treaties and regional courts or tribunals. At the international level, the issue of head of state immunity should be clarified in order to ensure that heads of state cannot act with impunity in committing crimes against international law and custom or human rights law. Only when these issues are addressed will there be a significant change to the trend amongst African regimes to act in a manner that is harmful to society.

On a continent with great potential, these regimes abuse their position in order to enrich themselves while impoverishing their citizens. If these trends were reversed, a prosperous Africa could take its rightful place in the international arena as a region in which governments and heads of state are held responsible and made accountable.

4

LAW, DEVELOPMENT AND RESPONSIBLE GOVERNANCE IN AFRICA

A Case Study of the Presidential Term Limits in Post-Conflict Burundi*

*Leah A Ndimurwimo***

Summary

The limitation of presidential term is amongst the issues that have raised concerns in Africa where incumbents of a number of African countries have shown their desires to remain in power or retain their tenure through political manipulations or changing the constitutions. Although there is a theoretical assurance in the democratic states that seek to embrace the universal constitutional principles of justice, democracy, freedom, equality, respect for rule of law and human rights, in practice the desired constitutional values in Africa are often being ignored.

The purpose of the 2005 Constitution in Burundi, for example, as clearly specified in the Preamble is to reaffirm, *inter alia*, put an end to the ongoing ethnic and political violence, human insecurity and instability. Yet, the interpretation of Articles 96 and 302 of the Constitution in light of the Constitutional Court of Burundi and East African Court of Justice's decisions have raised an important legal question, which ought be answered, contextualised and construed within the constitutional meaning. Owing to the historical accounts of militarisation and armed conflicts in Burundi, it is not clear whether or not the resort to *coup d'état* and armed violence as a response to the perceived "impugned decision" referred to in the case of *EACSOF v Attorney General of Burundi and Other* advanced the cause and the spirit of constitutionalism. In order to determine the extent of the law, development and responsible governance in Africa by using the post-conflict Burundi, this chapter attempts to critically analyse the fundamental provisions of the Post-conflict Constitution of 2005 relating to the presidential term limit as proposed in the Arusha Peace and Reconciliation Agreement of 2000.

---

*   This chapter is an updated version of the paper presented to the Nelson Mandela University and University of Johannesburg Faculties of Law Book Project Symposium, Port Elizabeth, 23-24 August 2018.

**   LLB (OUT); LLM (NMMU); LLD (NWU); Senior Lecturer, Faculty of Law, Nelson Mandela University.

4.1   INTRODUCTION

Since the turn of the millennium, there is a remarkable number of incumbent presidents who have managed to remain in office beyond their constitutionally mandated terms.[1] The current trend shows that there is a desire amongst incumbents to extend their presidential term limits through amending their constitutions. Such examples include the Chinese President Xi Jinping, Paul Kagame of Rwanda, Alvaro Uribe of Columbia and Algeria's Abdelaziz Bouteflika who have successfully taken the pathway of amending their constitutions. Furthermore, presidents like Vladimir Putin of Russia, Kagame and Uribe exemplify a study of Heads of State who were initially elected through democratic processes, but later chose to remain in power for a longer period, contrary to their original constitutional mandates.[2] This chapter confines itself to the efforts made to remain in office for longer than mandated in Africa by using examples of selected countries.

There have been attempts to deepen democracy by limiting presidential terms in Africa. Since the 1990s, there was a call to move away from one-party authoritarian states in order to embrace constitutionalism and good governance. The constitutions of the emerging democracies in Africa start with their affirmation of the universal values of justice, democracy, freedom, equality and respect for human rights. However, the construction of these emerging democracies in the continent remains a big challenge.[3] Incumbent presidents often come to power through legitimate democratic processes. However, later on, other dynamics come into play such as having a dominant political party, holding free but unfair elections and opting for a weaker rule of law that prevents their countries from being fully democratic states. Therefore, there has been a decline in respect of political and civil rights in countries like Algeria, Angola, Cameroon, Chad, Congo Republic, Democratic Republic of Congo (DRC), Egypt, Equatorial Guinea, Eritrea, Rwanda, Somalia, South Sudan, Sudan and Swaziland.[4] Similarly, other countries have been classified as "partly

---

1   Versteeg, Horley, Meng, Guim and Guirguis "The Law and Politics of Presidential Term Limit Evasion" 2020 120 *Columbia Law Review* 175.

2   Versteeg et al (n 1) 173.

3   See generally Akpojivi *Media Reforms and Democratization in Emerging Democracies of Sub-Saharan Africa* (2018). While evaluating the media reform processes and re-democratisation in Ghana and Nigeria's emerging democracies, Akpojivi argues that dependency approaches resulting from the transplanting of policy framework from the West into emerging democracies in Africa, the objectives of these reforms have not been achieved. In most cases Africa's democratic principles are based on the strategic choices that combine contextual and contingent variables. That means that the current trends show that Heads of State make calculations about their prospects of winning or losing in future competitive elections and these are considered as the primary source of electoral systems choice in Africa's emerging democracies. But contextual frameworks relating to the political legacies of varied authoritarian regimes tend to inform the political executives' institutional preferences that shape their choice of alternative electoral systems. See Mozaffar "Africa: Electoral Systems in Emerging Democracies" in Colomer (eds) *The Handbook of Electoral System Choice* (2004).

4   Fombad "An Overview of the Crisis of the Rule of Law in Africa" 2018 18 *African Human Rights Law Journal* 220-223.

free" which include Burkina Faso, Comoros, Kenya, Liberia, Madagascar, Malawi, Morocco, Mozambique, Niger, Nigeria, Seychelles, Tanzania, Togo and Zambia.[5]

In most African countries, the independence from colonial powers have been perceived as a failed project.[6] Many countries in Africa continue to struggle to consolidate democracy, constitutionalism and respect for the rule of law and human rights.[7] Noticeable examples include, but are not limited to, Burundi, Rwanda, DRC, Uganda, Cameroon and Zimbabwe (the late President Robert Mugabe was ousted from power in 2017 through military takeover), where incumbent presidents have indicated their intention to hang onto power through the violation of the Constitution or political manipulation of the Constitution in order to legalise their stay in power. In some instances, countries such as Somalia, Libya, Central African Republic and South Sudan are still entangled in the protracted armed conflicts and collapse of their constitutional orders. Others, like Zambia,[8] Tanzania[9] and South Africa,[10] although they are relatively peaceful and politically stable, yet, they have recently encountered the political upheavals and are in the process of reviewing their constitutions.[11] This suggests that there is a paradigm shift towards constitutional reforms in Africa. Although such constitutions may not share the same values, the tenets of constitutional values are shared across national legal systems.

In Burundi, for example, after three decades of Tutsi military regimes from 1966 to 1993 and 1996, internal and external factors of political instability and economic sanctions against Burundi pushed the country to consider democracy and

---

5   Fombad (4).

6   Prempeh "Africa's Constitutionalism Revival: False Start or New Dawn?" 2005 *International Journal of Constitutional Law* 469.

7   Kibert and Fombad "Transformative Constitutionalism and the Adjudication of Constitutional Rights in Africa" 2017 17 *African Human Rights Law Journal* 365.

8   The Mainza Chona Constitutional Review Commission of 1972 on institutionalisation of the One Party State. The Mvunga Commission which led to the promulgation of the 1991 Constitution which also reintroduced multi-party system and the limitation of the presidential term to five years renewable once. See also the Mwanakatwe Constitutional Review Commission of 1996, Mung'omba Constitutional Review Commission of 2003 and the Constitutional Amendment Bill of 2015.

9   Under President Jakaya Kikwete, Tanzania embarked on constitutional review processes. The Constitutional Review Act was enacted. This Act underwent three amendments in order to improve and broaden public participation. The first amendment was approved by the Parliament on 10 February 2012 and urged the Tanzanian Mainland and Island (Zanzibar) to engage and agree on fundamental matters pertaining to the constitutional review process that included having representatives from both sides of the Tanzanian Union. The second amendment of September 2013 dealt with the composition and operations of the Constituent Assembly and dissolution of the Constitutional Review Commission. The third Amendment of November 2013 dealt with, amongst others, the increase of members of the Constituent Assembly from 166 to 201. Also, the Referendum Act of 2014 was promulgated to enable a referendum to be held on 30 April 2015, but was prevented by the 2015 elections. See also the Nyalali Commission Report of 1991 on the adoption of a multi-party system and the Warioba National Constitutional Review Commission Report of 2012 on constitutional review in Tanzania since 1990s.

10   The Joint Constitutional Review Committee was established to review section 25 of the Constitution in South Africa on possible expropriation of land without compensation. See D Spies "Parliament Receives Over 700,000 Written Submissions on Land Expropriation" https://www.news24.com/SouthAfrica/News/parliament-receives-over-700-000-written-submissions-on-land-expropriation-20180624 (2018-06-24).

11   Kibert and Fombad (n 7) 365.

constitutionalism. The common doctrines of the separation of powers, rule of law, good governance and an independent judiciary were presumed to be respected. For the first time in the early 1990s, diverse political parties and government of Pierre Buyoya, a military official, started political dialogue that brought compromised peace and reconciliation agreements since 2000, specifically, the Arusha Peace and Reconciliation Agreement (the Arusha Peace Agreement).[12]

Contrary to the expectations of the flourishing rule of law, democracy and good governance, the postcolonial governments, like the case of Burundi, have been experiencing political instability, military *coups* and attempted *coups*,[13] authoritarianism, armed violence, corruption and gross violations of human rights.[14] For example, between 1960 and 2010, more than 200 successful and failed *coups* have been witnessed[15] across Africa – 104 in West Africa, 35 in Central Africa, 48 in Eastern Africa and 16 in Southern Africa.[16] Although in every *coup d'etat* or an attempted *coup d'etat* there seem to be justified reasons, repercussions are nonetheless evident, if Burundi can be cited amongst examples.[17]

The judicial interpretation of constitutional provisions generally are somehow inconsistent and tend to create judicial uncertainties. Reference is made to a few examples from other jurisdictions with respect to judicial interpretations of failure to abide by the constitutional principles. For example, in Kenya, the case of *Trusted Society of Human Rights Alliance v Attorney-General & Others*[18] dealt with invalidating various decisions of the president and Parliament for failing to comply with the Constitution. This decision was later overturned on appeal, but the appointments made by the president and approved by the National Assembly were considered ineffectual for months while the appeal was still pending. In the *Institute of Social Accountability & Another v National Assembly & 4 Others*[19] also, the court invalidated a popular law passed by the National Assembly and directed the government to remedy its faults. Similarly, in *The Very Right Rev Dr Jesse Kamau & Others v The Hon Attorney-General & Another*, it was observed that a timorous

---

12 The Arusha Peace Agreement was concluded on 28 August 2000 between Buyoya government, Tutsi-led military, seven Hutu parties and 10 Tutsi political parties, thus making a total of 19 parties to the agreement with diverse interests.

13 A small group's struggle to depose the established government fails which generally takes less than a week like what happened in Burundi in 2015.

14 Kibert and Fombad (n 7) 341.

15 Barka and Ncube "Political Fragility in Africa: Are Military Coups D'état a Never-Ending Phenomenon?" *African Development Bank* Report of 2012 https://www.afdb.org/fileadmin/uploads/afdb/Documents/Publications/Economic%20Brief%20-%20Political%20Fragility%20in%20Africa%20Are%20Military%20Coups%20d%E2%80%99Etat%20a%20Never%20Ending%20Phenomenon.pdf (2018-08-21).

16 See generally Japhet "Military Coups and Military Regimes in Africa" 1978 *South African Journal of Military Studies*; see also Giles C. "Sudan coup: Are military takeovers on the rise in Africa?" https://www.bbc.com/news/world-africa-46783600 (2019-04-11).

17 Barka and Ncube (n 15).

18 [2012] eKLR (HCK).

19 [2015] eKLR (HCK).

and unimaginative exercise of the judicial power of constitutional interpretation leaves the Constitution a stale and sterile document.[20] On interpretation of rights in particular, the court went on to note:

> The provisions touching fundamental rights have to be interpreted in a broad and liberal manner, thereby jealously protecting and developing the dimensions of those rights and ensuring that our people enjoy their rights, our young democracy not only functions but also grows, and the will and dominant aspirations of the people prevail. Restrictions on fundamental rights must be strictly construed.[21]

The reasoning behind the above cited Kenyan cases imply that the rights and duties established by substantive post-liberal alterations based on the constitutional designs in post-conflict societies like Burundi must be constrained by the past intellectual instincts and liberal judicial mind-set. Therefore, an approach that transcends legal formalism and positivism is necessary.[22]

Likewise, the Constitutional Court of South Africa in *Assign Services (Pty) Limited v National Union of Metalworkers of South Africa and Others*[23] for example, held that, legislation should be interpreted textually, contextually and purposefully. Consequently, under a transformative constitution, judges must, as a matter of necessity, justify their decisions not only by making reference to precedents and other legal authorities, but also by referring to certain overarching principles and values. Similarly, any attempts by the legislature to restrict the fundamental rights and freedoms must be strictly examined and justified. Therefore, the power to assess any measures restricting presidential term limits provided for in the Constitution must be vested in the judiciary.

The Constitutional Court of Burundi (CCB) and East African Court of Justice (EACJ) also had to deal with the issue of interpretation of the presidential limits provided for in the Constitution of Burundi in 2005 which proved to be uneasy task. Unlike most other cases of executive term limit evasion, it has been contended that Burundi's Constitution has never been amended, replaced, or ignored.[24]

While there were unsuccessful attempts to replace and, alternatively, amend the Constitution in March 2014, the case of Burundi is notably different from the common constitutional amendment processes that remove or soften term limits in

---

20   Nairobi HCMCA 890 of 2004 (unreported).

21   Above.

22   Klare "Legal Culture and Transformative Constitutionalism" 1998 *South African Journal on Human Rights* 146.

23   [2018] ZACC.

24   Ginsburg et al on the evasion of executive term limits in 2011 *William and Mary Law Review* 1807-1831.

other countries such as Uganda in 2005,[25] Congo-Brazzaville in 2015,[26] and Rwanda in 2015 so as to allow the incumbents to renew their presidential terms without arguably violating their respective constitutions.[27]

This chapter investigates the extent to which the principles of democracy and limitation to presidential terms in Africa are adhered to. It uses an example of Burundi where Burundian polities have developed from military rules to constitutional and democratic processes. The case of *East African Civil Society Organisations Forum (EACSOF) v Attorney General of Burundi and Others*[28] is considered in order to demonstrate how deteriorating political and social cohesion has been associated with maladministration in post-conflict Burundi. Articles 96 and 302 of the Constitution are used to explain the controversies surrounding the "third term presidential mandate" in Burundi. The chapter compares what is happening in the neighbouring countries with respect to the constitutionally entrenched presidential terms and succession. It concludes that one of the repercussions of ongoing human rights violations in post-conflict societies in Africa, Burundi in particular, is to engender the culture of impunity and the hindrance of national reconciliation, reconstruction and development. In addition, the concepts of democracy, promotion of human rights, and respect for the rule of law are analysed holistically. For that reason, this chapter refers to the constitutional interpretation by the CCB which was considered by the EACJ as discussed below under sections 4.3 and 4.4 of this chapter.

4.2 TWO FIVE-YEAR PRESIDENTIAL TERMS AND AGE LIMITS IN THE GREAT LAKES REGION OF AFRICA

The presidential term limit issue as raised in the *EACSOF* case has been demonstrated to be a contentious one in Africa. For example, both the CCB and EACJ in the Burundi case revealed the ambiguities that can be associated with the constitutional design of the presidential term limit. This chapter uses the examples

---

25 President Yoweri Museveni assumed executive powers from 1986 to date. After the protracted armed conflicts, the National Resistance Movement overthrew the previous repressive regimes, Museveni declared a transitional one-party government from 1986-1989 which was extended to 1996. For this period Museveni ruled Uganda without a Constitution, but rather through the NRM's Legal Notice 1 of 1986. In 1995, the Constitution of 1995 was adopted which provided for two five-year presidential and 75-year age limits respectively and elections were held. Museveni won and his mandatory presidential terms were supposed to end in 2005. However, a referendum on the presidential limit and restoration of multi-party democracy was approved. As a result Museveni was nominated as a presidential candidate for the 2006, 2011 and 2016 elections. Based on age Museveni would be disqualified as a president in 2019 and ineligible to run for the upcoming 2021 elections. Interestingly, the Constitution Amendment Bill No.2 of 2017 was brought before the Parliament on 20 December 2017, seeking the removal of the 75-year presidential age limits and became a law on 27 December 2017. This can allow Museveni to run for presidential candidacy in 2021.

26 *All Africa News* "Congo-Brazzaville: Referendum Passes Allowing President to Extend Rule" https://allafrica.com/stories/201510270558.html (2018-07-04).

27 Vandeginste "Legal Loopholes and the Politics of Executive Term Limits: Insights from Burundi" 2016 *Africa Spectrum* 43.

28 Case Number RCCB 303 decided on 5 May 2015.

from the neighbouring countries of Burundi to demonstrate inconsistencies in the application of the presidential term limits in Africa. For that reason, the countries of Tanzania, Uganda, DRC, Rwanda and Burundi are referred to in terms of two five-year presidential terms and age limits as well as the presidential alternance and the popular will.

4.2.1 Two five-year terms and age limits

Tanzania has complied with the two five-year presidential terms limit as stated in the Constitution[29] since the adoption of multi-party system in 1992.[30] In Uganda, when the National Resistance Movement (NRM) came to power, the two five-year presidential term limit was included in the Constitution of 1995 but was never implemented. The original Constitution stated that: a president is supposed to serve for two terms. But, this was scrapped through a referendum in 2005. Article 102 of the Constitution of Uganda states that the age limits for President should be between 35 to 75 years. This was removed by the Parliament after passing the Age Limit Bill.[31] The implication of the age limit law can now allow the 75-year-old President Yoweri Museveni to seek re-election for a sixth term in 2021, because the presidential term limit has recently been abolished together with the age limit. Rwanda, since the time the Rwandan Patriotic Front (RPF) assumed power in 1994, has now extended the presidential term limit from five to seven years.[32] In the DRC, after the expiry of the two five-year term limits, the President, Joseph Kabila. never changed the Constitution but still desired to stay in power and was unwilling to step down.[33] Although Kabila had a constitutional presidential mandate until 20 December 2016, this mandate was initially extended until the end of 2017. Then Kabila continued to remain in power until the presidential election was held in December 2018 when Felix Tshisekedi was elected and took over to become president of the DRC on 24 January 2019. In Burundi, through the referendum of May 2018, the Constitution has been changed like Rwanda's and has extended the term limit from five to seven years.

---

29   Article 42 of the Constitution of the United Republic of Tanzania of 1977 which is read together with section 9 of the Time of Assumption and Term of Office of President Act 15 of 1984.

30   See article 3 of the Tanzanian Constitution and Act No 4 of 1992 on the declaration of Tanzania as a multi-party state. See also the Nyalali Commission's Report of 1992, Ngasongwa "Tanzania Introduces a Multi-Party System" 1992 *Review of African Political Economy* 112-116.

31   BBC News "Uganda MPs Vote to Scrap Presidential Age Limit" 20 December 2017 https://www.bbc.com/news/world-africa-42434809 (2018-07-29).

32   Homolkova "Transnationalisation Potential of Electoral Violence in Burundi" 2017 *Journal of African Elections* 133. President Kagame's ability to contest elections for a further three terms suggests that future protests should not be discounted. His move has the potential of giving him an additional 15 years in office and disadvantages democracy, constitutionalism and responsible governance in Rwanda.

33   Kestler-D'Amours "DRC Violence Shows Kabila Determined to Stay in Power" January 2018 https://www.aljazeera.com/news/2018/01/drc-violence-shows-kabila-determined-stay-power-180101102949537.html (2018-09-29).

4.2.2 Five vs. seven years

Rwanda has changed its Constitution through referendum and this has been endorsed by the Parliament in 2017. The Rwandan constitutional referendum which was held on 18 December 2015 and included Rwandese citizens living abroad, voted on 17 December, and 98% of voters approved the seven-year term limit.[34]

Likewise, Burundi's change to the Constitution is one of the significant features. There are several arguments which have been put forward in that regard to the effect that the five-year term is not long enough or adequate for the government to implement the aspirations expressed in the election manifestos. Burundi being one of the poorest countries it cannot afford the election costs every five years as proven in 2015 when the government shouldered the costs of the 2015 elections, because the external donors like Burundi's former colonial power Belgium and the European Union (EU) boycotted the drive to fund elections.[35] Also, the government funding of the 2018 constitutional referendum's related costs has proven to be expensive. Like Rwanda, the Constitution of Burundi has been changed through referendum and the Parliament.[36]

The Independent National Electoral Commission, on 17 May 2018, confirmed that a majority number of Burundians voted in favour of a new Constitution. Overall, the referendum took place in a calm environment despite some alleged irregularities as reported by opposition and civil society representatives.[37] Given the approval of the new Constitution of Burundi, the United Nations has raised socio-economic and humanitarian concerns as many Burundians continue to live in refugee camps, especially in Tanzania, Rwanda, Uganda and the DRC.[38] But, what has been acknowledged, is the fact that the referendum to change the Constitution should reflect the will of the Burundians and should not have the negative impact of taking the country back to the political instability, human insecurity and the outrages of the 2015 elections. A call has been made on all political parties to engage in meaningful dialogues, which should include negotiations which aim towards peaceful, free, fair, transparent and inclusive participation in the 2020 elections.[39]

---

34   See *The Guardian* "Rwandan President Paul Kagame to Run for Third Term in 2017" 1 January 2016. https://www.theguardian.com/world/2016/jan/01/rwanda-paul-kagame-third-term-office-constitutional-changes (2018-07-29).

35   *BBC News* "Burundi's Nkurunziza Asks Public for Money for Election" 26 May 2015 https://www.bbc.com/news/world-africa-32886071

36   Institute for Security Studies "The AU Should Take a Stand on Burundi's Constitutional Review" 19 March 2018 https://issafrica.org/iss-today/the-au-should-take-a-stand-on-burundis-constitutional-review (2020-04-02); see also Reuters "Burundi Approves New Constitution Extending Presidential Term Limit" https://www.reuters.com/article/us-burundi-politics/burundi-approves-new-constitution-extending-presidential-term-limit-idUSKCN1IM1QG (2018-05-21).

37   The UN Security Council Report on the situation in Burundi S/PV.8268 of 24 May 2018 https://www.securitycouncilreport.org/atf/cf/%7B65BFCF9B-6D27-4E9C-8CD3-CF6E4FF96FF9%7D/s_pv_8268.pdf (2018-07-15).

38   Above.

39   Above.

4.2.3 Reflection of third termism in the African Great Lakes

The two five-year presidential term limit has proven to be an issue in both Rwanda and Burundi which are part of the African Great Lakes Region. Both countries, which have a long history of armed conflicts and had agreed on two five-year term limits, have now extended this to a two seven-year presidential term limit. They both used the Parliament to achieve their objectives. But, the question that remains is whether or not changes in the Constitution imply change of the presidential candidacy as raised in the *EACSOF* case.

4.2.4 Presidential alternancy and the popular will

The alternance of the presidents in line with the constitutional framework in Tanzania has been complied with. Tanzania managed to keep two five-year presidential terms as provided for in the Constitution and ultimately alternate the presidents since the independence from the British colonial rule. The only concerns that have been raised relate to the ruling party. Although it changed its name from Tanganyika African National Union (TANU) to Chama Cha Mapinduzi (CCM), it has remained in power since the independence to date. But, there are positive aspects because Tanzania remains economically and politically stable in comparison with its neighbouring countries of Rwanda, Burundi, DRC, Uganda and Kenya.

It must be noted that the presidencies in Burundi, Rwanda, Uganda and DRC are results of the armed struggle. President Kagame, for example, maintains that as long as the people of Rwanda want him to rule he will always be available.[40] But the EU and United States of America have argued that Kagame should step down in order to empower the younger generation. Thus, by implication, the people of Rwanda are keeping President Kagame in power as a form of gratitude for his military victory and apparent economic achievements. President Nkurunziza, on the other hand, after his second term, announced that he will not be available for the upcoming elections of 2020,[41] although during the 2018 referendum the opposition parties alleged that the incumbent wanted to entrench himself in power. But the ruling party's Secretary-General, Evariste Ndayishimiye, was elected as a presidential candidate in the May 2020 elections, he was sworn as a new President of Burundi in June 2020 after the sudden death of President Nkurunziza.[42]

---

40 *The Guardian* "Rwanda Votes to Give President Paul Kagame Right to Rule until 2034" https://www. theguardian.com/world/2015/dec/20/rwanda-vote-gives-president-paul-kagame-extended-powers (2018-02-08).

41 *News24* "Burundi President Surprises with Vow to Step Down in 2020" https://www.news24.com/Africa/ News/burundi-president-surprises-with-vow-to-step-down-in-2020-20180609 (2018-08-17). See also Mwakideu "Is Nkurunziza Ready to Relinquish Power?" https://mg.co.za/article/2020-01-28-is-burundi-president-pierre-nkurunziza-ready-to-relinquish-power/ (2020-01-28), the ruling party CNDD-FDD has elected an army general Evariste Ndayishimiye as its presidential candidate.

42 *News24* "Burundi's Evariste Ndayishimiye Sworn in as New President" https://www.news24.com/news24/ africa/news/burundis-evariste-ndayishimiye-sworn-in-as-new-president-20200618-2 (2020-07-11).

The Ugandan elections have been held many times, however, it seems that the incumbent is not ready to relinquish his presidential powers and has changed the presidential age and term limits for him to stay in power as supported by the Constitution. In the DRC, despite the expiry of the presidential term limit in 2016, President Kabila still remained in power, supported by the military although he eventually stepped down in 2018. The presidential term limits with specific reference to Burundi are discussed hereunder.

4.3   A CASE STUDY OF THE POST-CONFLICT BURUNDI

4.3.1 A history of the post-conflict Burundi

Before discussing various interpretations attributable to the above stated constitutional provisions, it is worth referring to a brief history of Burundi. After three decades of Tutsi military regimes from 1966 to 1993 and 1996, the United Nations (UN) adopted resolutions to intervene in the issue of Burundi.[43] Despite the international and regional initiatives which aimed at ending the armed conflicts, the fighting between the warring parties never stopped. Peace and reconciliation negotiations led to the conclusion of peace agreements like the Arusha Peace Agreement in 2000, but some of the Tutsi parties signed the Arusha Agreement with diverse reservations[44] while the Hutu parties like the *Conseil National pour le Défense de la Démocratie – Forces pour la Défense de la Démocratie* CNDD-FDD (the current ruling party) and the *Forces National de Libération* (FNL) did not sign the Agreement at all.[45] Hence, there was a need to engage in further peace negotiations which eventually benefited the CNDD-FDD and FNL by signing their own peace accords, such as the Pretoria Protocol on Political, Defence, Security and Power-Sharing of 2003 (the Pretoria Protocol) and the Dar es-Salaam Comprehensive

---

43   See the UN Security Council Resolutions 1325 (2000), 1820 (2008), 1888 (2009), 1889 (2009) and 1960 (2010) on women, peace and security, Resolutions 1674 (2006) and 1894 (2009) on the protection of civilians in armed conflicts, Resolutions 1612 (2005), 1882 (2009), 1998 (2011) and 2068 (2012) on children and armed conflicts and Resolution 2090 (2013) on extension of mandate of the UN Office in Burundi until 15 February 2014, Resolution 2248 (2015) on the UN Security Council's intention to consider additional measures against all Burundians who contribute to the perpetuation of violence and requested the Secretary-General to update the Council on the situation in Burundi within 15 days, Resolution 12174 (2015) a press statement noting the African Union decision to deploy an African Prevention and Protection Mission and calling on Burundian stakeholders to comply with it, Resolution 2303 (2016) on establishment of a UN police component in Burundi of 228 officers for a period of one year, Resolution S/2016/799 (2016) on the report of the Secretary-General to enable the UN to facilitate the deployment of AU human rights observers and military experts, and Resolution A/HRC/RES/36/2 (2017) on the Council resolution requesting the United Nations Office of the High Commissioner for Human Rights (OHCHR) to urgently dispatch a team of three experts to Burundi to collect information concerning human rights violations in cooperation with the government of Burundi and forward such information to the judicial authorities of Burundi.

44   Six out of 10 Tutsi political parties signed the Arusha Peace Agreement with reservations. See International Crisis Group (ICG) "Burundi's Peace Process: The Road Map from Arusha" 20 July 1998 https://www.refworld.org/docid/3ae6a6d10.html (2020-04-22).

45   Above.

Ceasefire and Peace Agreement of 2006.[46] As a result, the CNDD-FDD gained from the subsequent agreements and it assumed political power from 2005 to date.

4.3.2 Constitutional framework

After the conclusion of the Arusha Peace Agreement in 2000, the 2001 Constitution was adopted allowing the governance of the post-conflict Burundi. However, the Interim Constitution of 2004 repealed the 2001 Constitution and remained in force until the post-transition or Final Constitution of 2005 was adopted. The final Constitution was based on the French Model with some modifications to acknowledge ethnicity that plays a major role in Burundian politics.[47] It is through the constitutional framework that the salient constitutional-related issues attributable to the current constitutional crisis in Burundi ought to be addressed.

4.3.3 The flaws in the Arusha Peace Agreement and the Constitution

Upon examination of the peace and reconciliation initiatives as reiterated in the constitutional framework, it must be pointed out that some loopholes were evident in the above stated Arusha Peace Agreement, as well as in the 2005 Constitution. For example, ethnic quotas, i.e., Hutus, Tutsis and Twas, that is, 60% Hutu to 40% Tutsi in the executive, legislature and the judiciary and co-option of Batwa[48] which were provided for, while the ethnic composition in Burundi is 85% Hutus, 14% Tutsis and 1% Twas, raised concerns and have attracted legitimate criticisms. Furthermore, the ethnic quota which allowed 50/50 for Hutus and Tutsis, respectively, in the military have proven to be altogether impractical in the Burundian constitutional design.[49]

It is equally important to note that the rationale of ethnic quota requirements as mentioned above has far-reaching implications in the Burundian constitutional dispensation and their failure to provide comprehensive answers to the current constitutional crisis has exacerbated the situation. Accordingly, the proposed ethnic quotas have been removed under the constitutional referendum of May 2018 so that they can be determined under presidential directives.[50]

---

46 The Pretoria Protocol on Political, Defence, Security and Power-Sharing in Burundi 2003 (the Pretoria Protocol) and the Dar es-Salaam Comprehensive Ceasefire and Peace Agreement 2006. The Global Cease-Fire Agreement between the Transitional Government of Burundi and the CNDD-FDD 16 November 2003, and the Comprehensive Cease-Fire Agreement between the Government of Burundi and the Party for the Liberation of Hutu People-National Liberation Forces (PALIPEHUTU-FNL) 7 September 2006 were concluded and the subsequent agreements such as the Magaliesburg Agreement 2008 and Bujumbura Agreement 2009.

47 See the Preamble to the Burundian Post-transition Constitution of 2005.

48 Article 164 of the Post-transition Constitution of 2005.

49 Nantulya "After Burundi's Referendum, a Drive to Dismantle the Arusha Accords" 20 July 2018 https://africacenter.org/spotlight/after-burundis-referendum-a-drive-to-dismantle-the-arusha-accords/ (2018-11-17).

50 Nantulya (n 49).

Given the flaws which were evident in the peace agreements – to be precise, the Arusha Peace Agreement – the inadvertent consequences came to the light in the 2015 elections. The case of *EACSOF v Attorney General of Burundi and Others*[51] is a controversial one which instigated armed violence and highlighted, *inter alia*, the weaknesses of the Arusha Agreement as re-iterated in the Post-transition Constitution of 2005. The *EACSOF* case, which dealt with the interpretation of constitutional provisions concerning the presidential term limits,[52] whereby fourteen Senators in Burundi filed a motion before the court *a quo*, i.e., the CCB on 28 April 2015 wherein they were seeking an interpretation of Articles 96 and 302 of the Constitution.

The CCB for the first time was tasked to give clarity on the issues pertaining to the presidential term limit envisaged under the Arusha Peace Agreement[53] and the Constitution.[54] Amongst the issues raised before the CCB were: the lawfulness of the motion in terms of Article 230 (1) of the CCB's Constitution which provides that "[t]he Constitutional Court is referred to a matter by one-quarter of the members of the Senate", and most importantly, the interpretation of Articles 96 and 302 of the Constitution and the modalities of the referral of the matter relating to the interpretation of the Constitution.[55] A day before the handing down of the judgment, the Vice President of the CCB, a part of the minority judgment, fled Burundi alleging intimidation.[56] On 5 May 2015, the CCB in what is referred to as the "impugned decision"[57] held that Nkurunziza was eligible to run for the presidency of the country. Clearly, the "impugned decision" elicited political and security instability in Burundi in 2015.

4.3.4 Response to the Constitutional Court's decision

The "impugned decision" became the central thrust of the case whose consequences led to demonstrations, an attempted *coup d'état*,[58] internal displacement and a refugee crisis. A number of Burundian citizens fled the country again similarly to

---

51 An appeal to the East African Court of Justice, Appeal No 4 of 2016, whose judgment was handed down on 24 May 2018.

52 *EACSOF v Attorney General of Burundi and Other* [par 2].

53 After prolonged peace and ceasefire negotiations which were held in Tanzania under the mediation of former Tanzanian President Mwalimu Julius Nyerere. After his death, the former South African President Nelson Mandela took over. On 28 August 2000, in Arusha all the parties signed the Agreement with some reservations, especially Tutsi political parties, while Hutu parties like CNDD-FDD and FNL were not signatories. Law n°1/017 of 1 December 2000 on the adoption of the Arusha Peace Agreement was enacted.

54 Constitution of the Republic of Burundi of 2005.

55 As provided for under Article 228 (3) of Law No 1/010 of 18 March 2005 on promulgating the Constitution of Burundi.

56 *EACSOF v Attorney General of Burundi and Other* [par 5].

57 *EACSOF v Attorney General of Burundi and Other* [par 5].

58 Ndimurwimo and Mbao "Rethinking Violence, Reconciliation and Reconstruction in Burundi" 2015 *Potchefstroom Electronic Law Journal* 849-850.

what happened before in 1972 and the 1990s, and sought refuge in the neighbouring countries of Rwanda, DRC, Tanzania and Uganda.[59]

In spite of the CCB's careful consideration in arriving at its decision, it is important to note that the approval of President Pierre Nkurunziza's third term mandate in 2015 was criticised by opposition parties as well as the international community as unconstitutional and contrary to the spirit of the Arusha Agreement.[60] A fundamental issue attributable to the legality of Nkurunziza's third-term presidential candidacy lied on uncertainties found in the constitutional design in relation to the modalities on how the president should be elected.

Considering Article 302 of the Constitution *vis-à-vis* the "provisions relating to the first post transition period" and the vagueness of the use of the word "exceptionally" which appears to be independent of Article 96 were the key issues that had to be clarified. Articles 302 and 96 which intended to create an exceptional and special mandate for the presidential candidacy exposed the uncertainties which the CCB ought to expound. For example, it has been contended that, rather than objecting to the form of election provided for under Article 96 as the Arusha Agreement intended to be, the application of Article 302 was viewed as a delay in limiting the number of presidential terms by universal direct suffrage stated in Article 96. The CCB, in applying the broader interpretation, ruled out that the Arusha Agreement did not allow a third presidential term, but the drafters of the Constitution in 2005 wrongly interpreted the Arusha Agreement.[61]

Moreover, Article 302 of the Constitution is in conformity with Article 190 of the Electoral Code of April 2005. This Code, which was promulgated one month after the adoption of the Constitution in 2005, is seen as an exception to the principles enshrined in its Article 186 of the Code, which is also similar to the provisions of Article 96 of the Constitution envisioned by the Arusha Peace Agreement in 2000. It has been argued that the presidential term limit in Burundi occurred in a context of sustained militarism.[62] However, it must also be noted that the underlining historical factors of political and social injustices cannot be undermined either. In fact, the presidential "third term mandate" or "*troisième mandat*" vividly demonstrated a troubling governance trend in Burundi, notably, since the contested 2010 elections that paved the way for a return to probably a *de facto* one-party regime.[63]

---

59   UNHCR Briefing Notes "Burundi Refugee Numbers in Neighbouring Countries Reach 50,000 as Violence Continues" https://data2.unhcr.org/en/news/12771 (2015-05-08). The violence that accompanied the third-term crisis of Burundi resulted in at least 1,200 deaths and over 400,000 refugees between April 2015 and May 2017 according to estimates by the International Criminal Court (ICC) which has opened an investigation.

60   Homolkova (n 32).

61   Vandeginste (n 27) 54.

62   Vandeginste (n 27) 39-63.

63   Daley and Popplewell "The Appeal of Third Termism and Militarism in Burundi" 2016 *Review of African Political Economy*.

Based on the above, the following section seeks to analyse whether or not President Pierre Nkurunziza, who had served the post-transitional as a president in 2005 and 2010, was eligible for presidential candidacy in 2015. Another fundamental legal issue is whether the CCB's "impugned decision" in *EACSOF v Attorney General of Burundi and Others* advanced the development of legal norms and responsible governance in the post-conflict Burundi.

4.4   AN ANALYSIS OF THE EAST AFRICAN COURT OF JUSTICE'S DECISION

Given the unresolved issue before the CCB, the East African Civil Society Organisations Forum (EACSOF), which is a platform for Civil Society Organisations in East Africa brought an urgent application against President Pierre Nkurunziza's third term presidential campaign before the East African Court of Justice (the EACJ).[64] The EACJ had to determine whether or not the EACSOF had *locus standi*. The EACSOF based their *locus standi* on their pursuit to build a critical, knowledgeable and empowered civil society in the East African Community (EAC). For that reason, the EACSOF approached the EACJ in order to foster their confidence in articulating the grassroots, needs and interests to the EAC and its various organs, institutions and agencies. Thus, their *locus standi* lay within the objectives of the Treaty for the Establishment of the East African Community (the Treaty).[65]

As indicated above, the EACJ was established in terms of the Treaty. Initially, Kenya, Uganda and Tanzania were the first State Parties to ratify the Treaty. Thereafter, Burundi and Rwanda acceded to the Treaty on 18 June 2007 and became Members States of the EAC from 1 July 2007[66] and South Sudan joined the EAC in 2016. It is worth emphasising that the EAC's mandate in terms of the Treaty plays a major role in promoting democracy, rule of law and respect for human rights. The EACJ serves as a judicial body of the EAC. The Treaty's objectives confer powers on the EACJ to deal with a wide range of legal issues, including to develop policies and programmes that aim to widen and deepen cooperation amongst the Member States in political, economic, social and cultural fields, research and technology, defence, security and legal and judicial affairs, and other issues to their mutual benefit.[67] One of its explicit jurisdictions is the power to hear and determine disputes on the interpretation and application of the Treaty.[68]

On 6 July 2015, the applicants, EACSOF, sought orders for the stay Decree No. 100/177 of 9 June 2015 to postpone Burundi's presidential and senatorial elections

---

64   *EACSOF v Attorney General of Burundi and Other* Appeal No 4 of 2016. This was an appeal of the First Instance Division of The East African Court of Justice dated 29 September 2016.

65   Article 9 (e) of the EAC Treaty.

66   EAC "History of the EAC" https://www.eac.int/health/index.php?option=com_content&view=article&id =57&Itemid= (2018-10-22).

67   Chapter 8 of EAC Treaty.

68   Article 27 of the EAC Treaty.

of 15 and 24 June 2015 respectively, as well as the stay of the second respondent's decision, the Independent National Electoral Commission or *Commission électorale nationale indépendante* (CENI) dated 12 June 2015 which approved the nomination of Pierre Nkurunziza as a candidate in the presidential election. The urgent application further sought an order directing CENI and the government of the Republic of Burundi to postpone the presidential and senatorial elections.

The respondents were the Attorney-General of Burundi, CENI and the Secretary-General of the EAC. The EACSOF contended that the situation in Burundi required urgent attention and if no action was taken, President Nkurunziza would run for an unconstitutional third term of office. The applicants argued that the procedure used by the second respondent, CENI, in arriving at the decision to submit and accept the candidacy of President Nkurunziza, violated the Constitution and the Arusha Peace Agreement, both of which limit presidential tenure in Burundi to two terms.

It is imperative to state that the applicants' opinion in the interim orders raised serious and fair concerns in terms of the notions of democracy, the rule of law, transparency and constitutionalism.[69] On 14 July 2015, the urgent application was heard *ex parte*, but the EACJ declined to grant the orders sought. It transpired that Burundi's presidential election had been postponed to 21 July 2015, therefore the court ordered the application to be heard inter-parties.[70]

The presidential third term mandate issue was already decided in Burundi by the CCB. The question posed before the EACJ was whether the CCB had the final say on the matter, since Burundi is a Member State to the Treaty. Thus, the EACJ had to determine if it had the jurisdiction to review a constitutional matter that was already decided at the national level and dismiss the CCB's decision. At the same time, the EACJ had to determine whether or not the presidential nomination of Nkurunziza contravened Articles 5(3)(f), 6(d), 7(2), 8(1)(a) and (c), and 8(5) of the Treaty.[71] The respondents in their counter argument stated that the EACJ did not have jurisdiction to entertain the matter due to the fact that Article 30(3) of the Treaty, which states that "the Court shall have no jurisdiction under this Article where an act, regulation, directive, decision or action has been reserved under the Treaty to an institution of a State Party".[72]

It was stated that in Article 30(3) legal provision negates the jurisdiction of the court over matters that have been reserved under the Treaty to an institution of a State Party to the Treaty. The court referred to Article 9(4) and Article 27(1) of the Treaty and concluded that the Treaty does not expressly reserve the business of national

---

69   *EACSOF v Attorney General of Burundi and Others* 2-3.

70   Above par 3–4.

71   Above par 12.

72   Above par 13.

courts as one of those matters over which the EACJ has no jurisdiction.[73] However, the court used a purposive interpretation to determine whether it had jurisdiction. The court held that in matters relating to constitutional interpretation, it is excluded to entertain such matters as its jurisdiction is restricted to Treaty-related matters. Furthermore, that the EACJ had no jurisdiction to interpret the provisions of the Burundi Constitution or Arusha Peace Agreement for purposes of determining the correctness of the CCB's decision.

However, the EACJ, in elaborating more, stated that it is entirely different from the court reviewing the provisions of State Party's national law with a view to determining its compliance with the Treaty. The EACJ explicitly stated that it has jurisdiction to entertain the matter while referring to the latter scenario.[74] The EACJ observed further that, in the same vein, the court is not clothed with an appellate jurisdiction over the decisions of national courts. Article 23(3) of the Treaty specifically designates a court *a quo* in matters of Treaty interpretation. As such, the EACJ concluded that it was not persuaded that the EACSOF's application raised matters of the Treaty's interpretation.

Since the EACJ could not find jurisdiction over the CCB's "impugned decision", it was clear that the application was destined to fail. The respondents questioned the injury the applicants specifically stood to suffer in the event that the application was dismissed. The EACJ confirmed that even if it had to use the principle of convenience to determine whether the applicants' rights were worthy of protection, the court concluded that the applicants' rights did not outweigh the constitutional rights of the Burundians to vote. Reason being, the Constitution of Burundi prescribed the holding of the presidential election not later than one month before the expiration of the term of the incumbent president. Therefore, President Nkurunziza's term was set to expire on 26 August 2015, meaning that the presidential election had to be conducted at least before 26 July 2015. In essence, if the EACJ would have decided in favour of the applicants, it would have caused more harm to the Burundian citizens and the Constitution by denying them their democratic and constitutional right to vote in a timely manner for their president.

4.5   CRITICISM OF THE CCB AND THE EACJ DECISIONS

While reflecting on the law, development and responsible governance in the post-conflict Burundi, it is imperative to consider the political and social injustice of the past while upholding the fundamental rights of Burundian citizens which transcend civil and political rights. For example, the constitutionality of the Arusha Peace Agreement as echoed in Constitution provisions was tested in the courts of law for the first time by the CCB and the EACJ, ten years after the adoption of the

---

73   Above par 9.

74   Above par 16.

Constitution in 2005. Perhaps, if the dilemma of the presidential third term limits had been clarified before in the 2005 and 2010 elections, it would have prevented the undesirable consequences of the *"troisième mandat"* in the 2015 elections which took back the country to the history of bloodshed and armed violence. In other words, it would have resolved the issue of whether or not President Nkurunziza was eligible for re-election in 2015.

The EACJ acknowledged that although it may not be difficult to interpret Article 96 of the Constitution, the same cannot be said of Article 302. The court elaborated that the word "exceptionally" cast doubt on the real intentions of the drafters of the Constitution. The court went on and stated the following:

> [A]rticle 302 of the Constitution, given where it appears in the Constitution under provisions for the first post-transition period and the vagueness of the word "exceptionally" appears to be independent of Article 96 thereby creating a completely exceptional and special mandate which is unrelated to Article 96. Considering that the application of Article 302 can also delay the limiting number of presidential terms by universal direct suffrage provided for under Article 96. Moreover, the idea is in conformity with Article 190 of the Electoral Code of April 2005 which was approved one month after the promulgation of the Constitution which is similar to Article 302 of the Constitution as it states that it is the exception to the principles enshrined in Article 186 of the Electoral Code which is also similar to Article 96 of the Constitution. Though the Arusha Peace Agreement recommended that no President can serve more than two terms, the vague nature of Article 302 of the Constitution made a third term possible for a president who headed the first post-transition period. Considering that the applicants requested the Court to interpret Articles 96 and 302 of the Constitution and state if a renewal once of the term of the current president is in conformity with the Constitution. Considering that Article 302, for its part, came up with a special universal indirect suffrage mandate and had nothing to do with the mandate provided for in Article 96.[75]

The court's logical reasoning was flawless up to the point of interpreting Article 302 of the Constitution. The question posed was whether or not Article 7 of Protocol II of the Arusha Peace Agreement had a different meaning compared to Articles 96 and 302 of the Constitution.

Although Article 302 refers to the first presidential indirect universal suffrage as an "exceptional matter" because it was during the transitional phase, it does not mean the Articles of the Constitution must be read in isolation. Instead the Constitution ought to be read in whole so that Article 96 should complement Article 302.

It is imperative that even though President Nkurunziza's first term was elected under an indirect suffrage in terms of Article 302 in 2005, it would still have counted as a

---

term in respect of Article 96 of the Constitution. But, the EAC's mandate in terms of the Treaty is to promote constitutionalism. Therefore, the Treaty obliges the Member States to abide by the principles of good governance, including adherence to the principles of democracy, rule of law, accountability, transparency, social justice, equal opportunities, gender equality, as well as the recognition, promotion and protection of Human and Peoples' Rights.

Referring to the EACJ's rational thinking, it can be deduced that the EACJ did not fail in its mandate because it had no jurisdiction to interpret the matter which had already been decided under the national law of Burundi by the CCB. It seems, however, that all legal remedies were exhausted and President Pierre´ Nkurunziza was eligible to serve the third term. It is interesting to point out that the court never attempted 'for the sake of convenience' to interpret or even provide its opinion on Nkurunziza's third-term mandate. As it stands, it seems both CCB and EACJ were not ready to apply their minds and rule against Nkurunziza's perceived third-term mandate, contrary to the Arusha Peace Agreement and Constitution.

4.5.1 Article 96 vs. 302 debate

On the basis of the above, it is worth reflecting on the contents of both articles 96 and 302 which brought controversies in the "impugned decision". Article 96 provides that "the President of the Republic is elected by universal direct suffrage for a mandate of five years renewable one time".

Article 302 on the other hand stipulates:

> Exceptionally, the first President of the Republic of the post-transition period is elected by the National Assembly and the elected Senate convened in Congress, with a majority of two-thirds of the members. If this majority is not obtained on the first two ballots, further ballots are held immediately until a candidate obtains the votes equal to two-thirds of the members of the Parliament...

The interpretation that tends to trigger any given constitutional fallacy as the *EACSOF* case suggests, has to consider the nature of society and the objectives it seeks to achieve. Perhaps the fundamental issue to be mindful of is the intention of the legislature and the language used in both Articles 96 and 302 that ought to guide the judicial interpretation. While articulating on the contents of the above-stated articles, it can be construed that in most post-conflict society related cases the courts usually have to weigh up between the historical accounts of the past injustices and the political needs where the former may take precedent.

Interestingly, a referendum of changing the Constitution of Burundi in May 2018 proposed the change of presidential term limit from five years to seven years like Rwanda.[76] Out of 96% (4.7 million people) who registered to vote, 73% voted in

---

76   *IOL News* "'Yes' Votes Ahead in Burundi Constitutional Referendum" https://www.iol.co.za/news/africa/yes-votes-ahead-in-burundi-constitutional-referendum-15044270 (2018-05-18).

favour of amendment to the Constitution on extending the presidential term from five to seven years.[77]

Fairly, Burundi's third-term legal framework, as Vandeginste has revealed, was characterised by loopholes with an unintended uncertainty of the legal norm and an omission in the enforcement order.[78] This enabled the executive to maintain a legality which is derived from rule of adherence on legitimacy of executive powers.[79] Certainly, this shows how Burundi's national law and practice have been tested and measured against the constitutional framework. But Vandeginste, while referring to transitional justice, also pointed out that there is a remarkably sinister discrepancy between Burundi's policies and practice.[80]

4.5.2 Arusha Peace Agreement modalities

It is important to note that the Post-conflict Constitution of Burundi was adopted in 2005 based on the Arusha Peace Agreement modalities. Undeniably, the Arusha Peace Agreement as a founding document has an historical importance and a conceptual framework of trying to move Burundi from the culture of armed conflicts to peace and human security. For example, the explanatory memorandum of the Draft Constitution of 18 March 2005 referred to the Arusha Agreement and widely recognised the same as Burundi's foundational roadmap to peace and stability.[81] The parties resolved to put aside their political differences in order to promote the issues of their common understanding and interests of Burundian citizens. Furthermore, these parties reaffirmed and resolved to maintain peace, stability, justice, the rule of law, national reconciliation, unity and development. They also determined to put an end to the root causes underlying the recurrence of violence, bloodshed, insecurity, political instability, genocide and unfair discrimination of the past and to promote diversity.[82]

However, the ambiguities in the Arusha Peace Agreement itself have allowed the ruling party CNDD-DD government to disregard its relevance, specifically on the following aspects:

- It did not clearly address the presidential third-term issue.
- It has been viewed as a political agreement that was signed by the political parties with several reservations at the expense of interest of all Burundian citizens.

---

77 See *Sunday Times* "Burundi Approves New Constitution Extending Presidential Term Limit" https://www.timeslive.co.za/news/africa/2018-05-21-burundi-approves-new-constitution-extending-presidential-term-limit/ (2018-05-21).

78 Vandeginste (n 27) 43.

79 Beetham *The Legitimation of Power* (2013).

80 Vandeginste "Transitional Justice for Burundi: A Long and Winding Road Study" 2007 20. A paper presented at the International Conference on Building a Future on Peace and Justice, Nuremberg, 25-27 June 2007.

81 The Preamble to Protocol I of the Arusha Agreement that deals with the nature of the Burundi conflict, problems of genocide and exclusion and their solutions.

82 See articles 1-8 of Protocol I of the Arusha Peace Agreement.

- There were other subsequent peace and ceasefire agreements like the Pretoria Protocol of 2003 and the Dar es-Salaam Comprehensive Ceasefire and Peace Agreement of 2006 which brought an end to the armed conflicts in Burundi but which were not given the same constitutional status as those of the Arusha Peace Agreement.

- In terms of legal hierarchical norms, an agreement may not be superior to the Constitution which is supreme law of the country;[83] that means, a mere agreement should not be considered superior to the Constitution.

Similarly, the uncertainties posed by the combination of Articles 96 and 302 of the Constitution did not advance the spirit and letter of Arusha Peace Agreement. As such, it has been contended further that the proposal to amend the Burundi Constitution in 2014 did not seek to amend Article 96 which advocates for the two-term limit. However, the draft amendment logically proposed removing of the Constitution's Transitional Chapter XV, which includes Article 302.[84]

It has been argued further that the proposed constitutional amendment of 2014 was an attempt to delay the application of the term limit until 2020 as it fell one vote short of the required four-fifths majority in the National Assembly.[85] The relevance of this argument lies in the fact that the CCB's "impugned decision" was mindful of the historical factor of an unpleasing human rights track record since Burundi's independence in the wake of preparatory initiatives of the 2020 elections when the incumbent, President Nkurunziza, indicated he would step down as a head of state.[86]

It must be emphasised also that within the constitutional framework in Burundi, there is the need for setting up independent and impartial prosecution agencies in order to have an effective maintenance of democracy, rule of law and respect for human rights. As stated in the Guidelines on the Role of Prosecutors,[87] Member States to the UN and regional organisations like the African Union (AU), are under an obligation to uphold the principles of international and national criminal justice, supported by the Constitution. The Preamble to the Guidelines on the Role of Prosecutors states:

> The Guidelines should be respected and taken into account by governments within the framework of their national legislation and practice, and should

---

83   UN Security Council (2015a), Report of the Security Council Mission to the Central African Republic, Ethiopia and Burundi www.un.org/ga/search/view_doc.asp?symbol=S/2015/503 (2016-08-23). UN Peacebuilding Commission, regional actors also insisted on the supremacy of Burundi's Constitution.

84   Vandeginste (n 27) 43.

85   See the Chairman of the National Assembly at the time www.africania-news.com/partie2-nkurunziza-tente-de-modifier-la-constitution-et-echoue-de-justesse (2016-08-23).

86   Africa News "Burundi's president Pierre Nkurunziza made a surprise announcement on Thursday, saying he will not contest in the country's next presidential elections in 2020" http://www.africanews.com/2018/06/07/burundi-pierre-nkurunziza-says-he-will-not-run-for-president-in-2020/ (2018-10-22).

87   Guidelines on the Role of Prosecutors, Eighth United Nations Congress on the Prevention of Crime and the Treatment of Offenders 27 August to 7 September 1990 U.N. Doc. A/CONF.144/28/Rev.1 (1990) 189.

be brought to the attention of prosecutors, as well as other persons, such as judges, lawyers, members of the executive and the legislature and the public in general.[88]

According to the Guidelines, democracy must be in line with the national legal framework. For example, if substantive democracy can be complemented with procedural democracy, the problems of presidential term limits in Burundi could have been clarified, prioritised and resolved within the constraints of the law. Durotoye (2016) has analysed attempts made by autocratic leaders in Africa to abrogate presidential term limits.[89] Such an abrogation is usually done through dual strategies of co-optation[90] and intimidation.[91] Although the term "limit enforcement" has proven to be amongst the biggest challenges for limiting presidential power,[92] using presidential term limits generally can be an indicator for the institutionalisation of power.[93] In the context of the discussion above, it is prudent to suggest that the presidential term evasion attempts do not ignore the constitution completely. Instead, Heads of State in Africa generally show minimal respect for the constitution by using constitutional rules and procedures in order to evade term limits through amending the constitution.

4.6   CONCLUSION

The credibility and effectiveness of constitutionalism in modern societies depend upon the nature of the society and objectives it aims to achieve. It is imperative that constitutionalism and democracy in Burundi, for example, must involve, amongst other things, making choices and principles which Burundians may deem effective and operational. Certainly, constitutionalism in Burundi must reflect back and recall the country's history to shape Burundi's past, present and anticipate the country's future. As Nchalla has observed, the concept of constitutionalism is a prerequisite for the existence of a legitimate constitution.[94] The proponents of modern constitutionalism, for example, have considered that constitutionalism, from a theoretical point of view, is more concerned with rules, values and choices. However, in practice, it is a legal and political principle that is based on both rules

---

88   Above 189.

89   Durotoye "Resurgent Backsliding and Democracy in Africa" 2016 18 *International Journal of African and Asian Studies* 39.

90   A process of adding members to an elite group at the discretion of members of the body, usually to manage opposition and so maintain the stability and *status quo.*

91   Durotoye (n 89) 39.

92   Posner and Young "The Institutionalization of Political Power in Africa" 2007 *Journal of Democracy* 126.

93   See Tull and Simons "The Institutionalisation of Power Revisited: Presidential Term Limits in Africa" 2017 *Africa Spectrum* 79.

94   Nchalla "Tanzania's Experience with Constitutionalism, Constitution-making and Constitutional Reforms" in Mbondenyi and Ojienda (eds) *Constitutionalism and Democratic Governance in Africa: Contemporary Perspectives from Sub-Saharan Africa* (2013) 21.

and values.[95] As Backer has suggested, constitutional legitimacy is grounded in the development of a single system that is designed to give authoritative autonomy to the accustomed values of the community of nations that together make up the value systems of constitutionalism and constitutional legitimacy.[96]

The existence of a constitution that articulates democratic values and principles is not sufficient ground to establish a political system that is democratic.[97] However, it is equally accepted that a democratic constitution is a prerequisite for the development of democratic constitutionalism. That means, if there is a democratic constitution, a constant review of the compliance with democratic principles is of paramount importance in order to promote or to strengthen the transformative constitutionalism. The proposed amendments to the constitution in order to set a limit of two seven-year presidential terms,[98] must strive to take Burundi to another level of the country's reconciliation and reconstruction.

Over decades, the Tutsi-led military regimes and insurgent groups have been accused of committing serious international crimes. While reflecting on the law, development and responsible governance in post-conflict Burundi, accountability and responsibility for the past wrongs and putting an end to the culture of impunity in Burundi remain unfruitful. There is failure of the post-conflict government to cement national reconciliation and healing which could have brought about effective transformative constitutionalism and democracy. The CCB's impugned judgment in the case of *EACSOF v Attorney General of Burundi* demonstrate a call to limit the outrages of the ongoing armed conflicts in Burundi by pointing out the flaws of the constitutional provisions and Arusha Peace Agreement which have proven to be incompatible.

The CCB in the *EACSOF* case affirmed that the renewal, for at least one last time, of the presidential term of five years was not contrary to the Constitution. What remains unclear is whether the 2018 amendments to the Constitution, which have extended the presidential term to seven years like the neighbouring Rwanda, will continue to embrace the tenets of democracy and uphold constitutionalism.

Finally, the post-conflict government must be responsive to the political, social and economic needs of Burundian citizens while striving for true national reconciliation and reconstruction and avoiding the legacy of the military regimes which was revealed in the 2015 crisis that included an attempted *coup d'etat*. The popular will, *inter alia*, that allows the citizens to consider human security, peace, good governance, respect for human rights, rule of law and economic achievements like Tanzania, Rwanda

---

95   Above.

96   See Backer "From Constitution to Constitutionalism: A Global Framework for Legitimate Public Power Systems" 2009 *Penn State Law Review* 113.

97   Nchalla (n 94) 20.

98   Arabnews "UN Chief Takes Aim at Burundi Leader's Bid to Extend Rule" 6 February 2018 http://www.arabnews.com/node/1240851/world (2018-02-22).

and Burundi can be cited amongst examples. But, it seems that the popular will can also be easily usurped or overpowered by military and the Parliament as the DRC's and Uganda's experiences suggest. While constitutions are domestic instruments that should reflect and cater for local needs, it is evident that modern constitutions are nothing but *sui generis*.[99] Thus, the envisioned transformative constitutionalism of South Africa, for example, could provide a good model that could be used as an ideal one to fit the peculiar situation in Burundi, should there be political will to have responsible governance of the country.

---

99   Kibert and Fombad (n 7) 365.

5

SEXUAL AND GENDER-BASED VIOLENCE IN THE CONTEXT OF THE SYRIAN ARMED CONFLICT AND THE QUESTION OF INDIVIDUAL CRIMINAL RESPONSIBILITY FOR THE PERPETRATORS

*Mispa Roux**
*Kriyanka Reddi***

5.1 INTRODUCTION

In February 2011, peaceful protests in the Syrian Arab Republic began relating to poverty, corruption, the right to freedom of expression, and democratic rights. Soon thereafter, demands were made for the release of political prisoners, the general respect for fundamental human rights, as well as economic, legal and political reforms.[1] Within a month, more protests occurred after children were detained and tortured after allegedly portraying anti-Government graffiti on public buildings.[2] Soon after these events, Syrian armed forces responded violently by launching military operations throughout the state.[3] By 2017, more than 13.1 million people required urgent humanitarian and medical assistance, 6.1 million people were internally displaced, 2.9 million people were living in hard-to-reach areas and hundreds of thousands of civilians were trapped in besieged areas.[4] The humanitarian situation in Syria continues to deteriorate, and is becoming more severe and devastating.[5]

---

1   First Report of the Independent International Commission of Inquiry on the Syrian Arab Republic, Human Rights Council, A/HRC/S-17/2/Add.1 (23 November 2011) par 27 (First IICIS Report).

2   First IICIS Report (n 1) par 27.

3   First IICIS Report (n 1) par 27–28.

4   SC Res 2393 (2017), S/RES/2393 (2017), 19 December 2017 par 1.

5   SC Res 2393 (n 4).

*   LLB, LLM, LLD (International Law) (UJ); Senior Lecturer in Public Law, Faculty of Law, University of Johannesburg. Deputy Director of the South African Institute of Advanced Constitutional, Public, Human Rights and International Law (SAIFAC), a Centre of the University of Johannesburg.

** LLB, LLM (International Law) (UJ).

Since the inception of the civil war, the Syrian government's persistent stance has been that its use of force is necessary to retaliate against attacks from a number of non-state armed opposition groups and terrorist organisations.[6] What began as peaceful protests developed into a horrific humanitarian crisis and an extremely violent and complicated non-international armed conflict.[7] Parties to the conflict consist, on the one hand, of the Syrian government's armed forces together with its associated militias, and on the other hand, non-state armed opposition groups and extremist religious terrorist organisations (such as the Islamic State in Iraq and the Levant (ISIL) and Jabhat Fatah al-Sham).[8] Countless women, girls, men and boys have reported that they were victims of sexual and gender-based violence at the hands of all parties to the conflict,[9] and that it has occurred from the inception of the armed conflict.[10] Strong evidence indicates that sexual and gender-based violence lies central to the conflict, and is deliberately used as a weapon and method of warfare.[11] It has been widely acknowledged that violence against civilians in the Syrian armed conflict amounts to gross human rights violations, specifically genocide,[12] crimes against humanity, and war crimes.[13]

---

6   First IICIS Report (n 1) par 30 and 37.

7   Report of the Independent International Commission of Inquiry on the Syrian Arab Republic, Human Rights Council, A/HRC/37/72 (1 February 2018) (February 2018 IICIS Report); Report of the Secretary-General, Implementation of Security Council resolutions 2139 (2014), 2165 (2014), 2191 (2014), 2258 (2015), 2332 (2016), 2393 (2017) and 2401 (2018), S/2018/777, 22 August 2018.

8   S-G Report August 2018 (n 7) par 3 and 5. The UN Security Council specifically designated ISIL as a terrorist group in SC Res 2253 (2015), S/RES/2253 (2015), 17 December 2015. See further in this regard SC Res 2170 (2014), S/RES/2170 (2014), 15 August 2014; SC Res 2249 (2015), S/RES/2249 (2015), 20 November 2015.

9   Third Report of the Independent International Commission of Inquiry on the Syrian Arab Republic, Human Rights Council, A/HRC/21/50 (15 August 2012) 92 (Third IICIS Report).

10 SC Res 1960 (2010), S/RES/1960 (2010), 16 December 2010 1.

11 Report of the Independent International Commission of Inquiry on the Syrian Arab Republic, "I lost my dignity: sexual and gender-based violence in the Syrian Arab Republic", Human Rights Council, A/HRC/37/CRP.3 (8 March 2018) (SGBV IICIS Report); HRC Resolution, The human rights situation in the Syrian Arab Republic, A/HRC/RES/40/17 par 14–15 (HRC Resolution 40/17).

12 Independent International Commission of Inquiry on the Syrian Arab Republic, "They came to destroy: ISIS Crimes against the Yazidis", Human Rights Council, A/HRC/32/CRP.2 (15 June 2016) (IICIS Yazidi Report).

13 See further in general in this regard First IICIS Report (n 1) Second Report of the Independent International Commission of Inquiry on the Syrian Arab Republic, Human Rights Council, A/HRC/19/69 (22 February 2012) (Second IICIS Report); Third IICIS Report (n 9); Fourth Report of the Independent International Commission of Inquiry on the Syrian Arab Republic, Human Rights Council, A/HRC/22/59 (5 February 2013) (Fourth IICIS Report); Fifth Report of the Independent International Commission of Inquiry on the Syrian Arab Republic, Human Rights Council, A/HRC/23/58 (18 July 2013) (Fifth IICIS Report); Sixth Report of the Independent International Commission of Inquiry on the Syrian Arab Republic, Human Rights Council, A/HRC/24/46 (16 August 2013) (Sixth IICIS Report); Seventh Report of the Independent International Commission of Inquiry on the Syrian Arab Republic, Human Rights Council, A/HRC/25/65 (12 February 2014) (Seventh IICIS Report); Eighth Report of the Independent International Commission of Inquiry on the Syrian Arab Republic, Human Rights Council, A/HRC/27/60 (13 August 2014) (Eighth IICIS Report); Ninth Report of the Independent International Commission of Inquiry on the Syrian Arab Republic, Human Rights Council, A/HRC/28/69 (5 February 2015) (Ninth IICIS Report); Tenth Report of the Independent International Commission of Inquiry on the Syrian Arab Republic, Human Rights Council, A/HRC/30/48 (13 August 2015) (Tenth IICIS Report); Report of the Independent International Commission of Inquiry on the Syrian Arab Republic, Human Rights Council, A/HRC/33/55 (11 August 2016) (2016 IICIS Report); Report of the Independent International Commission of Inquiry on the Syrian Arab Republic,

The United Nations Security Council maintains that the only solution to the "humanitarian situation" is to be found in the political arena, specifically though a political transition supported by the current Syrian government.[14] The Security Council has strongly condemned the widespread violations of human rights by the Syrian authorities and expressed grave alarm at the "widespread use of torture, ill treatment, sexual and gender-based violence as well as all grave violations and abuses committed against children".[15] Sexual and gender-based violence perpetrated by ISIL, Jabhat Fatah al-Sham and entities associated with Al-Qaida has also been condemned by the Security Council, but in the greater scheme of human rights abuses and violations of humanitarian law that have occurred in the context of the conflict.[16] It further expressed outrage at the "unacceptable and escalating level of violence and the killing of well over a quarter of a million people, including tens of thousands of child casualties".[17] Notably, the Security Council stated that some violations "may amount to war crimes and crimes against humanity",[18] and stressed the need to end impunity and bring violators of human rights law and humanitarian law to justice. However, a draft Security Council resolution referring the situation to the Prosecutor of the International Criminal Court was vetoed,[19]

Human Rights Council, A/HRC/36/55 (8 August 2017) (2017 IICIS Report); February 2018 IICIS Report (n 7); Report of the Independent International Commission of Inquiry on the Syrian Arab Republic, Human Rights Council, A/HRC/39/65 (9 August 2018); Report of the Independent International Commission of Inquiry on the Syrian Arab Republic, Human Rights Council, A/HRC/40/70 (31 January 2019); Report of the Independent International Commission of Inquiry on the Syrian Arab Republic, Human Rights Council, A/HRC/42/51 (15 August 2019); Report of the Independent International Commission of Inquiry on the Syrian Arab Republic, Human Rights Council, A/HRC/43/57 (28 January 2020).

14 SC Res 2254 (2015), S/RES/2254, 18 December 2015 preamble and par 5 and 15; SC Res 2268, S/RES/2268, 26 February 2016 preamble and par 2, 7 and 8; SC Res 2336 (2016), S/RES/2336 (2016), 31 December 2016 preamble; SC Res (n 4) preamble and par 4. See further in this regard SC Res 2139 (2014), S/RES/2139 (2014), 22 February 2014; SC Res 2165 (2014), S/RES/2165 (2014), 14 July 2014; SC Res 2191 (2014), S/RES/2191 (2014), 17 December 2014; SC Res 2258 (2015), S/RES/2258 (2015), 22 December 2015; SC Res 2332 (2016), A/RES/2332 (2016), 21 December 2016. Since 2012, the Security Council has addressed five thematic concerns in its resolutions pertaining to the Syrian Arab Republic. The first concern, which has filtered through all Syrian-based resolutions, calls for a political solution to the situation in Syria. The second thematic concern involved condemning terrorism and violent extremism, preventing the funding to and travel of terrorist fighters, condemning trade with terrorist groups, expanding sanctions against Al-Qaida, the Islamic State and their associates; and finally requiring member states to take measures to prevent terrorist attacks in Islamic State- controlled areas. The third concern focused on monitoring the use of chemical weapons in Syria, identifying the perpetrators using chemical weapons and attempting to eradicate the use thereof. The fourth concern addressed the urgent need for humanitarian aid, authorised passage for humanitarian aid and cross-border relief delivery, demanded the lifting of sieges and authorised the monitoring of the humanitarian situation. Finally, the final thematic concern involved the establishment of monitoring mechanisms mandated to monitor and report on violations of human rights and humanitarian law in Syria.

15 SC Res 2165 (n 14).

16 SC Res 2170 (n 8) par 2 and 3.

17 SC Res 2332 (n 14).

18 SC Res 2191 (n 14) par 1.

19 SC Draft Res 348, S/2014/348, 22 May 2014 https://www.securitycouncilreport.org/atf/cf/%7b65BFCF9B-6D27-4E9C-8CD3-CF6E4FF96FF9%7d/s_2014_348.pdf (2018-09-01); SC Res 2332 (n 14) par 1 and 4. See par 4.1 below for a discussion on the role of the Security Council and the ICC.

and repeated recommendations by various UN organs and entities echoing this have been ignored.[20]

Despite this Security Council deadlock, several other United Nations organs and entities have also focused on human rights abuses and violations of humanitarian law in the Syrian conflict.[21] The General Assembly condemned all forms of torture, systematic and widespread sexual and gender-based violence, rape, as well as other forms of ill treatment by both the Syrian authorities and opposition groups.[22] It also specifically condemned the gross and systematic abuse of women's and children's rights, and sexual and gender-based violence, including the enslavement and sexual exploitation of women and girls by ISIL.[23] With regard to the persistent and widespread use of sexual violence, abuse and exploitation occurring in state-controlled detention centres, the General Assembly expressed concern at the "prevailing climate of impunity for sexual violence crimes".[24]

In early 2018, the High Commissioner for Human Rights warned that "the perpetrators of these crimes must know they are being identified; that dossiers are being built up with a view to their prosecution; and that they will be held accountable for what they have done".[25] The High Commissioner reiterated that the situation in Syria should be referred to the International Criminal Court and urged all states to support the International, Impartial and Independent Mechanism[26] in order to ensure future prosecutions.[27] In her 2018 report, the Special Representative of the Secretary-General on Sexual Violence in Conflict stated that the majority of conflict-related sexual and gender-based violence is currently committed by non-state actors,[28] noting that "[d]espite extensive documentation of patterns of conflict-

---

20   GA Res 71/248, International, Impartial and Independent Mechanism to Assist in the Investigation and Prosecution of Persons Responsible for the Most Serious Crimes under International Law Committed in the Syrian Arab Republic since March 2011, A/RES/71/248, 11 January 2017 2.

21   See (n 14). See further discussion in par 1 below.

22   GA Res 72/191, *Situation of human rights in the Syrian Arab Republic*, A/RES/72/191, 19 December 2017 at 7.

23   GA Resolution 72/191 (n 22) 8.

24   GA Resolution 72/191 (n 22) 8.

25   "Those responsible for war crimes in Syria 'will be held accountable for what they have done' says UN rights chief", United Nations News Report, 2 March 2018 https://news.un.org/en/story/2018/03/1003981 (2018-07-23) (UN News Report).

26   GA Res 71/248, International, Impartial and Independent Mechanism to Assist in the Investigation and Prosecution of Persons Responsible for the Most Serious Crimes under International Law Committed in the Syrian Arab Republic since March 2011, A/RES/71/248, 11 January 2017. In terms of this resolution, the Independent Mechanism, with the Independent International Commission of Inquiry on the Syrian Arab Republic, is mandated to "collect, consolidate, preserve, and analyse evidence" pertaining to violations of international humanitarian law and human rights violations, as well "prepare files in order to facilitate and expedite fair and independent criminal proceedings".

27   UN News Report (n 25).

28   Report of the Secretary-General on Conflict-Related Sexual Violence, S/2018/250, 23 March 2018, par 3 (S-G Report on Sexual Violence).

related sexual violence, not a single perpetrator has faced prosecution, either in the Syrian Arab Republic or abroad".[29]

In August 2011, the UN Human Rights Council established the Independent International Commission of Inquiry on the Syrian Arab Republic[30] with the mandate

> to investigate all alleged violations of international human rights law since March 2011 in the Syrian Arab Republic, to establish the facts and circumstances that may amount to such violations and of the crimes perpetrated and, where possible, to identify those responsible with a view to ensuring that perpetrators of violations, including those that may constitute crimes against humanity, are held accountable.[31]

The Commission of Inquiry works in close cooperation with the International, Impartial and Independent Mechanism to assist in the Investigation and Prosecution of Persons Responsible for the Most Serious Crimes under International Law committed in the Syrian Arab Republic since March 2011,[32] which was established in December 2016 in an unprecedented move by the General Assembly. The mandate of the Syria Mechanism is

> to collect, consolidate, preserve and analyse evidence of violations of international humanitarian law and human rights violations and abuses and to prepare files in order to facilitate and expedite fair and independent criminal proceedings, in accordance with international law standards, in national, regional or international courts or tribunals that have or may in the future have jurisdiction over these crimes, in accordance with international law.[33]

29   S-G Report on Sexual Violence (n 28) par 78.

30   HRC Resolution, Situation of Human Rights in the Syrian Arab Republic, S-17/1, 22 August 2011. The Human Rights Council decided in 2019 to extend the mandate of the Commission of Inquiry for another year. See further HRC Resolution 40/17 (n 11) par 55.

31   HRC Res S-17/1 (n 30) par 13.

32   First Report of the International, Impartial and Independent Mechanism to Assist in the Investigation and Prosecution of Persons Responsible for the Most Serious Crimes under International Law Committed in the Syrian Arab Republic since March 2011, transmitted by the Secretary-General to the General Assembly, Seventy-second Session, Agenda Item 34(a), Prevention of Armed Conflict, A/72/764, 28 February 2018 (First Syria Mechanism Report); Second Report of the International, Impartial and Independent Mechanism to Assist in the Investigation and Prosecution of Persons Responsible for the Most Serious Crimes under International Law Committed in the Syrian Arab Republic since March 2011, transmitted by the Secretary-General to the General Assembly, Seventy-third Session, Provisional Agenda Item 34, Prevention of Armed Conflict, A/73/295, 3 August 2018; Third Report of the International, Impartial and Independent Mechanism to Assist in the Investigation and Prosecution of Persons Responsible for the Most Serious Crimes under International Law Committed in the Syrian Arab Republic since March 2011, transmitted by the Secretary-General to the General Assembly, Seventy-third Session, Agenda Item 34, Prevention of Armed Conflict, A/73/741, 13 February 2019; Fourth Report of the International, Impartial and Independent Mechanism to Assist in the Investigation and Prosecution of Persons Responsible for the Most Serious Crimes under International Law Committed in the Syrian Arab Republic since March 2011, transmitted by the Secretary-General to the General Assembly, Seventy-fourth Session, Provisional Agenda Item 31, Prevention of Armed Conflict, A/74/313, 22 August 2019.

33   GA Res 71/248 (n 20) par 4.

However, notwithstanding extensive international condemnation of gross human rights violations, calls for accountability of the perpetrators[34] and isolated humanitarian efforts by third states,[35] the commission of gross human rights violations in Syria by all parties to the conflict has continued unabated and with complete impunity.[36] At the time of writing, the situation of armed conflict in Syria has not been referred to the ICC Prosecutor,[37] and is neither under "preliminary examination"[38] nor a "situation under investigation"[39] by the ICC.[40] International convention law, customary law, and jurisprudence all define acts of sexual and gender-based violence during situations of armed conflict as international crimes, in particular as genocide, crimes against humanity, and war crimes.[41] Further, the obligation to prosecute perpetrators of international crimes is *erga omnes* in nature, and is imposed on Syria, third states and member states of the United Nations.[42]

Two factors that have had an immense stifling impact on the proper investigation and prosecution of sexual and gender-based violence in Syria, are under-reporting and delayed reporting.[43] A question that must also be considered is that of

---

34   See for example Statement by the President of the Security Council, *The Situation in the Middle East*, S/PRST/2011/16, 3 August 2011; First IICIS Report (n 1); SC Res 2139 (n 14); SC Res 2165 (n 14); SC Res 2191 (n 14); SC Res 2258 (n 14); and SC Res 2332 (n 14); SC Res 2396 (2017), S/RES/2396 (2017), 21 December 2017; GA Res 71/248 (n 20); GA Res 72/191 (n 22); Report of the Secretary-General, *Implementation of the Resolution establishing the International, Impartial and Independent Mechanism to Assist in the Investigation and Prosecution of Persons Responsible for the Most Serious Crimes under International Law Committed in the Syrian Arab Republic Since March 2011*, A/71/755, 19 January 2017 par 6, 10 and 31; Report of the Secretary-General, *Implementation of the Resolution establishing the International, Impartial and Independent Mechanism to Assist in the Investigation and Prosecution of Persons Responsible for the Most Serious Crimes under International Law Committed in the Syrian Arab Republic Since March 2011*, A/71/755/Add.1, 16 August 2017; "Syria: Criminal Justice for Serious Crimes under International Law", Human Rights Watch (17 December 2013) https://www.hrw.org/news/2013/12/17/syria-criminal-justice-serious-crimes-under-international-law#intro (2018-07-23) (HRW Syria news report); "These are the crimes we are fleeing: Justice for Syria in Swedish and German Courts", Human Rights Watch (October 2017) 34-35 https://www.hrw.org/report/2017/10/03/these-are-crimes-we-are-fleeing/justice-syria-swedish-and-german-courts (2018-07-23) (HRW Universal Jurisdiction Report); "The state of the world's human rights", Amnesty International Report 2017/18 349-353 https://www.amnesty.org/download/Documents/POL1067002018ENGLISH.PDF (2018-08-16).

35   US/UK-led humanitarian intervention in Syria: reasons were about the use of chemical weapons.

36   S-G Report on Sexual Violence (n 28) par 78; HRW Syria news report (n 34).

37   SC Draft Res 348 (n 19).

38   Preliminary examinations, International Criminal Court https://www.icc-cpi.int/pages/pe.aspx (2018-07-19).

39   Situations under investigation, International Criminal Court https://www.icc-cpi.int/pages/situations.aspx (2018-07-19).

40   Article 12(3) of the ICC Statute. See further discussion in par 4.1 below.

41   *The Prosecutor v Jean-Paul Akayesu* (2 September 1998) ICTR Case No ICTR-96-4-T (Judgment and Sentence); *The Prosecutor v Anto Furundžija* (10 September 1998) ICTY Case No IT-95-17/1-T (Judgment). See further in general Eboe-Osuji *International Law and Sexual Violence in Armed Conflict* (2012) and Roux "Sexual violence during armed conflict and reparation: paying due regard to a unique trauma" 2015 *African Yearbook on International Humanitarian Law* 87.

42   Roux "The *erga omnes* obligation to prevent and prosecute gross human rights violations with special emphasis upon genocide and persecution as a crime against humanity" 2012 *African Yearbook on International Humanitarian Law* 98. See further par 4 below.

43   2016 IICIS Report (n 13) 16; SGBV IICIS Report (n 11) par 5.

individual criminal responsibility of the various actors for the commission of international crimes.

Under-reporting and delayed reporting result from the deep social stigma attached to victims, tied in with a culture of silence and denial.[44] In the Syrian context, cultural, social and religious beliefs, as well as notions on marriage, honour, fidelity and the sexuality of women and girls, all have a powerful influence on the social stigma attached to victims of sexual and gender-based violence.[45]

The question of individual criminal responsibility in Syria for sexual and gender-based violence is further complicated by several other factors. Historically, the focus of international criminal justice has been on holding senior government officials of totalitarian governments individually criminally responsible,[46] resulting from the fact that international crimes are mostly committed by "totalitarian governments in power, government armed forces and other armed factions supporting the government's ideology".[47] As will be shown in this chapter, it is also the case in the Syrian armed conflict where government armed forces are responsible for committing sexual and gender-based violence during ground operations, house raids, at checkpoints, and during detention,[48] amounting to crimes against humanity[49] and war crimes.[50]

International law recognises that genocide, crimes against humanity, and war crimes need not *only* be committed by tyrannical governments, but can be perpetrated by non-state actors, too.[51] In the Syrian armed conflict, members of non-state armed opposition groups and terrorist organisations[52] have and continue to perpetrate

---

44 2016 IICIS Report (n 13) 16.

45 Fourth IICIS Report (n 13) 75.

46 London Charter for the International Military Tribunal to be held at Nuremberg (London Charter); Statute of the International Criminal Tribunal for Rwanda (ICTR Statute); Statue of the International Criminal Tribunal for the Former Yugoslavia (ICTY Statute); Statute for the Special Court for Sierra Leone (SCSL Statute); Law on the Extraordinary Chambers in the Courts of Cambodia (ECCC Law).

47 Roux "Early warning of gross human rights violations: an international law perspective" 2011 4 *Tydskrif vir die Suid-Afrikaanse Reg* 650 660. See further Masło "The attribution of international criminal responsibility for serious violations of human rights and international humanitarian law to senior leaders" in Krzan (ed) *Prosecuting International Crimes: A Multidisciplinary Approach* (2016) 81 82-83.

48 SGBV IICIS Report (n 11) par 3 and 7–50.

49 SGBV IICIS Report (n 11) par 110, 119–120 and 122–123.

50 SGBV IICIS Report (n 11) par 108 and 121.

51 Article IV of the Convention on the Prevention and Punishment of Genocide (Genocide Convention); article 7(2)(a) of the Rome Statute of the International Criminal Court (ICC Statute); common article 3 of the Geneva Conventions; article 1 of Protocol II to the Geneva Conventions.

52 Extremist, terrorist organisations party to the Syrian non-international armed conflict are Jabhat Fatah al-Sham and the Islamic State in Iraq and the Levant (ISIL).

sexual and gender-based violence, amounting to war crimes;[53] and in the case of the ISIL,[54] to genocide,[55] crimes against humanity[56] and war crimes.[57]

The International Criminal Court is increasingly holding non-state actors individually criminally responsible for international crimes.[58] Those persons accused of committing sexual and gender-based violence were charged[59] and found guilty[60] of committing war crimes and crimes against humanity; with sexual and gender-based violence being considered within the wider scheme of these crimes, and not as crimes *per se*.[61] Evidence collected, both by the International Commission of Inquiry on Syria and the Syria Mechanism, indicates that sexual and gender-based violence are priorities in the accountability-process of all actors in the Syrian armed conflict, regardless of their affiliation or status.[62] At this stage of the conflict, it is crucial that perpetrators are charged with sexual and gender-based violence either as crimes *per se*, or charged with committing sexual and gender-based violence as forms or categories of genocide, crimes against humanity and war crimes.[63] This view is consistent with existing jurisprudence of the Rwandan[64] and Yugoslavian Tribunals,[65] as well as the ICC Office of the Prosecutor's 2014 Policy Paper on Sexual and Gender-based Crimes.[66]

The purpose of the chapter is essentially to engage with the challenge of individual criminal responsibility of the various actors for committing sexual and gender-based violence in the Syrian armed conflict amounting to genocide, crimes against humanity and war crimes. This is important because an *erga omnes* obligation is imposed on the international community to prosecute international crimes.[67] If this

53 SGBV IICIS Report (n 11) par 125–127.

54 IICIS Yazidi Report (n 12).

55 IICIS Yazidi Report (n 12) par 100–165.

56 IICIS Yazidi Report (n 12) par 166–168.

57 IICIS Yazidi Report (n 12) par 169–173.

58 *The Prosecutor v Bosco Ntaganda* (22 August 2006) ICC Case No ICC-01/04-02/06 (First Warrant of Arrest); *The Prosecutor v Bosco Ntaganda* (13 July 2012) ICC Case No ICC-01/04-02/06 (Second Warrant of Arrest); *The Prosecutor v Thomas Lubanga Dyilo* (14 March 2012) ICC Case No ICC-01/04-01/06 (Trial Chamber I Judgment); *The Prosecutor v Thomas Lubanga Dyilo* (1 December 2014) ICC Case No ICC-01/04-01/06 A 4 A 6 (Appeals Chamber Judgment); *The Prosecutor v. Dominic Ongwen* (8 July 2005) ICC Case No ICC-02/04-01/15 (Warrant of Arrest).

59 *Ntanganda* (n 58); *Ongwen* (n 58).

60 *Lubanga* (n 58) par 1358.

61 2014 Policy Paper on Sexual and Gender-Based Crimes, Office of the Chief Prosecutor of the International Criminal Court, June 2014 par 1 https://www.icc-cpi.int/iccdocs/otp/OTP-Policy-Paper-on-Sexual-and-Gender-Based-Crimes--June-2014.pdf (2018-08-17) (2014 OTP Policy Paper on Sexual and Gender-based Crimes). See discussion in par 3.1 below.

62 SGBV IICIS Report (n 11); First Syria Mechanism Report (n 32) par 23–25 and 31.

63 2014 OTP Policy Paper on Sexual and Gender-based Crimes (n 61) par 72–73.

64 *Akayesu* (n 41).

65 *Furundžija* (n 41).

66 2014 OTP Policy Paper on Sexual and Gender-based Crimes (n 61) par 72–73.

67 Roux (n 42).

obligation is breached, impunity for the commission of international crimes will be enjoyed,[68] and the victims thereof will not obtain justice.[69] As will be shown below, individual criminal responsibility of all actors to the Syrian conflict is challenging in and of itself, but the accountability of non-state actors, which will include members of armed groups and terrorist organisations, has unique challenges. The fact that Syria is not a state party to the ICC Statute,[70] and the political impasse of the Security Council in referring the situation to the ICC Prosecutor,[71] only serve to compound these issues. Further, for each of the different international crimes, a different test and evidence is used to ensure individual criminal responsibility of the different actors. It is therefore crucial to engage with these issues to establish whether it is possible to hold the various actors individually criminally responsible.

The chapter will firstly contextualise sexual and gender-based violence in the Syrian armed conflict, through a discussion of the various actors committing these international crimes.[72] It will be shown that while state and non-state actors alike are committing these crimes, these violent acts may amount to different international crimes, whether war crimes, crimes against humanity, or genocide. Reports that will be relied upon indicate that nearly all actors are using sexual and gender-based violence as a very specific weapon and method of warfare. The chapter will then turn to the reasons behind under-reporting and delayed reporting of sexual and gender-based violence, namely the deep social stigma in Syrian society, resulting from culture and religion.

The chapter will then consider the question of individual criminal responsibility for acts amounting to genocide, crimes against humanity, and war crimes.[73] This will be done mainly by engaging with the requirement of an "organisational policy" for crimes against humanity, and a "plan or policy" for war crimes, as these requirements add to the difficulty of holding non-state actors accountable for these crimes. The chapter will conclude by highlighting various possibilities to overcome the challenges to individual criminal responsibility, specifically in light of fulfilling the *erga omnes* obligation to prosecute international crimes,[74] and thereby avoiding impunity for it.[75] The possible solutions that will be discussed focus on individual criminal responsibility at the ICC, the establishment of criminal jurisdiction by national courts of third states, and the establishment of either an international or regional *ad hoc* or hybrid court or tribunal.

---

68   Roux (n 42).

69   February 2018 IICIS Report (n 7) par 13.

70   State Parties to the Rome Statute https://asp.icc-cpi.int/en_menus/asp/states%20parties/Pages/the%20 states%20parties%20to%20the%20rome%20statute.aspx (2018-09-06).

71   SC Draft Res 348 (n 19).

72   See par 2 below.

73   See par 3 below.

74   Roux (n 42) 102.

75   See par 4 below.

The work of the International Commission of Inquiry and the Syria Mechanism is crucial to ensuring international criminal justice at the international, national and regional levels, and therefore, it is essential that the international community and all parties to the conflict cooperate with these organs.[76] It is, however, only in prosecuting *all* types of actors for sexual and gender-based violence, including non-state actors, that progress will be made in avoiding impunity for these atrocities, as well as provide remedies to victims, thereby restoring their dignity.[77]

5.2 SEXUAL AND GENDER-BASED VIOLENCE AS AN INTERNATIONAL CRIME: THE CONTEXT OF THE SYRIAN ARMED CONFLICT

In his seminal work, *International Law and Sexual Violence in Armed Conflicts*, International Criminal Court Judge Chile Eboe-Osuji states that "it is no longer a matter for reasonable debate that a high frequency of sexual violence during armed conflicts is very much an integral part of the wider and regular waves of armed conflicts".[78] The United Nations recognised that sexual and gender-based violence is a "defining" distinguishing feature of modern warfare, and is consistently used as a weapon and method of warfare.[79] For the most part, women and girls bear the brunt of sexual and gender-based violence during armed conflict,[80] but men and boys aren't completely safe from this form of violence either, as will be shown to be the case in the Syrian context.[81]

Eboe-Osuji argues that three theories can be discerned that lay bare the primary motives behind sexual violence during armed conflict, which can all be perceived in the Syrian context:[82] the "theory of inevitability",[83] the "theory of opportunism",[84] and the "theory of deliberate policy".[85] The core of the theory of inevitability supports the argument "that armed conflicts do mysterious things to the psyche of male fighters"[86] and therefore, that such savage violence is to be blamed on the evolutionary differences between women and men.[87] However, it is true that "not

---

76   GA Res 71/248 (n 20) par 6.

77   Roux (n 41) 94-110.

78   Eboe-Osuji (n 41) 65.

79   United Nations *Women, Peace and Security*, Study Submitted by the Secretary-General pursuant to Security Council Resolution 1325 (2000), United Nations 2002, 2 http://www.un.org/womenwatch/daw/public/eWPS.pdf (2018-08-19) par 7 (Women, Peace and Security S-G Study).

80   Eboe-Osuji (n 41) 65-66.

81   SGBV IICIS Report (n 11) par 43–50.

82   Eboe-Osuji (n 41) 72.

83   Eboe-Osuji (n 41) 72-81.

84   Eboe-Osuji (n 41) 81-83.

85   Eboe-Osuji (n 41) 83-94.

86   Eboe-Osuji (n 41) 72.

87   Eboe-Osuji (n 41) 75-81. Eboe-Osuji states at 81 that "the evolutionary theory of rape should heighten, rather than diminish, the duty upon military hierarchies to put efficient systems in place to prevent rapes during war, having trained, armed and deployed men whom they ought to have known or suspected as

all soldiers rape",[88] and that evolutionary theories behind rape in fact *reinforce* the obligation on superiors to prevent sexual violence by their subordinates.[89] The second theory, opportunism, lies in the inability of soldiers to control their sexual urges, and that they take advantage of the complete turmoil that ensues from a situation of armed conflict.[90] Eboe-Osuji disagrees with this theory, arguing that it "begs the question ... of how well international law is laid down and construed to protect women – or contain the evil of sexual violence – during armed conflicts".[91]

The third theory is highly relevant for purposes of this chapter, namely that sexual and gender-based violence during armed conflict is committed as a result of a deliberate policy.[92] A deliberate policy can materialise either explicitly, or in a more implied way where commanders and superiors systematically overlook the commission of sexual and gender-based violence and fail to prosecute its perpetrators.[93] An explicit policy is evidenced when it is used as a weapon and method of warfare during armed conflict, which manifests in different ways, depending on whether the victims are women or men.

Sexual violence against women is committed with an intention to humiliate and degrade them, specifically when they are associated with the enemy or are members of a targeted group. In some societies, sexual and gender-based violence is considered a "crime of honour"[94] whereby the community as a whole is targeted, leading to its "social degradation".[95] Men of the enemy camp or male members of the targeted group are humiliated, as sexual violence is used as a tool of domination and emasculation: "to violate the women is also to rape the souls of their men".[96] One of the most unsettling shapes that the humiliation of sexual violence may take, is by becoming imprinted "in an enduring way, into the social fabric and psyche of the subjugated group".[97] Women are raped repeatedly while detained to ensure their impregnation,[98] resulting in permanently changing the "ethnic composition",[99]

---

having evolved to rape women at any available opportunity. Failure to put such systems in place should result in criminal responsibility on the part of superiors for the resulting rapes."

88   Eboe-Osuji (n 41) 75.

89   Eboe-Osuji (n 41) 75.

90   Eboe-Osuji (n 41) 81.

91   Eboe-Osuji (n 41) 83.

92   Eboe-Osuji (n 41) 83-94.

93   Eboe-Osuji (n 41) 83-94.

94   Eboe-Osuji (n 41) 83.

95   Human Rights Watch "Shattered lives: sexual violence during the Rwandan genocide and its aftermath" September 1996 2 https://www.hrw.org/legacy/reports/1996/Rwanda.htm (2018-09-06) (HRW Shattered Lives).

96   Eboe-Osuji (n 41) 84.

97   Eboe-Osuji (n 41) 85.

98   Eboe-Osuji (n 41) 84.

99   Article 7(2) (f) of the ICC Statute.

or genetic make-up of children of the enemy or targeted group, in particular in societies where the biological father's genetics determine the child's.[100]

Lastly, two further ways in which a policy of sexual and gender-based violence can explicitly be used as a weapon and method of warfare is by terrorising the enemy and members of the targeted group into defeat, or as a method of torture during detention or interrogation.[101] Terrorising and torture is in and of itself humiliating,[102] and further, both may amount to the intentional causing of "serious bodily or mental harm",[103] "great suffering, or serious injury to body or to mental or physical health",[104] as well as inflicting "severe pain or suffering, whether physical or mental".[105]

The way in which a deliberate policy to commit sexual and gender-based violence during armed conflict can manifest implicitly, is through "systematic connivance or condonation" by superiors, which Eboe-Osuji explains as follows:[106]

> Systematic *condonation* of sexual violence occurs when the military or political hierarchy systematically turns a blind eye to its troops' commission of sexual violence or systematically avoid prosecution, notwithstanding legal proscriptions against sexual violence. Such attitudes from the hierarchy certainly have the effect of encouraging impunity in soldiers who would rape women during war. Systematic *connivance* in sexual violence means tacit encouragement of troops to commit sexual violence. It is sufficiently bad, and no less evil, that condonation or connivance occurs at all, and not at a systematic level: but the presence of such attitudes in systematic patterns is what converts the evil to one of policy.[107]

Systematic connivance and condonation is demonstrated when it is more acceptable to superiors that subordinates direct repressed aggression and resentment resulting from "the pathetic circumstances of soldiers"[108] towards women, as the "foregoing has a potential to implode into loss of morale or explode into mutiny or both".[109] It is further believed that sexual violence is "necessary for combat performance", a notion that has existed since antiquity in the guise that women of the enemy or targeted group are the spoils of war, the "prize for victory in war".[110] Lastly, connivance and condonation is considered as the "social glue that aids in the bonding process of

---

100 Eboe-Osuji (n 41) 84. See further in this regard *Akayesu* (n 41) par 121; S-G Report on Sexual Violence (n 28) par 13–14.

101 Eboe-Osuji (n 41) 85-86.

102 Roux (n 41) 93.

103 Article II (b) of the Genocide Convention.

104 Article 7(1) (k) of the ICC Statute.

105 Article 1(1) of the Convention against Torture and Other Cruel, Inhuman and Degrading Treatment or Punishment; and articles 7(1) (f) and 7(2) (e) of the ICC Statute.

106 Eboe-Osuji (n 41) 86.

107 Eboe-Osuji (n 41) 86-87 (own emphasis).

108 Eboe-Osuji (n 41) 89.

109 Eboe-Osuji (n 41) 90.

110 Eboe-Osuji (n 41) 90-91.

esprit de corps of men-at-arms", fed by sexual violence against women.[111] Combined, these factors contribute to impunity for sexual and gender-based violence, that superiors consider an "authorised transgression" by subordinates.[112]

To turn to sexual and gender-based violence committed in the context of the Syrian armed conflict, it has been reported since 2011 that members of government armed forces and associated militias have committed these atrocities during house raids, at government checkpoints, or while being detained in government-controlled detention centres.[113] Government forces allegedly targeted women because of their familial link to actual or perceived male members of opposition armed groups.[114] The detention of female relatives, and the implication that she would be raped when in detention, appeared designed to either humiliate that woman and her family, or alternatively force the surrender of male relatives linked to armed opposition groups.[115] In some detention centres, officials threatened to rape detainees or their relatives in order to exact information from them.[116] In one report, a nine-year-old girl, whose father was suspected of being a member of a non-state armed opposition group, was raped by government forces.[117] On numerous occasions, women reported that they were not only raped, but also tortured by officials, often being subjected to electrocution or to being burned with cigarettes, lighters or melted plastic.[118] Male detainees have also reported that either they personally, or their cellmates, were raped with objects, including knives, and that others had received electric shocks to their genitals.[119] Several reports indicated that rape and sexual assault of both men and women were perpetrated at checkpoints located in the areas of Aleppo, Damascus, Dara'a, Homs and Latakia.[120]

The Commission of Inquiry on Syria reported that most accounts of sexual and gender-based violence occurred in state-run detention centres, or had been perpetrated by soldiers or check-point officials.[121] Acts of rape, sexual torture and other acts of sexual violence by government forces and associated militia against men, women and children were committed on a systematic and widespread scale.[122] The Commission concluded as early as 2013 that factual evidence supported the finding that sexual and gender-based violence committed in the context of the

---

111   Eboe-Osuji (n 41) 92.

112   Eboe-Osuji (n 41) 93.

113   2016 IICIS Report (n 13) 16; SGBV IICIS Report (n 11) par 3 and 7–50.

114   Tenth IICIS Report (n 13) 8.

115   Tenth IICIS Report (n 13) 8.

116   2016 IICIS Report (n 13) 16.

117   2016 IICIS Report (n 13) 16.

118   Fourth IICIS Report (n 13) 75; 2016 IICIS Report (n 13) 16.

119   2016 IICIS Report (n 13) 16.

120   Seventh IICIS Report (n 13) 12.

121   Fourth IICIS Report (n 13) par 97.

122   Fourth IICIS Report (n 13) par 106–110.

armed conflict amounted to war crimes and crimes against humanity,[123] and has repeatedly reiterated this conclusion, most recently in March 2018.[124] It found that criminal acts

> were committed in pursuance of a [state] policy to target civilians broadly perceived as associated with the opposition, evidenced by the systematic occurrence of crimes across geographic areas. The existence of a State policy is further demonstrated by the fact that significant State resources were employed in the commission of the crimes and the way in which numerous State institutions throughout the country actively participated and coordinated operations at various levels of the sequential conduct, during which custodial deaths and other crimes occurred. Military and civilian courts consistently failed to order investigations into cases where detainees appearing before a judge were visibly ill treated, sometimes displaying severe injuries, and in cases of deaths in custody.[125]

Sexual and gender-based violence by members of non-state armed opposition groups and terrorist organisation, Jabhat Fatah al-Sham, reflect the second theory discerned by Eboe-Osuji, namely opportunism.[126] The Commission of Inquiry on Syria did not find evidence of a policy of sexual and gender-based violence by these groups,[127] but considered the use of sexual and gender-based violence by these groups as means to terrorise and exploit the opposition and for purposes of "sectarianism".[128] The Commission concluded that acts amounting to rape, sexual torture and sexual violence perpetrated by these groups were "in violation of common article 3 of the Geneva Conventions and constitute war crimes".[129] Over the course of the conflict, women and children were targeted for kidnapping, and were later used in prisoner exchanges for women and fighters detained by the state.[130]

Sexual and gender-based violence by extremist terrorist organisation ISIL is by far the most disturbing. In 2016, the Independent International Commission of Inquiry on Syria concluded that ISIL committed the crime of genocide, crimes against humanity and war crimes against the Yazidis,[131] and that crimes against humanity were committed against Sunni Muslim women living in ISIL-controlled areas.[132] The

---

123   Fourth IICIS Report (n 13) par 110.

124   SGBV IICIS Report (n 11) par 109–110. See further Thematic Report of the Independent International Commission of Inquiry on the Syrian Arab Republic, "Out of sight, out of mind: deaths in detention in the Syrian Arab Republic", Human Rights Council, A/HRC/31/CRP.1 (3 February 2016) par 98 (IICIS Thematic Report).

125   IICIS Thematic Report (n 124) par 89.

126   Eboe-Osuji (n 41) 81- 83.

127   SGBV IICIS Report (n 11) par 52 and 58–71.

128   SGBV IICIS Report (n 11) par 52, 55, 57, 61 and 66.

129   Seventh IICIS Report (n 13) 12.

130   Tenth IICIS Report (n 13) 9.

131   IICIS Yazidi Report (n 12) par 100–173.

132   2016 IICIS Report (n 13) 16-17.

Commission reported that thousands of Yadizi women and girls had been "sold" in the Syrian governorates of Allepo, Dayr az-Zawr, Hasakah, Homs and Raqqah.[133] These Yazidi women and girls had reportedly endured sexual enslavement, brutal rape, severe beatings and gang rape if they attempted to escape from Islamic State fighters.[134]

In 2014, within days of members of ISIL entering Sinjar, a region located in northern Iraq in close proximity to the Syrian border,[135] unimaginable atrocities against the Yazidi community were committed. They were systematically captured and forcibly transferred to Syria.[136] In 2016, the Commission reported that around 3,200 Yazidi women and girls were captives of ISIL in areas under their control in Syria.[137] The Commission found that ISIL had

> committed, and continues to commit, the crime of genocide, as well as multiple crimes against humanity and war crimes, against the Yazidis. The genocide committed against the Yazidis has not primarily been accomplished through killings, though mass killings of men and women have occurred. Rather ISIS seeks to destroy the Yazidis in multiple ways, as envisaged by the drafters of the 1948 Genocide Convention. ISIS has sought, and continues to seek, to destroy the Yazidis through killings; sexual slavery, enslavement, torture and inhuman and degrading treatment, and forcible transfer causing serious bodily and mental harm; the infliction of conditions of life that bring about a slow death; the imposition of measures to prevent Yazidi children from being born, including forced conversion of adults, the separation of Yazidi men and women, and mental trauma; and the transfer of Yazidi children from their own families and placing them with ISIS fighters, thereby cutting them off from beliefs and practices of their own religious community, and erasing their identity as Yazidis.[138]

The Commission determined that, through its public statements and conduct, ISIL and its members demonstrated an intention to destroy in whole or in part the Yazidis of Sinjar in particular, where the majority of the world's Yazidi population live.[139] In one interview, a woman, who was held captive for about a year, reported that they

> were driven into Raqqah city at night and held in a building there. I was there for three weeks before I was sold. Throughout that time, [ISIL] fighters were coming to buy women and girls. All of us were Yazidi. I think I was sold about 15 times in all. It is hard to remember all those who bought me.[140]

---

133 2016 IICIS Report (n 13) 17.

134 Tenth IICIS Report (n 13) 9; 2016 IICIS Report (n 13) 17.

135 IICIS Yazidi Report (n 12) par 1. Sinjar is home to the majority of the Yazidi population. The Yazidi are a religious community that the Islamic State considers infidel.

136 IICIS Yazidi Report (n 12) par 1–4.

137 IICIS Yazidi Report (n 12) par 6.

138 IICIS Yazidi Report (n 12) par 201–202.

139 IICIS Yazidi Report (n 12) par 1.

140 IICIS Yazidi Report (n 12) par 42.

Another survivor, a 12-year-old girl who was held captive for about seven months, stated that they were first registered, and thereafter ISIL

> took our names, ages, where we came from and whether we were married or not. After that, [ISIL] fighters would come to select girls to go with them. The youngest girl I saw them take was about 9 years old. One girl told me that 'if they try to take you, it is better that you kill yourself'.[141]

As mentioned above, within Syrian society, a deep social stigma, in addition to a culture of silence and denial, surround sexual and gender-based violence committed during the armed conflict.[142] In a 2002 study by the United Nations Secretary-General, it was noted that "[w]omen and girls are often viewed as bearers of cultural identity and thus become prime targets (during armed conflict). Gender-based and sexual violence have increasingly become weapons of warfare",[143] and "[t]he specific experience of women and girls in armed conflict is linked to their status in societies".[144] In nearly all cultures, high emphasis is placed on a woman's "sexual virtue":[145] rape not only humiliates the woman, but everyone associated with her.[146] These sentiments ring true in the Syrian context, where society is still extremely patriarchal, and intensely influenced by religious and cultural dogma.[147]

It can be argued that Eboe-Osuji's third theory concerning a deliberate policy to commit sexual and gender-based violence during armed conflict and the ways in which it materialises either explicitly or implicitly[148] may find application in the Syrian context. This is especially true when considering the social stigma surrounding sexually violent crimes within this society,[149] as well as the fact that no form of accountability has transpired for the commission of these crimes.[150] It is comparable to the Rwandan genocide and the Yugoslavian armed conflicts where sexual and gender-based violence were also used as a weapon and method of warfare against women from the targeted groups,[151] whereas in Syria victims include men and boys associated with the enemy or targeted groups.[152] In Syria, perpetrators exploit the social stigma, extreme humiliation, and victims' fear of being ostracised from their communities should sexual violence committed against them become public, in order to commit these crimes with carnal abandon.[153]

---

141 IICIS Yazidi Report (n 12) par 42.

142 See par 1 above.

143 Women, Peace and Security S-G Study (n 79) par 7.

144 Women, Peace and Security S-G Study (n 79) par 6.

145 S-G Report on Sexual Violence (n 28) par 13.

146 HRW Shattered Lives (n 95) 2.

147 Fourth IICIS Report (n 13) 75; SGBV IICIS Report (n 11) par 5–6, 93–102.

148 Eboe-Osuji (n 41) 83-94.

149 Fourth IICIS Report (n 13) 75; SGBV IICIS Report (n 11).

150 See (n 34).

151 See further in this regard Akayesu (n 41); Furundžija (n 41); HRW Shattered Lives (n 95).

152 SGBV IICIS Report (n 11) par 43–50.

153 S-G Report on Sexual Violence (n 28) par 19.

To illustrate, in one incident, the Commission of Inquiry on Syria was informed that a female victim of sexual assault was murdered by her brother-in-law in order to "preserve the honour of the family".[154] The Commission also received reports that some female victims had been abandoned by their husbands after they had been raped,[155] and many women committed suicide after being raped.[156] Some women reported to the Commission that being the victim of sexual assault and the dishonour associated therewith is a fate worse than death.[157] Directing sexual and gender-based violence against men and boys associated with the enemy or targeted group becomes a humiliating display of domination and emasculation,[158] with many reports indicating that men and boys are terrorised and tortured during detention by members of government and associated militias in particular.[159]

The combined impact of these factors is that it plays a dominant role in stifling the proper investigation and prosecution of these crimes.[160] The under-reporting and delayed reporting of sexual and gender-based violence is a direct result of the extreme social stigma, humiliation, and the victims' fear of being ostracised.[161] Lastly, the trauma and stigma suffered materialises in different ways on different victims, with male victims and children born as a result of rape facing distinctive difficulties, which often take years to manifest.[162]

The next part will engage with the various possibilities that exist for states in the international community to hold perpetrators individually criminally responsible for sexual and gender-based violence, whether at international, regional or national levels. The *erga omnes* obligation to investigate and prosecute these crimes forms the basis for this, and the obligation is imposed on Syria, third states and member states of the United Nations.[163]

Before the possibilities of individual criminal responsibility will be discussed, it will, however, be necessary to engage with the meaning and question of individual criminal responsibility. What makes the question of individual criminal responsibility complicated, is whether non-state actors, including members of terrorist organisations, can also be held individually criminally responsible for genocide, crimes against humanity and war crimes. This issue is of particular relevance for the Syrian armed conflict, as many non-state actors in the conflict have and continue to commit international crimes.

---

154   Third IICIS Report (n 9) 91.

155   Third IICIS Report (n 9) 91.

156   Third IICIS Report (n 9) 91.

157   Fourth IICIS Report (n 13) 75.

158   Eboe-Osuji (n 41) 84.

159   2016 IICIS Report (n 13) par 104; SGBV IICIS Report (n 11) par 43–50.

160   2016 IICIS Report (n 13) par 104; SGBV IICIS Report (n 11) par 5.

161   S-G Report on Sexual Violence (n 28) par 19.

162   S-G Report on Sexual Violence (n 28) par 19.

163   Roux (n 42).

5.3   THE QUESTION OF INDIVIDUAL CRIMINAL RESPONSIBILITY OF NON-STATE ACTORS FOR INTERNATIONAL CRIMES

It is an accepted international criminal law principle that only individual, natural persons can be prosecuted: state entities cannot be "tried" and "punished" in a criminal manner.[164] For an organisation or state entity to be declared criminal, its criminal status must be determined in terms of a binding international treaty or statute. The London Charter of the International Military Tribunal held at Nuremberg expressly provided for the Nazi Party and certain organisations to be declared criminal.[165] The London Charter provided that mere membership of a criminal organisation could be regarded as a criminal act, even if participation in that group was involuntary.[166] The Nuremberg Tribunal stated that in light thereof that a declaration of criminality of organisations and armed groups will "fix the criminality of its members", that the definition of a criminal organisation

> should exclude persons who had no knowledge of the criminal purposes or acts of the organisation and those who were drafted by the State for membership, unless they were personally implicated in the commission of (crimes against peace, war crimes and crimes against humanity) as members of the organisation. Membership alone is not enough to come within the scope of these declarations.[167]

The Leadership Corps of the Nazi Party itself was subsequently declared criminal in nature by the Nuremberg Tribunal,[168] and organisations declared criminal included the *Geheime Staatspolizei* (Gestapo) and the *Sicherheitsdients des Reichsführer SS* (SD),[169] as well as the *Schutzstaffeln der Nationalsozialistischen Deutschen Arbeiterpartei* (SS).[170] However, the requirement to prosecute an individual member on the basis of membership of the Nazi Party and the latter organisations, was that the member had to have had "knowledge that (the Party or organisation) was being used for the commission" of criminal acts, or that the individual was "personally implicated as member" of the Party or organisation.

---

164   Commentary to Article 58 par 2 at 363-364 of the International Law Commission's Commentary to the Articles on the Responsibility of States for Internationally Wrongful Acts, *Report of the International Law Commission, Official Records of the General Assembly, Fifty-third Session*, 23 April–1 June and 2 July–10 August 2001, Supplement 10 (A/56/10), par 4 at 365 (2001 ILC Report); *Application of the Convention on the Prevention and Punishment of the Crime of Genocide (Bosnia and Herzegovina v Serbia and Montenegro)* 26 February 2007 ICJ Reports 1 (Judgment), par 170–174 at 64-66.

165   Articles 9(1) and 10 of the London Charter.

166   Articles 9(1) and 10 of the London Charter. See further Cassese *International Criminal Law* (2012) 34.

167   Judicial Decisions: International Military Tribunal (Nuremberg), Judgment and Sentences, reprinted in January 1947, 41 *American Journal of International Law* 172 251.

168   *Nuremberg Judgment* (n 167) 255-256.

169   *Nuremberg Judgment* (n 167) 261-262.

170   *Nuremberg Judgment* (n 167) 266-267.

All international criminal law instruments adopted since the London Charter expressly provide for the individual criminal liability of natural persons only.[171] Acts by military organisations and armed forces or groups cannot therefore automatically be attributed to each individual member of the organisation by mere fact of an individual's membership thereto: for a member of an organisation to be held individually criminally responsible, such member has to bear personal responsibility for a particular act or omission.[172]

In general, individual criminal responsibility indicates "the responsibility of individual persons, including state officials, under certain rules of international law for conduct such as genocide, war crimes and crimes against humanity".[173] Individual criminal responsibility will only follow if a person has breached the law, participated in the commission of a crime, displayed some form of mental participation in committing the offence, or was culpably negligent or deliberately omitted to prevent criminal acts committed by subordinates, and the omission can be attributed to the individual.[174]

The ICC Statute stipulates that a "natural person" shall be criminally responsible and liable to punishment if that person commits an international crime, individually or jointly, with or through another person,[175] or attempts to or orders, solicits or induces the commission of a crime,[176] or facilitates, aids, abets, provides the means for or otherwise assists in the attempt or commission of a crime.[177] Furthermore, a person may be held criminally liable if that person, intentionally and knowingly, contributes to the attempt or commission of a crime involving a group of people acting with a common purpose aimed at furthering the criminal objectives of the group.[178]

At the International Criminal Court, the official capacity of heads of state and government, as well as members of government and parliament, will not exempt criminal responsibility; therefore, immunity does not bar the court from exercising its jurisdiction over any individual.[179] Additionally, the court is entitled to hold military commanders and persons effectively acting as military commanders criminally responsible for crimes committed by forces under that commander's

---

171　Article IV of the Genocide Convention; Article II of the Convention on the Non-Applicability of Statutory Limitations to War Crimes and Crimes against Humanity; Article 6 of ICTY Statute; Article 5 of the ICTR Statute; Article 25 of the ICC Statute; Article 29 of the ECCC Law.

172　Cassese (n 166) 34.

173　Commentary to article 58 of the 2001 ILC Report (n 164).

174　Cassese (n 166) 33 and 34. See further *The Prosecutor v Duško Tadić* 15 July 1999 ICTY IT-94-1-A (Judgment), par 186.

175　Article 25 (3)(a) of the ICC Statute.

176　Article 25 (3)(b) of the ICC Statute.

177　Article 25 (3)(c) of the ICC Statute.

178　Article 25 (3)(d) of the ICC Statute.

179　Article 27 of the ICC Statute.

effective military command and control or effective authority and control.[180] Military commanders may only be held responsible if firstly, the commander knew or should have known that military forces were committing or about to commit crimes,[181] and secondly, if the commander did not "take all necessary and reasonable measures within his or her power to prevent or repress their commission or to submit the matter to the competent authorities for investigation and prosecution".[182]

The position in international criminal law since the Nuremberg Tribunal regarding individual criminal responsibility for state officials,[183] military commanders and superiors[184] is therefore clear. However, the ICC Statute includes further require-ments for perpetrators of crimes against humanity and war crimes in its definitions, specifically that these crimes must be committed "pursuant to or in furtherance of a state or organisational policy"[185] or "as part of a plan or policy".[186] The definition of genocide in terms of the Statute includes the genocidal policy generally, without describing the type of perpetrators specifically: perpetrators of genocide are included in terms of the provisions dealing with the principles of international criminal law relating to individual criminal responsibility.[187] This is in contrast to the Genocide Convention, where it is explicitly provided that genocide can be committed by "constitutionally responsible rulers, public officials or private individuals".[188]

The additional requirements for perpetrators of crimes against humanity and war crimes in terms of the ICC Statute has undergone much scrutiny amongst academics,[189] and has formed the subject matter of a number of cases both at the *ad hoc* Tribunals[190] and at the ICC.[191] It was also addressed by the International Law Commission as part of its long-term programme of work on crimes against

---

180 Article 28 of the ICC Statute.

181 Article 28(1)(a)(i) of the ICC Statute.

182 Article 28(1)(a)(ii) of the ICC Statute.

183 See for example article IV of the Genocide Convention, and articles 7(2)(a) and 27 of the ICC Statute.

184 Article 28 of the ICC Statute.

185 Article 7(2)(a) of the ICC Statute.

186 Article 8(1) of the ICC Statute.

187 Articles 22-33 of the ICC Statute.

188 Article 4 of the Genocide Convention.

189 See further in this regard Bassiouni *The Legislative History of the International Criminal Court* (2015) 151-152; Cassese and Gaeta *Cassese's International Criminal Law* (2013) 91; Dugard *International Law: A South African Perspective* (2011) 178; Hansen "The policy requirement in crimes against humanity: lessons from and for the case of Kenya" 2011 43 6 *The George Washington International Law Review* 13-15; Schabas "State policy as an element of international crimes" 2008 *Journal of Criminal Law and Criminology* (Spring) 952-982 974; Triffterer and Ambos (eds) *Rome Statute of the International Court: A Commentary* 3 ed (2016) 246-250.

190 *The Prosecutor v Duško Tadić* (7 May 1997) ICTY Case No IT-94-1-T (Opinions and Judgment); *Akayesu* (n 41); *The Prosecutor v Thihomir Blaškić* (3 March 2000) ICTY Case No IT-95-14-T (Judgment); *Kunarac* (n 247).

191 *Situation in the Republic of Kenya* (31 March 2010) ICC Case no ICC-01/09 (Decision pursuant to Article 15 of the Rome Statute on the authorisation of an investigation into the Situation in the Republic of Kenya) (*ICC Kenya Authorisation Decision*); Karanga; Ruto; Ntaganda; Kony; Lubanga; Ongweni.

humanity in general.[192] The debate has resulted from the various actors who commit acts amounting to crimes against humanity, namely state actors, state-like actors and non-state actors, and is of particular relevance to Syria considering the various actors involved in the armed conflict.

Both Cassese and Dugard considered that, for an act to amount to a crime against humanity, it had to form part of a governmental policy or a widespread, systematic practice of atrocities tolerated, condoned or acquiesced in by a government or *de facto* authority.[193] In contrast, Bassiouni argued that because the ICC Statute's definition of crimes against humanity expressly refers to "state policy", the words "organisational policy" should not be interpreted to mean that the policy can be that of any organisation involving non-state actors,[194] thus asserting that the jurisdiction of the ICC does not extend to non-state actors.[195] In turn, Schabas suggested that although non-state actors are able to perpetrate crimes against humanity, non-state actors are less likely to evade prosecution because "most states are both willing and able to prosecute the terrorist groups, rebels", and that it is therefore unnecessary to include the policy of non-state actors in the ambit of the policy requirement.[196] Burns argued that an organisational policy "can undoubtedly include state organs and will extend to para-military units of a state, organised rebel groups within a state, or even unorganised rebel groups so long as there is a sufficient core that develops such a policy for the group".[197] He concluded that non-state actors "may in principle fulfil the organisational requirement and therefore be subjected to the jurisdiction of the ICC".[198] Finally, in their commentary to the ICC Statute, Triffterer and Ambos supported the "functional approach" which infers "the requirements of an organisation within the meaning of article 7(2)(a) from the context element, i.e., this organisation's capacity to wage a widespread or systematic attack against the civilian population".[199] They stated further that

> [c]learly the policy need not be one of a State. It can also be an organisational policy. Non-state actors or private individuals who exercise *de facto* power can constitute the entity behind the policy. This provision in the article reflects the contemporary position that individuals not linked to a state or its authorities can commit crimes under international law.[200]

---

192 Report of the International Law Commission, Sixty-fifth Session, 6 May–7 June and 8 July–9 August 2013, *Official Records of the General Assembly, Sixty-eight Session, Supplement No. 10* (A/68/10), par 170 (2013 ILC Report).

193 Cassese and Gaeta (n 189) 91; Dugard (n 189) 178.

194 Bassiouni (n 189) 151-152; Hansen (n 189) 14.

195 Bassiouni (n 189) 151-152; Hansen (n 189) 13.

196 Schabas (n 189) 952-982, 974.

197 Hansen (n 189) 14.

198 Hansen (n 189) 15.

199 Triffterer and Ambos (n 189) 250.

200 Triffterer and Ambos (n 189) 246.

The decisions of the ICTY, the ICTR and the ICC have varied: in some instances, the requirement of policy was expressly required, in others it was inferred from the circumstances, or it was not required at all. The Statutes of the ICTY[201] and the ICTR[202] did not explicitly require an organisational policy-requirement in their respective definitions of crimes against humanity, which became apparent in the judgments and opinions of these courts.[203] In *Tadić*, the Trials Chamber of the Yugoslavian Tribunal interpreted the phrase "directed against any civilian population" to mean that "the acts must occur on a widespread or systematic basis, that there must be some form of a governmental, organisational or group policy to commit these acts and that the perpetrator must know of the context within which his actions are taken".[204] Thus, the ICTY in *Tadić* called for the existence of a state or organisational policy to be present as an element of the crime, and held that

> the [ICTY] is not bound by past doctrine but must apply customary international law as it stood at the time of the offences. In this regard the law in relation to crimes against humanity has developed to take into account forces which, although not those of the legitimate government, have *de facto* control over, or are able to move freely within, defined territory. The Prosecution ... argues that under international law crimes against humanity can be committed on behalf of entities exercising *de facto* control over a particular territory but without international recognition or formal status of a *de jure* state, or by a terrorist group or organisation. The judgment concludes by stating that a policy is required to constitute a crime against humanity, but it need not be the policy of a state.[205]

In turn, the *Blaškić* judgment stated that a plan "need not necessarily be declared expressly, clearly or precisely but that such plan may be surmised from the occurrence of a series of events".[206] In *Kunarac*, the ICTY Appeals Chamber held that "neither the attack nor the acts of the accused needs to be supported by any form of policy or plan" and that nothing under customary international law required proof of a policy or plan to commit international crimes.[207] Accordingly,

> proof that the attack was directed against a civilian population and that it was widespread or systematic, are legal elements of the crime. But to prove these elements, it is not necessary to show that they were the result of the existence of a policy or plan. It may be useful in establishing that the attack was directed against a civilian population and that it was widespread or systematic (especially the latter) to show that there was in fact a policy or

---

201   Article 5 of the ICTY Statute.

202   Article 3 of the ICTR Statute.

203   First Report on Crimes Against Humanity, Sean D Murphy (Special Rapporteur), *Report of the International Law Commission, Official Records of the General Assembly, Sixty-seventh Session* 4 May–5 June and 6 July–7 August 2015 (A/CN.4/680) 17 February 2015, par 138 (Murphy's First Report).

204   *Tadić* (n 190) par 644.

205   *Tadić* (n 190) par 654–655. See further Hansen (n 189) 15.

206   *Blaškić* (n 190) par 203–204. See further Shaw *International Law* (2009) 437.

207   *Kunarac* (n 190) par 98.

plan, but it may be possible to prove these things by reference to other matters. Thus, the existence of a policy or plan may be evidentially relevant, but it is not a legal element of the crime.[208]

In the *Akayesu* judgment at the Trial Chamber of the Rwandan Tribunal, it was held that the

> concept of 'widespread' may be defined as massive, frequent, large scale action, carried out collectively with considerable seriousness and directed against a multiplicity of victims. The concept of 'systematic' may be defined as thoroughly organised and following a regular pattern on the basis of a common policy involving substantial public or private resources. There is no requirement that this policy must be adopted formally as the policy of a state. There must however be some kind of preconceived plan or policy.[209]

The requirement of an organisational policy for the commission of a crime against humanity and whether this will include non-state actors, has been interpreted in a great amount of detail by the International Criminal Court. The ICC Elements of Crimes elaborates on the requirement in article 7(2)(a) of the Statute by stating that the "policy to commit such attack requires that the State or organisation actively promote or encourage such an attack against a civilian population".[210]

The most interesting argument thus far has been that of the ICC's Pre-trial Chamber II in the *Kenya Authorisation Decision*.[211] In this case, the majority opted for a progressive functional approach and determined that "the formal nature of the group and level of organisation should not be the defining criterion",[212] and that the question is rather whether or not a group has "the capability to perform acts which infringe on basic human values".[213] In order to determine whether a specific group meets the requirement of an "organisation" in terms of the ICC Statute, the majority held that it must be decided "on a case-by-case basis",[214] taking the following into account:

> (i) whether the group is under a responsible command, or has an established hierarchy; (ii) whether the group possesses, in fact, the means to carry out a widespread or systematic attack against a civilian population; (iii) whether

---

208 *Kunarac* (n 190) par 98.

209 *Akayesu* (n 41) par 580.

210 Elements of Crimes, International Criminal Court, Official Records of the Assembly of States Parties to the Rome Statute of the International Criminal Court, First session, 3–10 September 2002, https://www.icc-cpi.int/NR/rdonlyres/336923D8-A6AD-40EC-AD7B-45BF9DE73D56/0/ElementsOfCrimesEng.pdf (2018-08-19).

211 *ICC Kenya Authorisation Decision* (n 191).

212 *ICC Kenya Authorisation Decision* (n 191) par 90. See further Holvoet "The state or organisational policy requirement within the definition of crimes against humanity in the Rome Statute: an appraisal of the emerging jurisprudence and the implementation practice by ICC states parties" in *International Crimes Database Brief 2* (October 2013) at 4 http://www.internationalcrimesdatabase.org/upload/documents/20131111t105507-icd%20brief%20%202%20-%20holvoet.pdf (2018-08-19).

213 *ICC Kenya Authorisation Decision* (n 191) par 90.

214 *ICC Kenya Authorisation Decision* (n 191) par 93.

the group exercises control over part of the territory of a State; (iv) whether the group has criminal activities against the civilian population as a primary purpose; (v) whether the group articulates, explicitly or implicitly, an intention to attack a civilian population; (vi) whether the group is part of a larger group, which fulfils some or all of the abovementioned criteria.[215]

The majority concluded that,

had the drafters of the Statute intended to exclude non-State actors from the term 'organisation', they would not have included this term in article 7(2)(a) of the Statute. The Chamber thus determines that organisations not linked to a State may, for the purposes of the Statute, elaborate and carry out a policy to commit an attack against a civilian population.[216]

However, in a dissenting opinion, Judge Kaul[217] stated that an "organisation" within the meaning of article 7(2)(a) should extend to state-like organisations, but that it is unconvincing to extend the meaning to include non-state actors[218] with "the capability to perform acts which infringe on basic human values" as interpreted by the majority.[219] He argued that further thought is required, or the consequence will be that the concept of crimes against humanity is applied to any infringement of human rights,[220] and that "although acts of low-level government officials are attributable to the state, only actors at the "high level" are capable of establishing a policy".[221] He further developed certain characteristics that are able to turn a private organisation into an entity with state or quasi-state abilities,[222] including a

collectivity of persons which was established and acts for a common purpose over a prolonged period of time, which is under responsible command or adopted a certain degree of hierarchical structure, including, as a minimum, some kind of policy level with the capacity to impose the policy on its members and to sanction them and which has the capacity and means available to attack any civilian population on a large scale.[223]

Thus, in meeting these requirements, an organisation has the potential of being termed a "state-like" actor. He found that non-state actors, specifically organised crime groups, criminal gangs and organised armed civilians, do not fall within the criteria discussed above and are unable to carry out a policy as required by

---

215 *ICC Kenya Authorisation Decision* (n 191) par 93.

216 *ICC Kenya Authorisation Decision* (n 191) par 92. See further Holvoet (n 212) 10.

217 *Situation in the Republic of Kenya* (31 March 2010) ICC Case no ICC-01/09 (Decision pursuant to Article 15 of the Rome Statute on the authorisation of an investigation into the Situation in the Republic of Kenya), Dissenting Opinion of Judge Hans-Peter Kaul, par 31 (*Kenya Kaul Dissenting Opinion*).

218 *Kenya Kaul Dissenting Opinion* (n 217) par 53.

219 *ICC Kenya Authorisation Decision* (n 191) par 90.

220 *Kenya Kaul Dissenting Opinion* (n 217) par 53.

221 *Kenya Kaul Dissenting Opinion* (n 217) par 43.

222 *Kenya Kaul Dissenting Opinion* (n 217) par 51.

223 *Kenya Kaul Dissenting Opinion* (n 217) par 51.

Article 7 of the Statute.[224] In this respect, Judge Kaul put forward the arguments that organisations should at least partake in some characteristics of the state,[225] that setting a high threshold for the term "organisation" avoids the trivialisation of the crimes contained in the Statute,[226] and that historically States are primarily the parties that adopt policies, either formally or in practice, in order to attack a civilian population, as opposed to non-state actors.[227]

The approach of the majority in the *Kenya Authorisation Decision*[228] is similar to the one supported by the International Law Commission over the years.[229] In 2013, by including "crimes against humanity" as part of its long-term programme of work,[230] the ILC set the purpose that an international treaty "on the prevention and punishment of crimes against humanity"[231] would result from its work. Between 2015 and 2017, the ILC provisionally adopted draft articles on crimes against humanity.[232] Notably, the definition of crimes against humanity in draft article 3 replicates article 7 of the ICC Statute, barring three non-substantive amendments relating to the context of the articles.[233] Draft article 3(2)(a) provides that an "[a]ttack directed against any civilian population" means a course of conduct involving the multiple commission of acts ... against any civilian population, pursuant to or in furtherance of a State or organisational policy to commit such attack".[234]

In his First Report on Crimes Against Humanity, Special Rapporteur Sean Murphy discussed the 'policy' requirement[235] as well as the question of whether non-state actors could be held individually criminally responsible for crimes against humanity.[236] He stated that, considering the language of article 7(2)(a) of the ICC Statute, specifically by including "state or organisational policy", that "article 7 expressly contemplates crimes against humanity by non-state perpetrators".[237] He further supported the above and other ICTY, ICTR and ICC cases where a similar

224 *Kenya Kaul Dissenting Opinion* (n 217) par 52.
225 *Kenya Kaul Dissenting Opinion* (n 217) par 51.
226 *Kenya Kaul Dissenting Opinion* (n 217) par 55.
227 *Kenya Kaul Dissenting Opinion* (n 217) par 61.
228 *ICC Kenya Authorisation Decision* (n 191).
229 Murphy's First Report (n 203) par 139–150.
230 2013 ILC Report (n 192).
231 Murphy's First Report (n 203) par 13 and section II in general.
232 Report of the International Law Commission, Sixty-seventh Session, 4 May–5 June and 6 July–7 August 2015, *Official Records of the General Assembly, Seventieth Session, Supplement No.10* (A/70/10), Chapter VII (2015 ILC Report); Report of the International Law Commission, Sixty-eighth Session, 2 May–10 June and 4 July–12 August 2016, *Official Records of the General Assembly, Seventy-first Session, Supplement No.10* (A/71/10) Chapter VII (2016 ILC Report); Report of the International Law Commission, Sixty-ninth Session, 1 May–2 June and 3 July–4 August 2017, *Official Records of the General Assembly, Seventy-second Session, Supplement No.10* (A/72/10) Chapter IV (2017 ILC Report).
233 Murphy's First Report (n 203) par 8, 21–25, 122–124 and 176–177 in particular, and section VI in general.
234 2015 ILC Report (n 232) par 116.
235 Murphy's First Report (n 203) par 138–144.
236 Murphy's First Report (n 203) par 144–150.
237 Murphy's First Report (n 203) par 147.

approach was implemented.[238] The ILC subsequently endorsed Murphy's First Report,[239] commenting that the reason for provisionally adopting draft article 3, in particular by mirroring the wording of article 7 of the ICC Statute, is because "policy" may "potentially (emanate) from a non-State organisation", therefore "the definition set forth in paragraphs 1 to 3 of draft article 3 does not require that the offender be a State official or agent".[240] The ILC hereby confirmed that including non-state actors under the concept of an organisation "is consistent with the development of crimes against humanity under international law".[241]

As mentioned above, the ICC Statute also requires that, in order for violence committed during an armed conflict to amount to war crimes, it must be committed "as part of a plan or policy".[242] The position in terms of international humanitarian law and individual criminal responsibility for war crimes is determined by common article 3 of the Geneva Conventions,[243] article 1 Protocol II,[244] in addition to applicable provisions in the ICC Statute.[245] The threshold in terms of the former provides that "each party" to a non-international armed conflict is bound by the Conventions, whereas the requirements for article 1 Protocol II is that "organised armed groups" must be "under responsible command", exercise "control over a part of its territory as to enable them to carry out sustained and concerted military operations and to implement this Protocol".[246]

The question whether non-state actors are capable of committing war crimes also came before the Yugoslavian Tribunal in *Kunarac*, where the ICTY Appeals Chamber held the following regarding war crimes and the policy requirement:

> What ultimately distinguishes a war crime from a purely domestic offence is that a war crime is shaped by or dependent upon the environment – the armed conflict – in which it is committed. It need not have been planned or supported by some form of policy. The armed conflict need not have been causal to the commission of the crime, but the existence of an armed conflict must, at a minimum, have played a substantial part in the perpetrator's ability to commit it, his decision to commit it, the manner in which it was committed or the purpose for which it was committed. Hence, if it can be established, as

---

238 Murphy's First Report (n 203) par 148–150.

239 2015 ILC Report (n 232).

240 2015 ILC Report (n 232), Commentary to draft article 3 par 31 at 69.

241 2015 ILC Report (n 232), Commentary to draft article 3 par 22 at 65-66 and par 29–33 at 68-70.

242 Article 8(1) of the ICC Statute.

243 Geneva Convention (I) for the Amelioration of the Condition of the Wounded and Sick in Armed Forces in the Field of 12 August 1949; Geneva Convention (II) for the Amelioration of the Condition of Wounded, Sick and Shipwrecked Members of Armed Forces at Sea, 12 August 1949; Geneva Convention (III) relative to the Treatment of Prisoners of War, 12 August 1949; Geneva Convention (IV) relative to the Protection of Civilian Persons in Time of War, 12 August 1949.

244 Protocol Additional to the Geneva Conventions of 12 August 1949, and relating to the Protection of Victims of Non-International Armed Conflicts (Protocol II), 8 June 1977.

245 See articles 8, 25, 27 and 28 of the ICC Statute.

246 Article 1 of Additional Protocol II (n 244).

in the present case, that the perpetrator acted in furtherance of or under the guise of the armed conflict, it would be sufficient to conclude that his acts were closely related to the armed conflict.[247]

An additional factor complicating the Syrian armed conflict, is the involvement of extremist terrorist organisations.[248] It was noted by the UN Special Representative to the Secretary-General on Sexual Violence that, to date, "not a single member of ISIL … has been prosecuted for offenses of sexual violence".[249] International humanitarian law is not usually applicable to acts of terrorism, and these acts will only be covered "when they are committed within the framework or as part of an armed conflict".[250] However, terrorist acts are prohibited by international criminal law,[251] and if committed within the context of an armed conflict, it will constitute "war crimes that must be universally prosecuted".[252] This means that international crimes committed in the context of the Syrian armed conflict, in particular by ISIL and Jabhat Fatah al-Sham, will be subject to international criminal law, and members of these organisations can be held individually criminally responsible.

The position held in this chapter therefore supports the so-called "functional approach" regarding the requirement of an "organisational policy" by groups perpetrating crimes against humanity, as well as the "plan or policy" required for war crimes.[253] Therefore, all non-state actors that are parties to the non-international armed conflict in Syria, including members of the terrorist organisations[254] such as ISIL[255] and Jabhat Fatah al-Sham,[256] may be subjected to individual criminal prosecution. The reason for this is that all these non-state actors have "the capability to perform acts which infringe on basic human rights",[257] and, should the factors

---

247 *The Prosecutor v Dragoljub Kunarac* (12 June 2002) ICTY Case No IT-96-23 & IT-96-23/1-A. *Kunarac* par 58.

248 S-G Report August 2018 (n 7) par 3 and 5.

249 S-G Report on Sexual Violence (n 28) par 20.

250 Sassòli, Bouvier and Quintin "How Does Law Protect in War? Cases, Documents and Teaching Materials on Contemporary Practice" 2011 *International Humanitarian Law, Volume I: Outline of International Humanitarian Law Third Edition* (March) 128.

251 Sassòli et al (n 250) 128.

252 Sassòli et al (n 250) 128.

253 Triffterer and Ambos (n 189) 250.

254 See further in this regard *Tadić* (n 190) par 654–655.

255 "The Islamic State of Iraq and al-Sham (ISIS)", The Syria Institute http://syriainstitute.org/wp-content/uploads/2015/09/ISIS-Cheat-Sheet-final.pdf (2018-03-26). The Islamic State (also known as the Islamic State of Iraq and al-Sham (ISIS), the Islamic State of Iraq in the Levant (ISIL) or Daesh), is a multinational terrorist organisation consisting of tens of thousands of Syrian and Iraqi forces. It is estimated that there are between 17,000 and 31,000 Islamic State fighters in Syria, at least half of whom are foreigners.

256 "Jabhat al-Nusra", The Syria Institute http://syriainstitute.org/wp-content/uploads/2015/11/JN-Cheat-Sheet-final.pdf (2018-03-26). Jabhat Fatah al-Sham (formerly known as the Al-Nusra Front for the People of the Levant or Jabhat al-Nusra) is a Sunni extremist armed group, which allegedly links to Al-Qaida to the Syrian Arab Republic. The group was established in mid-2011 and claimed responsibility for several attacks against state officials and government forces. It is estimated that Jabhat Fatah al-Sham has just under 10,000 members, most of whom are Syrian.

257 *ICC Kenya Authorisation Decision* (n 191) par 90.

of an "organisation" as articulated by the majority in the *Kenya Authorisation Decision* be met,[258] such actors would qualify as organisations capable of forming and carrying out their own policies. Further, evidence gathered by the Commission of Inquiry and the Mechanism for Syria indicate that all parties to the Syrian armed conflict are committing war crimes and crimes against humanity,[259] and in the case of ISIL, genocide.[260] In its reports, the Commission further refers to the various policies of the Syrian government's armed forces and associated militias[261] as well as ISIS[262] to commit these crimes. Lastly, the functional approach is supported as it ensures accountability for both state and non-state actors, ensures legal certainty, and prevents the arbitrary application of international law.

There are a number of possibilities for the individual criminal responsibility of perpetrators of genocide, crimes against humanity, and war crimes in the Syrian armed conflict. The next part will describe these possibilities, which will consist of prosecution at the International Criminal Court, national criminal prosecution of members of the various parties to the conflict, as well as the possibility of establishing an international or regional *ad hoc* or hybrid tribunal. Each one of the possibilities to hold perpetrators individually criminally responsible faces particular obstacles, which will be discussed in turn.

5.4   INDIVIDUAL CRIMINAL RESPONSIBILITY FOR SEXUAL AND GENDER-BASED VIOLENCE: THE POSSIBILITIES

The *erga omnes* obligation to prosecute international crimes is imposed on the responsible state, third states, and member states of international treaties.[263] It is important to note the difference between signatory states and non-signatory states to international instruments establishing courts or tribunals: constitutive documents only impose obligations upon member or signatory states. However, in terms of the *erga omnes* obligation, violations of such a nature will impose obligations upon all states in the international community, regardless of whether that state supports or opposes the obligation.

The practical effect of the *erga omnes* obligation to prosecute international crimes is that the primary responsibility to exercise international criminal jurisdiction over sexual and gender-based violence is imposed first and foremost on the Syrian Arab

---

258   *ICC Kenya Authorisation Decision* (n 191) par 93.

259   See further in general in this regard First IICIS Report (n 1); Second IICIS Report (n 13); Third IICIS Report (n 9); Fourth IICIS Report (n 13); Fifth IICIS Report (n 13); Sixth IICIS Report (n 13); Seventh IICIS Report (n 13); Eighth IICIS Report (n 13); Ninth IICIS Report (n 13); Tenth IICIS Report (n 13); 2016 IICIS Report (n 13); 2017 IICIS Report (n 13).

260   IICIS Yazidi Report (n 12) par 1; SGBV IICIS Report (n 11) par 111–113.

261   Fourth IICIS Report (n 13) par 106–110 and 75–78; IICIS Thematic Report (n 124) par 98; SGBV IICIS Report (n 11) par 109–110.

262   IICIS Yazidi Report (n 12) par 1; SGBV IICIS Report (n 11) par 111–113.

263   Roux (n 42) 117.

Republic. The most ideal situation is therefore for the Syrian government to exercise primary jurisdiction over international crimes committed on its territory during the armed conflict by holding perpetrators of international crimes individually criminally responsible in its own national courts: "the proximity of the evidence, the knowledge of the accused and the victims, and the better perspective which it has on all circumstances surrounding the crime"[264] all serve to add to the utopian ideal of the fulfilment of this primary responsibility by Syria. At the time of writing, however, no such international criminal jurisdiction has been established by Syria, indicating either its inability or unwillingness to do so.[265] The *erga omnes* obligation to prosecute international crimes will in this case be imposed on third states and member states of the International Criminal Court, in addition to Syria, as will be illustrated below.

5.4.1   The International Criminal Court

The ICC has jurisdiction over the "most serious crimes" of concern to the international community.[266] Further, the ICC is to prosecute "those most responsible" for international crimes, therefore, to hold those in leadership positions individually criminally responsible: national courts are expected to prosecute mid- and lower-level accused.[267] The ICC operates strictly in terms of the principle of complementarity:[268] it will only exercise jurisdiction if unwillingness or inability is illustrated by national courts with the required jurisdiction.[269] The impact hereof is that the jurisdiction of the Court is subordinate to national jurisdictions; it "complements" the domestic criminal justice systems" regarding international crimes.[270] The principle of comple-

---

264 Ryngaert "Applying the Rome Statute's complementarity principle: drawing lessons from the prosecution of core crimes by states acting under the universality principle" 2008 19 *Criminal Law Forum* 153 158-159. See also Ratner, Abrams and Bischoff *Accountability for Human Rights Atrocities in International Law: Beyond the Nuremberg Legacy* (2009) 176.

265 Article 17 of the ICC Statute.

266 Preamble and articles 1 and 5 of the ICC Statute.

267 Triffterer and Ambos (n 189) 19. See further Bellelli "The establishment of the system of international criminal justice" in Bellelli *International Criminal Justice: Law and Practice from the Rome Statute to Its Review* (2010) 5 56; Bergsmo *Criteria for Prioritising and Selecting Core International Crimes Cases* (2009); Clark "The development of international criminal law" in Eboe-Osuji (ed) *Protecting Humanity: Essays in International Law and Policy in Honour of Navanethem Pillay* (2010) 367 368.

268 Preamble and article 1 of the ICC Statute. See also in this regard Lattanzi "Concurrent jurisdictions between primacy and complementarity" in Bellelli *International Criminal Justice: Law and Practice from the Rome Statute to Its Review* (2010) 181 188-190; Sadat "Understanding the complexities of international criminal tribunal jurisdiction" in Schabas and Bernaz *Routledge Handbook of International Criminal Law* (2011) 197 200-202; Stahn "Complementarity: A Tale of Two Notions" 2008 19 *Criminal Law Forum* 87; Wolfrum "Prosecution of international crimes by international and national criminal courts: concurring jurisdiction" in *Studi di Diritto Internazionale in Onore di Gaetano Arangio-Ruiz, Volume III* (2004) 2199 2201, 2203, 2204-2209.

269 Article 17 of the ICC Statute.

270 Ambos "Prosecuting international crimes at the national and international level: between justice and *realpolitik*" in Kaleck, Ratner, Singelnstein and Weiss (eds) *International Prosecution of Human Rights Crimes* (2007) 55 64-65. See also Wouters "The obligation to prosecute international law crimes" in *Proceedings of the Bruges Colloquium: The Need for Justice and Requirements for Peace and Security, 9–10 September 2004* (2004) 17 20-21.

mentarity further requires states to establish national jurisdiction over international crimes because the principal duty to prosecute gross human rights violations lies first and foremost with national courts.[271]

The Office of the Prosecutor of the ICC recognised that sexual and gender-based violence fall within the category of "most serious crimes" of concern to the international community.[272] In its 2014 Policy Paper on Sexual and Gender-Based Crimes, the ICC Prosecutor affirmed its "commitment ... to paying particular attention to sexual and gender-based crimes in line with Statutory provisions"[273] by making the investigation and prosecution of these crimes a priority.[274] The Policy Paper further stated that "sexual and gender-based crimes [can be charged] explicitly as crimes *per se*"[275] where sufficient evidence exists, or as forms[276] or different categories[277] of genocide, crimes against humanity and war crimes. The purpose of cumulative charges is to "reflect the severity and multi-faceted character of these crimes fairly, and to enunciate their range supported by the evidence in each case",[278] and further, that it will "properly describe, *inter alia*, the nature, manner of commission, intent, impact, and context".[279]

Most international calls for the individual criminal responsibility of perpetrators of sexual and gender-based violence in the Syrian armed conflict have stated that the International Criminal Court is the most appropriate to prosecute these international crimes.[280] In its March 2018 report on sexual and gender-based violence in Syria, the International Commission of Inquiry unambiguously recommended "as a matter of urgency" that the UN Security Council refer the situation in Syria "to the International Criminal Court or an *ad hoc* tribunal, bearing in mind that, in the context of the Syrian Arab Republic, only the Security Council is competent to refer the situation", and that it should "support the recommendations" of the Commission.[281] The Syrian Mechanism is also specifically mandated to "assist" in investigating and prosecuting genocide, crimes against humanity and war crimes

---

271 Article 17 of the ICC Statute; Ratner et al (n 264) 254; Bellelli "Obligation to cooperate and duty to implement" in Bellelli *International Criminal Justice: Law and Practice from the Rome Statute to Its Review* (2010) 211 212-214; Chung "The punishment and prevention of genocide: the International Criminal Court as a benchmark of progress and need" 2007-2008 40 *Case Western Reserve Journal of International Law* 227 228-229.

272 Preamble and articles 1 and 5 of the ICC Statute; 2014 OTP Policy Paper on Sexual and Gender-based Crimes (n 61) par 1.

273 2014 OTP Policy Paper on Sexual and Gender-based Crimes (n 61) par 6.

274 2014 OTP Policy Paper on Sexual and Gender-based Crimes (n 61) par 6 and 14.

275 2014 OTP Policy Paper on Sexual and Gender-based Crimes (n 61) par 72.

276 2014 OTP Policy Paper on Sexual and Gender-based Crimes (n 61) par 72.

277 2014 OTP Policy Paper on Sexual and Gender-based Crimes (n 61) par 73.

278 2014 OTP Policy Paper on Sexual and Gender-based Crimes (n 61) par 72.

279 2014 OTP Policy Paper on Sexual and Gender-based Crimes (n 61) par 73.

280 See (n 34).

281 SGBV IICIS Report (n 11) par 135.

at "national, regional or international courts or tribunals that have or may in the future have jurisdiction over these crimes",[282] and its work is "complementary" to the Commission.[283]

However, individual criminal prosecution of perpetrators of international crimes during the Syrian armed conflict at the International Criminal Court faces many obstacles. Firstly, Syria is not a member state of the ICC.[284] Of course, ideally Syria could become a state party to the Rome Statute, and self-refer the case to the ICC.[285] Failing which, two other options are available to enable the ICC to establish international criminal jurisdiction: a United Nations Security Council referral of the situation,[286] or the initiation of an investigation *proprio motu* by the ICC Prosecutor of Syria as a non-member state that accepts the jurisdiction of the Court by way of declaration.[287]

With regard to obtaining a UN Security Council referral to the ICC: the veto power has been successfully and consistently used by Russia and China in preventing any notable type of involvement in the Syrian situation, making this option highly improbable.[288] The first recommendation made to the Security Council to refer the situation in Syria to the International Criminal Court was in January 2013 by the United Nations High Commissioner for Human Rights.[289] The Commission of Inquiry reiterated this recommendation soon after in February 2013,[290] yet, to this day draft resolutions "have never made it past the floor of the Security Council".[291] This is in stark contrast to the swift response of the Security Council in adopting a resolution referring the situation in the Sudan to the ICC in March 2005,[292] after it was recommended to do so by the International Commission of Inquiry on Darfur in January 2005.[293]

An investigation *proprio motu* by the Prosecutor of the ICC also proves to be problematic. As stated above, at the time of writing there was no public indication that the situation in the Syrian Arab Republic is either under preliminary

---

282   GA Res 71/248 (n 20) par 10.

283   First Syria Mechanism Report (n 32) par 30.

284   State Parties to the Rome Statute (n 70).

285   Articles 13(a) and 14 of the ICC Statute.

286   Article 13(b) of the ICC Statute.

287   Articles 12, 13(c) and 15 of the ICC Statute.

288   Adams "Failure to Protect: Syria and the UN Security Council", Global Centre for the Responsibility to Protect, Occasional Paper Series no 5 March 2015 19 www.globalr2p.org/media/files/syriapaper_final.pdf (2017-04-16). See further SC Draft Res 348 (n 19).

289   Fourth IICIS Report (n 13) par 18.

290   Fourth IICIS Report (n 13) par 180.

291   February 2018 IICIS Report (n 7) par 11.

292   SC Res 1593 (2005), S/RES/1593 (2005), 31 March 2005 par 1.

293   *Report of the International Commission of Inquiry on Darfur to the United Nations Secretary-General Pursuant to Security Council Resolution 1564 of 18 September 2004,* 25 January 2005, 145 http://www.un.org/news/dh/sudan/com_inq_darfur.pdf (2018-09-14).

examination or investigation at the International Criminal Court.[294] The Rome Statute permits the Prosecutor to engage in a *proprio motu* investigation into the Syrian Arab Republic[295] to establish whether reported acts amount to crimes falling within the jurisdiction of the ICC.[296] Depending on the seriousness and reliability of the information received, the Prosecutor must find a reasonable basis upon which to proceed with an investigation.[297] Further, article 12 of the ICC Statute describes "preconditions to the exercise of jurisdiction", which may find application to Syria: a non-member state may accept the ICC's jurisdiction by way of declaration "with respect to the *crime in question*".[298] A first reading hereof seems encouraging, as it is thought that perhaps Syria can choose to accept the ICC's jurisdiction with regard to the commission of genocide by ISIL against the Yazidi,[299] thereby partially fulfilling its *erga omnes* obligation to prosecute international crimes, while still avoiding accountability for its own governmental officials for crimes against humanity and war crimes. However, the stark reality is that the ICC Assembly of State Parties have interpreted "crime" in article 12(3) to mean "situation":[300] Rule 44(2) of the ICC Rules of Procedures and Evidence provides that, should a state accept the ICC's jurisdiction, "the Registrar shall inform the State concerned that the declaration under article 12, paragraph 3, has as a consequence the acceptance of jurisdiction with respect to the *crimes* referred to in article 5 of relevance to the *situation*".[301] The implication hereof is that a state therefore has to accept the Court's jurisdiction with regard to a situation *as a whole*, and may not do so with regard to a single crime which falls within the jurisdiction of the Court.

The prospects of successfully holding perpetrators of sexual and gender-based violence, committed in the Syrian armed conflict, individually criminally responsible at the ICC therefore seems extremely bleak. At this point, a strong argument can be made that Syria is illustrating a clear unwillingness or inability to prosecute international crimes committed on its territory, therefore imposing the *erga omnes* obligation to prosecute international crimes on third states. The next part will consider that a more promising possibility in holding perpetrators individually criminally responsible would be to explore national prosecutions by third states.

---

294 Preliminary examinations at the ICC (n 38); Situations under investigation at the ICC (n 39).

295 ICC Statute, article 15.

296 ICC Statute, article 15(2).

297 Rule 104 of the ICC Rules of Procedure and Evidence http://www.icc-cpi.int/iccdocs/PIDS/legal-texts/ RulesProcedureEvidenceEng.pdf (2018-08-19). See further Schabas *The International Criminal Court: A Commentary on the Rome Statute, Oxford Commentaries on International Law* (2010) 321. Should the ICC Prosecutor find a reasonable basis upon which to proceed with an investigation, there is an obligation to obtain the consent of the Pre-Trials Chamber of the ICC prior to engaging in an 'investigation proper'.

298 Article 12(3) of the ICC Statute (own emphasis).

299 IICIS Yazidi Report (n 12) par 1, 201–202.

300 Triffterer and Ambos (n 189) 684-688.

301 Rule 44(2) of the ICC Rules of Procedure and Evidence (own emphasis).

Third states will be obliged to establish national jurisdiction over perpetrators of international crimes in Syria, either in terms of domesticating the ICC Statute, or in terms of the *erga omnes* obligation.

5.4.2 The exercise of national jurisdiction

Municipal legislation granting jurisdiction to national courts over international crimes either enacts legislation in terms of international treaty obligations, such as the obligation to incorporate the ICC Statute into national legislation, or grants national courts universal jurisdiction over international crimes.[302] When a state enacts legislation incorporating an international convention or treaty into municipal law, the state is acting in terms of an international obligation in terms of the treaty, whereas when a state enacts legislation granting the state universal jurisdiction, that state is acting "voluntarily", therefore acting in terms of international principles of a "permissive" nature.[303] It is therefore important to differentiate between, on the one hand, the option available to states to exercise universal jurisdiction,[304] and, on the other, the obligation to enact legislation to grant jurisdiction to national courts over international crimes in terms of treaty obligations.

In *ad hoc* Judge Van den Wyngaert's dissenting opinion to the *Arrest Warrant* case, she pointed out that there is "no generally accepted definition of universal jurisdiction in conventional or customary international law",[305] however,

> [d]espite uncertainties that may exist concerning the definition of universal jurisdiction, one thing is very clear: the *ratio legis* of universal jurisdiction is based on the international reprobation for certain very serious crimes such as war crimes and crimes against humanity. Its *raison d'être* is to avoid impunity, to prevent suspects of such crimes finding a safe haven in third countries.[306]

---

302 Butler "The growing support for universal jurisdiction in national legislation" in Macedo *Universal Jurisdiction: National Courts and the Prosecution of Serious Crimes Under International Law* (2006) 67-68.

303 Gaeta "National prosecution of international crimes: international rules on grounds of jurisdiction" in *Studi di Diritto Internazionale in Onore di Gaetano Arangio-Ruiz, Volume III* (2004) 1923 1924-1926.

304 Akande and Shah "Immunities of state officials, international crimes, and foreign domestic courts" 2011 21 *European Journal of International Law* 815 834-838; Steven "Genocide and the duty to extradite or prosecute: why the United States is in breach of its international obligations" 1998-1999 39 *Virginia Journal of International Law* 425 439-443.

305 *Arrest Warrant of 11 April 2000 (Democratic Republic of the Congo v Belgium)* 14 February 2002 ICJ Reports 137 (Dissenting Opinion of ad hoc Judge Van den Wyngaert) par 44. The ICJ did not furnish clarity on the legality of universal jurisdiction, especially in view of the divergent views of the judges in the Case. See further in general in this regard *Arrest Warrant of 11 April 2000 (Democratic Republic of the Congo v Belgium)* 14 February 2002 *ICJ Reports* 1 (Judgment); *Arrest Warrant of 11 April 2000 (Democratic Republic of the Congo v Belgium)* 14 February 2002 *ICJ Reports* 35 (Separate Opinion of President Guillaume); *Arrest Warrant of 11 April 2000 (Democratic Republic of the Congo v Belgium)* 14 February 2002 *ICJ Reports* 46 (Dissenting Opinion of Judge Oda); *Arrest Warrant of 11 April 2000 (Democratic Republic of the Congo v Belgium)* 14 February 2002 *ICJ Reports* 63 (Joint Separate Opinion of Judges Higgens, Kooijmans and Buergenthal).

306 Dissenting Opinion of *ad hoc* Judge Van den Wyngaert (n 305) par 46.

It was further acknowledged by Judge Van den Wyngaert that states have domesticated the principle in "very different ways" and, in many instances, it will in actual fact amount to the extraterritorial exercise of jurisdiction, rather than universal jurisdiction in a strict sense.[307] Nevertheless, a benefit of establishing jurisdiction in terms of the principle of universal jurisdiction, in addition to avoiding impunity, is that any perpetrator of international crimes can be prosecuted, irrespective of whether they are a state or non-state actor, where the crime was committed, or whether the perpetrator or the victim holds the nationality of the prosecuting state.[308]

It is this latter benefit of universal jurisdiction that is important when considering other public international law principles that will also allow third states to establish national criminal jurisdiction over international crimes, namely, the principles of territoriality, protection of the state, active nationality and passive personality.[309] The territoriality principle "allows a state to exercise jurisdiction concerning the status of persons or things within the state's territory, over conduct that occurs, in whole or in part, within the state's territory, and over extraterritorial conduct that has a substantial effect within the state's territory"[310] This principle is an extension of the territorial, sovereign equality of states.[311] In turn, the principle of the protection of the state allows a state to exercise jurisdiction over acts that affect the safety and security of the state.[312] These two principles would find application to Syria, because Syria is the responsible and territorial state in respect of international crimes committed by its governmental armed forces and affiliated groups, and further, because international crimes committed by non-state armed opposition groups and extremist terrorist organisations threaten the safety and security of the Syrian Arab Republic.

Two other general principles of public international law also find application in the Syrian context. Firstly, the principle of active nationality allows a state to exercise jurisdiction over its own nationals who committed crimes abroad.[313] This would

---

307 Dissenting Opinion of *ad hoc* Judge Van den Wyngaert (n 305) par 44.

308 Universal criminal jurisdiction with regard to the crime of genocide, crimes against humanity and war crimes, Resolution by the Seventeenth Commission of the Institut de Droit International, Kraków Session, 2005, Article 1 http://www.idi-iil.org/app/uploads/2017/06/2005_kra_03_en.pdf (2018-09-10).

309 Brownlie "The obligation to extradite for the repression of international crimes under customary law" in Salerno *Diritti Dell'Uomo, Estradizione ed Espulsione: Atti del Convegno di Studio Organizzato dall'Università di Ferrara per Salutare Giovanni Battaglini (29-30 Ottobre 1999)* (2003) 300-307. See also in this regard *The Princeton Principles on Universal Jurisdiction*, Princeton Project on Universal Jurisdiction (2000) http://lapa.princeton.edu/hosteddocs/unive_jur.pdf (2018-09-10); *Case of the SS "Lotus"* 7 September 1927 *Publications of the PCIJ Series A No. 10* 1 (Collection of Judgments); Cryer *Prosecuting International Crimes: Selectivity and the International Criminal Law Regime* (2005) 84; Steven (n 304) 430; Ratner et al (n 264) 177-178.

310 Steven (n 304) 432. See further Brownlie (n 309) 301-303.

311 Brownlie (n 309) 301; Crawford *Brownlie's Principles of Public International Law* (2012) 447-455; Cryer, Friman, Robinson and Wilmshurst *An Introduction to International Criminal Law and Procedure* (2010) 87 537 589; Tanzi "Remarks on sovereignty in the evolving constitutional features of the international community" in Arsanjani, Cogan, Sloane and Wiessner (eds) *Looking to the Future: Essays on International Law in Honor of W. Michael Reisman* (2011) 299.

312 Brownlie (n 309) 304-305.

313 Brownlie (n 309) 303-304.

mean that third states will be able to apply criminal jurisdiction over their nationals that participate in the Syrian armed conflict and who commit international crimes.[314] Secondly, the principle of passive personality allows a state to exercise jurisdiction over crimes committed abroad that harmed one of its nationals.[315] In terms hereof, third states would be able to exercise criminal jurisdiction over crimes committed in Syria against its nationals, if this would be the case.

At the time of writing, the only states that have established national criminal jurisdiction in relation to the Syrian armed conflict are Sweden and Germany. Swedish and German courts have engaged in the prosecution of various Syrian nationals on the basis of universal jurisdiction, as well as German nationals on the basis of active personality.[316] In their ongoing and completed cases, the Swedish and German courts have engaged in prosecutions pertaining to war crimes, including aggravated assault, extrajudicial executions, desecration of corpses, engaging in acts of torture and kidnapping, bearing membership in terrorist organisations and violating national military weapons control laws.[317] Thus far, the individuals who have been prosecuted are linked to armed groups affiliated with the Free Syrian Army, armed groups opposed to the Syrian government, members of the Syrian Army, and members of terrorist organisations ISIL and Jabhat Fatah al-Sham.[318] However, none of the accused where charged with sexual and gender-based violence in the Syrian armed conflict.

Finally, it has to be mentioned that a possible impediment to the prosecution of senior government officials at the national courts of foreign states is the principle of state immunity. The question of "immunity of state officials from foreign criminal jurisdiction" was included in the International Law Commission's long-term programme of work in 2006,[319] which resulted in a number of reports.[320] In 2019,

---

314 The Security Council has urged states in a number of resolutions to establish their national jurisdiction over nationals that participate in terrorist activities, specifically in Syria. See for example in this regard SC Res 2170 (n 8) par 5 and 8; SC Res 2249 (n 8) par 4–5; SC Res 2253 (n 8) par 12.

315 Brownlie (n 309) 304.

316 HRW Universal Jurisdiction Report (n 34).

317 HRW Universal Jurisdiction Report (n 34) 34-35.

318 HRW Universal Jurisdiction Report (n 34) 34-35.

319 Report of the International Law Commission, Fifty-eighth Session, 1 May–9 June and 3 July–11 August 2006, *Official Records of the General Assembly, Fifty-eighth Session, Supplement No.10* (A/61/10) Annex A, par 1–13.

320 Report of the International Law Commission, Fifty-ninth Session, 7 May–5 June and 9 July–10 August 2007, Official Records of the General Assembly, Fifty-ninth Session, Supplement No.10 (A/62/10) par 376; Preliminary Report on Immunity of State Officials from Foreign Criminal Jurisdiction, Roman Anatolevich Kolodkin (Special Rapporteur) Report of the International Law Commission, Sixtieth Session, 5 May–6 June and 7 July–8 August 2008, Official Records of the General Assembly, Sixtieth Session, Supplement No.10 (A/63/10) Chapter X; Second and Third Reports on Immunity of State Officials from Foreign Criminal Jurisdiction, Roman Anatolevich Kolodkin Special Rapporteur, Report of the International Law Commission, Sixty-third Session, 26 April–3 June and 4 July–12 August 2011, Official Records of the General Assembly, Sixty-third Session, Supplement No.10 (A/66/10) Chapter VII; Preliminary Report on Immunity of State Officials from Foreign Criminal Jurisdiction, Concepción Escobar Hernández, Special Rapporteur, Report of the International Law Commission, Sixty-fourth Session, 7 May–1 June and 2 July–3 August 2012, Official Records of the General Assembly, Sixty-fourth Session,

the International Law Commission provisionally adopted draft articles, with parts 2 and 3 of particular importance for the question of the individual criminal responsibility of Syrian government officials at national courts of foreign states.[321] Parts 2 and 3 provide for immunity *ratione personae* and immunity *ratione materiae*: draft articles 3 and 4 confirm the position that "heads of state, heads of government and ministers of foreign affairs" will enjoy absolute immunity at national courts of foreign states during their term of office.[322] Despite the impediment that the principle of immunity may pose to the prosecution of Syrian government officials, ILC draft article 7 confirms that immunity *ratione materiae* may not apply for genocide, crimes against humanity, war crimes and torture.[323] However, the ILC draft articles have not been finally adopted at the time of writing.

5.4.3 The establishment of an international or regional ad hoc or hybrid tribunal

It has to be briefly mentioned that another possibility, also envisioned by the Syria Mechanism[324] to address impunity in the Syrian Arab Republic is the establishment of an international or regional *ad hoc* or hybrid criminal tribunal for international crimes committed in the armed conflict since 2011. However, it is anticipated that this may also face some obstacles, depending on the type of tribunal that is settled for: an *ad hoc* tribunal in the style of the ICTY and the ICTR, or alternatively a hybrid tribunal in the style of the SCSL and the ECCC. Both the ICTY and ICTR *ad hoc* tribunals were established by way of Security Council resolutions.[325] However,

---

Supplement No.10 (A/67/10) Chapter VI; Second Report on Immunity of State Officials from Foreign Criminal Jurisdiction, Concepción Escobar Hernández, Special Rapporteur, Report of the International Law Commission, Sixty-fifth Session, 6 May–7 June and 8 July–9 August 2013, Official Records of the General Assembly, Sixty-fifth Session, Supplement No.10 (A/68/10) Chapter V; Third Report on Immunity of State Officials from Foreign Criminal Jurisdiction, Concepción Escobar Hernández, Special Rapporteur, Report of the International Law Commission, Sixty-sixth Session, 5 May–6 June and 7 July–8 August 2014, Official Records of the General Assembly, Sixty-sixth Session, Supplement No.10 (A/69/10) Chapter V (Hernández Third Report); Fourth Report on Immunity of State Officials from Foreign Criminal Jurisdiction, Concepción Escobar Hernández, Special Rapporteur, Report of the International Law Commission, Sixty-seventh Session, 4 May–5 June and 6 July–7 August 2015; Fifth Report on Immunity of State Officials from Foreign Criminal Jurisdiction, Concepción Escobar Hernández, Special Rapporteur, Report of the International Law Commission, Sixty-eighth Session, 2 May–10 June and 4 July–12 August 2016, Official Records of the General Assembly, Sixty-eighth Session, Supplement No.10 (A/71/10) Chapter XI; Sixth Report on Immunity of State Officials from Foreign Criminal Jurisdiction, Concepción Escobar Hernández, Special Rapporteur, Report of the International Law Commission, Seventieth Session, 30 April–1 June and 2 July–10 August 2018, Official Records of the General Assembly, Seventieth Session, Supplement No.10 (A/73/10) Chapter XI (Hernández Sixth Report); Seventh Report on Immunity of State Officials from Foreign Criminal Jurisdiction, Concepción Escobar Hernández, Special Rapporteur, Report of the International Law Commission, Seventy-first Session, 29 April–7 June and 8 July–9 August 2019, Official Records of the General Assembly, Seventy-first Session (A/CN.4/729).

321 Seventh Report on Immunity of State Officials from Foreign Criminal Jurisdiction, Concepción Hernández (Special Rapporteur), *Report of the International Law Commission, Official Records of the General Assembly, Seventy-first Session,* 8 July–9 August 2019 (A/CN.4/729), 18 April 2019, Annex I (Hernández Seventh Report).

322 Hernández Seventh Report (n 321) Draft Articles 3 and 4.

323 Hernández Seventh Report (n 321) Draft Article 7.

324 GA Res 71/248 (n 20) par 4; First Syria Mechanism Report (n 32) par 8 and 12.

325 SC Res 827 (1993), S/RES/827 (1993), 25 May 1993; SC Res 955 (1994), S/RES/955 (1994), 8 November 1994. See further ICTY Statute; ICTR Statute.

with regard to the way in which Russia and China have used their veto power in blocking an ICC-referral, the realisation of this possibility seems unlikely. Should a hybrid tribunal in the style of the SCSL or the ECCC be settled for,[326] it is foreseeable that the involvement of the Syrian government could prove problematic, in the same way that the Cambodian government's involvement proved problematic in the establishment of the ECCC.[327]

5.5   CONCLUSION

The non-international armed conflict in the Syrian Arab Republic has been unabating since 2011, and perpetrators of genocide, crimes against humanity and war crimes have enjoyed complete impunity.[328] The sense of frustration of the Commission of Inquiry on Syria regarding the lack of accountability for international crimes is palpable because it has been documenting and reporting these atrocities for over six years, without any adequate response from those empowered to bring about justice:

> The Commission has diligently and meticulously documented, analysed, verified and presented to the Human Rights Council, the Secretary-General, the Security Council, the General Assembly, regional bodies and the international community information about this tragedy that could have been halted. Instead, the involvement of a variety of regional and international actors and sponsors has enabled the prolongation and escalation of the conflict rather than brought it to an end. Over time, the Commission has reported on systematic violations of human rights and international humanitarian law, including arbitrary arrests, torture in detention, enforced disappearances, sexual and gender-based violence, attacks on medical facilities, schools and markets, indiscriminate attacks and intentional attacks against civilians. No party has abided by its obligations, either under international humanitarian or human rights law, to protect civilians, the infrastructure that facilitates civilian life and livelihoods or specially protected sites that form the backbone of their communities. Humanitarian aid has been instrumentalized as a weapon of war with siege warfare and denial of life-giving assistance used to compel civilian communities and parties to the conflict alike to surrender or starve. As a Commission of inquiry, the primary tasks of the commissioners have been to document all serious human rights violations and war crimes, expose those responsible, seek to bring perpetrators to account for their crimes and help the victims to achieve justice. Efforts to promote criminal

---

326 GA Resolution 57/228, *Khmer Rouge Trials*, A/RES/57/228, 27 February 2003; GA Resolution 57/228, *Khmer Rouge Trials B*, A/RES/57/228 B, 22 May 2003; SC Res 1315 (2000), S/RES/1315 (2000) 14 August 2000. See further SCSL Statute; ECCC Law.

327 The Commission on Human Rights Resolution 1997/49, *Situation of Human Rights in Cambodia*, Office of the High Commissioner for Human Rights, 58th Meeting, 11 April 1997, par 8–12; *Report of the Special Representative of the Secretary-General for Human Rights in Cambodia, Mr Thomas Hammarberg, Submitted in accordance with Commission Resolution 1997/40* UN Doc.:E/CN.4/1998/95 (20 February 1998); Commission on Human Rights Resolution 1998/60, *Situation of Human Rights in Cambodia*, Office of the High Commissioner for Human Rights, 52nd Meeting, 17 April 1998.

328 S-G Report on Sexual Violence (n 28) par 78; HRW Syria news report (n 34).

accountability through the International Criminal Court have not been successful so far, despite the best efforts of the Human Rights Council, the Commission, a large number of Member States committed to the promotion of international justice and countless civil society groups. Attempts to refer the situation in the Syrian Arab Republic to the International Criminal Court have never made it past the floor of the Security Council. More success may be achieved through recourse to universal jurisdiction and we welcome the fact that the number of such cases before a variety of national jurisdictions is on the rise.[329]

As illustrated above, prosecution at the International Criminal Court would be the most appropriate, but is repeatedly prevented, both as a result of the non-membership of Syria of the ICC Statute, and the lack of political will to overcome the impasse at the Security Council.[330] While the Security Council has validly and consistently called for a political solution to the Syrian conflict, a political solution cannot be achieved in isolation: the only way in which impunity for international crimes will be avoided, and victims assisted in obtaining justice, is by prosecuting state and non-state actors for committing genocide, crimes against humanity, and war crimes.[331] International jurisprudence on the individual criminal responsibility of non-state actors for international crimes, in particular of members of extremist terrorist organisations, is non-existent, and a judgment by the ICC in this regard would be groundbreaking.

Although the state with primary jurisdiction over international crimes is the state where these crimes have been committed in the first place, the judicial systems in such states are hardly ever in the position to prosecute such crimes successfully,[332] as is the case in Syria. It therefore has to be reiterated that it is crucial for third states to prosecute international crimes at their national courts,[333] whether it is in terms of their treaty obligations to domesticate international criminal law, or in terms of the public international law principles of jurisdiction.[334]

The establishment of national jurisdiction over international crimes by third states is not without its challenges, but there are several factors that make national prosecution favourable. International adjudication is extremely expensive, in contrast to national

---

329   February 2018 IICIS Report (n 7) par 9–11.

330   See par 4.1 above.

331   Roux (n 41) 94-110.

332   Gioia "State sovereignty, jurisdiction, and 'modern' international law: the principle of complementarity in the International Court" 2006 19 *Leiden Journal of International Law* 1095 1106-1109; Orentlicher "The future of universal jurisdiction in the new architecture of transnational justice" in Falk, Elver and Hajjar (eds) *Human Rights: Critical Concepts in Political Science: Volume III* (2008) 63 81; Schabas "National courts finally begin to prosecute genocide, the 'crime of crimes'" 2003 1 *Journal of International Criminal Justice* 3943.

333   S-G Report on Sexual Violence (n 28) par 6.

334   See par 4.2 above.

courts.[335] It is also difficult to establish an international court or tribunal, specifically in a politically-charged situation like Syria.[336] International courts and tribunals "are distant from and inaccessible to the affected populations",[337] whereas justice is "seen to be done" if criminal trials take place in the state where gross human rights violations were committed: "the entire process becomes more deeply connected with the society, providing it with the potential to create a strong psychological effect on the population".[338] If international courts and tribunals are not situated within the state where atrocities took place, it is more difficult to use the prosecution as a reconciliation and peace-building tool. The vast numbers of perpetrators involved in the commission of international crimes also make it impossible for international fora to prosecute everyone who played a role in the commission of these crimes.[339] Therefore, an advantage of domestic courts is that they can deal with greater numbers of accused: lower-level accused should be charged by national courts, albeit within the responsible state, or within third states. International courts and tribunals should try only the highest-level accused and those involved in formulating the policy to commit genocide, crimes against humanity and war crimes.

The work of international bodies (such as the Commission of Inquiry on Syria, the Syria Mechanism, the Human Rights Council, the High Commissioner for Human Rights, the Special Representative to the Secretary-General for Children and Violence, and the UN Special Representative to the Secretary-General on Sexual Violence) in raising awareness, investigating and gathering information and evidence has to be lauded. These UN organs and entities are laying down the groundwork for courts and tribunals, whether international, regional or national, to hold perpetrators individually criminally responsible for international crimes committed in the Syrian armed conflict. In particular, the organs' and entities' approach to and sensitive attention placed on sexual and gender-based violence committed during the conflict is also highly significant, especially in light of the deep social stigma and culture of silence and denial that surround these crimes within Syrian society.[340] It is therefore vital for the international community to cooperate with these UN organs and entities to continue their work, despite the political deadlock at the Security Council.

Finally, it is impossible that all women, men and children will report sexual and gender-based violence committed against them in the Syrian armed conflict, in the same way that it is impossible to hold every perpetrator individually criminally responsible for their international crimes. However, individual criminal prosecution

---

335 Ratner et al (n 264) 203.

336 Ratner et al (n 264) 176.

337 Ratner et al (n 264) 252.

338 Ratner et al (n 264) 203.

339 Ratner et al (n 264) 195-196. Ratner states that an estimated 800,000 persons participated in the Rwandan genocide: by 2008 an estimated 10,000 perpetrators had been tried in domestic courts and 70,000 persons had been brought before *gacaca* courts.

340 See par 1 above.

of key perpetrators of these international crimes will go a long way in acknowledging the tragedy that befell this nation, and in punishing those responsible for the humiliation and terror caused during the conflict. This will fulfil the *erga omnes* obligation to prosecute international crimes,[341] and thereby impunity for these horrific crimes will be avoided.[342]

---

341 Roux (n 42).

342 Roux (n 42).

6

THE LIFE ESIDIMENI TRAGEDY

A Terrible Tale of Death, Torture and Disappearance of Utterly Vulnerable Mental Health Care Users

*Deon Erasmus**

6.1 INTRODUCTION

On 29 September 2015, the Gauteng Department of Health ("the Department") terminated a contract with Life Esidimeni, which had been in operation for over 30 years. In terms of the contract, Life Esidimeni supplied caring facilities to mental health care users in several psychiatric homes it operated.[1] As the contract was terminated on a six-month notice period, all mental health care users had to be moved out of the Life Esidimeni facilities by 31 March 2016. This led to random mass discharges of patients. The closure date of the facilities was later extended to 30 June 2016. The decision to terminate the contract necessitated the moving of 1,711 patients between October 2015 and the end of June 2016. These mental health care users were moved to hospitals and non-governmental organisations selected by the Department and some were returned to their family homes.[2]

The three reasons for the termination of the contract advanced by the Department were a policy requirement to deinstitutionalise mental health care users, concerns raised by the Auditor-General regarding the duration of the contract and budgetary constraints.[3]

---

1   *Families of Mental Health Care Users Affected by the Gauteng Mental Marathon Project (Claimants) and National Minister of Health of the Republic of South Africa and Others (Respondents)* par 23 http://www. saflii.org/images/LifeEsidimeniArbitrationAward.pdf (2018-11-15). Hereinafter "Award".

2   Award par 24.

3   Award par 27.

---

*   B Juris, LLB (UPE); LLD (UFS); Professor and Head of the Department of Criminal and Procedural Law, Faculty of Law, Nelson Mandela University.

The Department did not heed concerns raised and warnings expressed by families of the mental health care users, civil society, professional bodies and clinical personnel within the Department, before and after the termination of the contract, as to the protection of the rights and meeting of the needs of the removed mental health care users. The then member of the Executive Council, Ms Mahlangu, the Head of Department, Dr Slebano and Head of the Mental Health Directorate, Dr Manamela, proceeded with the mass removals of patients, without any involvement and consultation with the families concerned or concerned health professionals. These irrational decisions resulted in the death of at least 144 patients, excluding the 44 patients still missing. About 1,400 patients survived the gruelling conditions they had to endure after their forced removal from Life Esidimedi facilities.[4]

In this chapter, the "harrowing account of the death, torture and disappearance of utterly vulnerable mental health care users in the care of an admittedly delinquent provincial government" will be discussed with reference to Fineman's vulnerability theory and the need for a responsive state.[5] Issues concerning constitutional damages and the reaction to the arbitration award will in addition be discussed.

6.2   THE ARBITRATION HEARING

The Life Esidimeni Arbitration was established pursuant to a recommendation of the Health Ombud's report into the matter.[6] The dispute was referred to a single arbitrator, retired Deputy Chief Justice Dikgang Moseneke ("the arbitrator") subject to a written arbitration agreement signed on 8 September 2017 in terms of the provisions of the Arbitration Act 42 of 1965. The arbitration proceedings started on 9 October 2017 and ended on 9 February 2018. The hearings, at which 60 witnesses testified, ran for 45 days, including two days of legal arguments.[7]

The core dispute that had to be determined was the nature and extent of equitable redress, including compensation due to mental health care users and their families who were negatively affected by the closure of the Life Esidimeni mental health care facilities.[8] The State admitted unqualifiedly that it was liable to compensate the affected mental health care users and their families individually or as a group.[9]

The State contended that it was liable to compensate the families of the deceased and the surviving mental health care users or their families for their estimated

---

4   Award par 25.

5   See par below.

6   "Report into the circumstances surrounding the deaths of mentally ill patients: Gauteng Province" recommendation 17 https://www.sahrc.org.za/home/21/files/Esidimeni%20full%20report.pdf (2018-11-15).

7   Award par 4.

8   Award par 5.

9   Award par 6.

funeral expenses and common law general damages as a result of pain, suffering and emotional shock. An all-inclusive amount of R200 000 was tendered for that purpose.[10]

The claimants in general advanced that, apart from the general damages for which the State is obviously liable, it should also be liable for constitutional damages, as a result of the "pervasive, egregious, uncaring and wanton violations" of the constitutional rights of the mental health care users and their families.[11]

The arbitrator found that the patients died under unlawful circumstances, as they were placed at non-governmental organisations at the instance, request and authority of the State. The NGOs willingly became agents for the State and had to care for the patients against payment of subsidies and remuneration. Both the State and its agents acted recklessly, uncaringly and contrary to the legislative framework protecting mental health care users. The State was the primary bearer of the duty of care and other constitutional duties applicable to the patients and their families. The outsourcing of these duties to ill-equipped and ill-prepared NGOs amounted to a blatant, unlawful and life-threatening disregard of the State's constitutional and statutory duties which was the cause of multiple deaths and torture.[12]

The three State officials mentioned above testified at the arbitration hearing that they had no reason to believe that the displaced mental health care users would die or suffer severe ill treatment and torture. The arbitrator held that this response was so improbable that it had to be false.[13] The reasons for the termination of the contract were rejected by the arbitrator and described as "neither cogent nor rational".[14] Evidence was led at the hearing that de-institutionalisation was expensive and ordinarily not a cost-saving measure.[15] The mental health care users as well as the NGOs to which they were transferred were not adequately prepared for the move.[16]

In the following section, the details of the award issued by the arbitrator will be set out.

6.3   THE ARBITRATION AWARD

On 19 March 2018, the arbitrator made the following monetary award:[17]

1. The Government (as represented by the National Minister of Health, the Premier of Gauteng and MEC of Health: Gauteng Province) was ordered to

---

10   Award par 10. Some claimants accepted this offer.
11   Award par 10.
12   Award par 79.
13   Award par 26.
14   Award par 28.
15   Award par 29.
16   Award par 31.
17   Award par 226.

pay an agreed amount of R20 000 to each of the claimants listed in respect of funeral expenses.[18]

2.   The Government was ordered to pay R180 000 to each of the claimants in respect of general damages for shock and psychological trauma.

3.   The Government was ordered to pay R1 000 000 to each of the claimants as appropriate relief and compensation for its "unjustifiable and reckless breaches of section 1(a), (c) and (d), section 7, section 10, section 12(1)(d) and (c), section 27(1)(a) and (b) and section 195(1)(a), (b), (d), (e), (f) and (g) and multiple contraventions of the National Health Act 61 of 2003 and the Mental Health Care Act 17 of 2002 that caused the death of 144 mental health care users and the pain, suffering and torture of 1 418 mental health care users who survived and their families".

4.   The parties also agreed to have a place of remembrance or monument erected for the victims of the Gauteng Mental Health Marathon Project and counselling for the bereaved family members. The purpose of this monument must serve as a reminder to future generations of the human dignity and vulnerability of mental health care users.

5.   Government was further ordered to provide the Health Ombud and the claimants or their legal representatives with a recovery plan with the purpose to achieve a systemic change in the provision and delivery of mental health care in Gauteng. This recovery plan had to be delivered within 6 months of the publication of the award and thereafter every 6 months until the conclusion of the recovery plan.

6.   The arbitrator in addition ordered that the conduct of certain of the professional health officers should be reported to their respective professional bodies.

7.   The Government was lastly ordered to pay the party and party legal costs of all the claimants.

In the following section, the legislative framework within which the duties and responsibilities of the Government relating to the care of mental health care users will be set out and discussed.

6.4   THE LEGISLATIVE FRAMEWORK

The National Health Act 61 of 2003 and the Mental Health Care Act 17 of 2002 are the primary legislative instruments applicable to mental health care users. These acts aim to give effect to the progressive realisation of the constitutional right of access to health care services. Section 27 of the Constitution provides that every person has the right to have access to health care services, including reproductive health care, and also states that no person may be refused emergency treatment. According to

---

18   Those who accepted the offer of the Government of R200 000 previously were excluded from this award.

section 7(2) of the Constitution, the government must respect, protect, promote and fulfil the rights set out in the Bill of Rights.

In relation to health care services, this means that government must *respect* the right of access to health care services by not unfairly or unreasonably obstructing access to existing health care services, whether in the public or private sector; *protect* the right by developing and implementing a comprehensive legal framework to ensure access to health care services and *promote* the right by creating a legal framework ensuring that individuals realise these rights themselves.[19]

In terms of the National Mental Health Policy Framework and Strategic Plan,[20] an important objective of the policy is the promotion and protection of the human rights of people living with mental illness.[21]

The government also has international law obligations regarding the rights of mental health users. The Universal Declaration of Human Rights,[22] for instance, declares that no one shall be subjected to torture or cruel, inhumane or degrading treatment or punishment[23] and guarantees the right to security in the event of sickness or disability.[24]

The African Charter on Human and People's Rights[25] provides in article 16 that every individual shall have the right to enjoy the best attainable state of physical and mental health and states that parties are under an obligation to take the necessary measures to protect the health of their people.

In terms of the preamble to the Convention on the Rights of Persons with Disabilities,[26] parties must promote, protect and ensure the full and equal enjoyment of all human rights and fundamental freedoms by all persons with disabilities and promote respect for their inherent dignity.

The United Nations Principles for the Protection of Persons with Mental Illness and for the Improvement of Mental Heath Care[27] sets the standard of the best available mental health care within the health and social care system, which includes the right

---

19   "The Constitution and public health policy" 33 https://section27.org.za/wp- content/uploads/2010/04/Chapter2.pdf (2018-11-20).

20   2013-2020. The framework had become national policy after extensive consultation and the adoption of the Ekurhuleni Declaration on Mental Health in April 2012.

21   Framework par 5 https://www.health-e.org.za/wp-content/uploads/2014/10/National-Mental-Health-Policy-Framework-and-Strategic-Plan-2013-2020.pdf (2018-11-20).

22   Adopted by the UN General Assembly resolution 217A(III) on 10 December 1948.

23   Art 5.

24   Art 25(1).

25   Adopted by the General Assembly of the OAU on 27 June 1981 and entered into force on 21 October 1986, ratified by South Africa on 10 October 1997.

26   Adopted at the UN Headquarters on 13 December 2006 Preamble.

27   Adopted by the UN GA on 17 December 1991 as Resolution 46/19.

to be treated with humanity and respect for the inherent right to human dignity and protection from physical or other abuse and degrading treatment.

From the aforementioned legal framework, it is clear that the State has the duty to care for and protect the rights of mental health care users. In the next section, the position of mental health care users will be discussed within the framework of Fineman's vulnerability theory.

6.5   FINEMAN'S VULNERABILITY THEORY

In current human rights rhetoric, "vulnerability" is normally referred to in collective terms. Vulnerable groups should be afforded special protection, it is argued, because their rights are perceived to be particularly at risk of being violated. The rights of these vulnerable groups are consolidated in group-differentiated categories of rights, due to specific character traits or specific experiences the group members share.[28]

Some groups, such as children, due to their relative immaturity and developing character, are viewed by default as requiring special protection.[29] Vulnerability is mostly associated with concepts such as victimhood, deprivation, dependence or pathology. So, for example, in health discourse persons infected with HIV-AIDS are classified as a "vulnerable population". Other examples include those living in poverty or confined to state institutions, such as prisons and mental health care facilities. Fineman[30] correctly submits that children and the elderly are "prototypical examples" of sympathetic vulnerable groups.

Fineman[31] defines the human condition as one of universal and continuous vulnerability. She describes vulnerability as a condition which arises from our human embodiment, which is exposed to an omni-present possibility of being exposed to harm, injury and misfortune. The influence of these factors may vary in intensity and may occur accidentally or intentionally. Individuals may attempt to lessen the occurrence of these risks or mitigate the impact thereof, but the possibility of them occurring cannot be eliminated and therefore they are beyond human control.[32]

This has the result that there is an ever-present possibility that humans may become dependent on others as a result of biologically-based catastrophes such as diseases or epidemics. Humans are in addition vulnerable to physical forces occurring in the environment they live in, such as fire, floods, drought and famine.[33]

---

28   "The protection of vulnerable individuals in the context of EU policies on border checks, asylum and immigration" http://www.fp7-frame.eu/wp-content/uploads/2016/08/Deliverable-11.3.pdf (2018-11-25).

29   Above.

30   Fineman "The vulnerable subject: anchoring equality in the human condition" 2008 *Yale Journal of Law and Feminism* 1 8.

31   Fineman "Vulnerability and inevitable inequality" *Oslo Law Review* 133.

32   Fineman (n 30) 9.

33   Above.

Human vulnerability is experienced by each individual in a unique manner as each individual is positioned in a different way "within a web of economic and institutional relationships".[34] Due to the fact that individuals cannot avoid the state of vulnerability, humans turn to societal institutions to assist and protect them against their inherent vulnerability. She argues that society cannot eliminate human vulnerability but can and does address human vulnerability by introducing programmes, institutions and structures for that purpose. Any vulnerability analysis will thus include individual and institutional components.[35]

She develops the theory further by stating that human vulnerability and the need for connection and the care generated in the process motivates humans to reach out and form a society. This brings "individuals into families, families into communities and communities into societies, nation states, and international organizations".[36]

The state legitimised and empowered social institutions. These institutions can assist some to recover quickly from their difficulties while other institutions impact negatively on the recovery process. The state accordingly must accept responsibility for the conduct of these institutions.[37]

Fineman[38] argues that the actions of state-empowered institutions should be scrutinised as to their role in providing assets in ways that may, even though not intentionally, unfairly privilege certain persons or groups. Just as is the case with individuals, institutions are also vulnerable both to internal and external forces. Empowered institutions are capable of being captured or corrupted. They can be harmed or grow too big and become ineffective. These institutions nevertheless have a pivotal role to play in addressing the vulnerability of individuals. It is thus imperative that they exercise their powers in a non-discriminatory manner so as neither to favour nor disadvantage individuals or groups. What is important is that the institutions should be structured in such a way that they can respond fairly to the shared human vulnerability. If they fail in exercising this duty fairly, the state would have to rectify the position by either justifying the unequal treatment or acting positively to adjust the institutional arrangements.[39] Lessig is of the view that institutional corruption occurs when an ostensibly legal or current ethical strategy of an institution has the effect that it undermines the effectiveness of the institution by weakening its ability to achieve its purpose. This may lead to the weakening of the institution's purpose or the public's trust in the institution.[40]

---

34 Fineman (n 30) 10.

35 Above.

36 Fineman "Equality, autonomy, and the vulnerable subject in law and and politics" in Fineman and Grear (eds) *Vulnerablility: Reflections on a new ethical foundation for law and politics* 13-22.

37 Kohn "Vulnerability theory and the role of government" 2014 *Yale Journal of Law & Feminism* 1 6.

38 Fineman (n 30) 18.

39 Fineman (n 30) 19.

40 Lessig "Institutional corruption defined" 2013 *Journal of Law, Medicine and Ethics* 3 2.

The vulnerability theory accordingly argues for the development of a more responsive state. The state is constituted for the common benefit of all and not for a select few. The state thus has the obligation to ensure that its empowered institutions do not unduly privilege any group over another.[41]

The vulnerability theory of Fineman provides a useful theoretical framework to explain the role of the state in the protection of the rights of vulnerable groups, such as mental health care users. It is submitted that mental health care users who are cared for in state-empowered institutions or NGOs who are appointed by the state to care for mental health care users are a vulnerable population. Due to their vulnerability, the state should be responsive to their needs. It is clear that the decisions taken by the state officials during and after the move of the mental health care users and their reaction to the catastrophic consequences is indicative of institutional corruption within these state-empowered institutions.[42] This calls for a scrutiny of the structure and actions of these institutions in order that they may be more responsive to the needs of mental health care users. This will necessitate serious adjustments of the institutional arrangements and leadership structures thereof.

These adjustments of institutional arrangements can only be achieved through political and administrative accountability. Public office bearers and government officials should act in the best interests of society.[43]

In the following section, the nature and application of constitutional damages as a measure of redress for the violation of constitutional rights will be set out, with reference to the arbitration award.

6.6   CONSTITUTIONAL DAMAGES AS A MEASURE OF REDRESS

The Government resisted the claims for constitutional damages on two grounds. It firstly argued that once a claimant has been compensated under common law, she or he may not rely on the Constitution to seek redress.[44]

In terms of section 38 of the Constitution, anyone listed in the section, who alleges that a right in the Bill of Rights has been infringed upon or threatened, has the right to approach a competent court, which court may grant appropriate relief, including a declaration of rights. In the case of *Fose v Minister of Safety and Security*,[45] the Constitutional Court entertained a claim for exemplary damages against the Minister of Police as a result of alleged torture committed by members of the police service.

---

41   Fineman "The vulnerable subject and the responsive state" 2011 *Emory Law Journal* 251 273-4.

42   Lessig (n 37) 3.

43   https://www.news24.com/MyNews24/political-accountability-denied-20170317 (2020-03-11). The aspect of responsiveness and accountability is futher discussed in par 7 below.

44   Award par 212.

45   1997 3 SA 786 (CC).

Before evidence was led, the case served before the Constitutional Court for it to determine whether a claim for punitive damages was a competent claim in terms of the Constitution. The plaintiff instituted a delictual claim for damages. The court had to decide whether the plaintiff was entitled to constitutional damages, inclusive of punitive damages, in addition to ordinary delictual damages.[46]

The court held that "appropriate relief" would include a claim for damages, but that it was not appropriate in this case to award punitive damages. The court was of the view that in many cases the common law will be broad enough to provide all the relief that would be appropriate for the particular breach of constitutional rights. Each case would depend on its own facts.[47] The court, however, indicated that the courts have a responsibility and should "force new tools" and shape innovative remedies to achieve proper enforcement of constitutional rights via the courts.[48] It is submitted that the approach of the court to award constitutional damages was conservative and that the court viewed the common law remedies as the starting point when considering damages for the infringement of constitutional rights.

In *MEC Department of Welfare, Eastern Cape v Kate*,[49] constitutional damages were awarded to the plaintiff as a result of the systemic failure by the Eastern Cape Provincial Government to honour its constitutional obligation to pay social grants to those who qualify for it. Mrs Kate applied for a disability grant in April 1996, but was only informed in August 1996 that her grant was approved. She claimed the amount that had accrued to her since the approval of her application, plus interest. The High Court awarded interest, including interest from the date that her application was made. The plaintiff was not entitled to interest for this period, as the debt did not accrue to her upon making application for the grant. The Supreme Court of Appeal awarded constitutional damages based on the fact of the systemic and continued failure of the provincial government to deliver social grants.[50]

The court was mindful of the fact that Mrs Kate suffered direct financial loss as the grant was destined to be consumed and not invested but the loss for her was "just as real".[51] The court commented that to be held in poverty is a cursed condition and that apart from the physical discomfort of her deprivation her human dignity was reduced. Being unlawfully deprived of a grant that is required for her daily survival amounts to an unnecessary extended endurance of her condition as long as the unlawful deprivation continues. The court indicated that there is no empirical

---

46 Compare Neethling and Potgieter *Neethling-Potgieter-Visser Law of Delict* (2015) 4-5 267-278. See also O'Regan "Fashioning constitutional remedies in South Africa: some reflections" 2011 *Advocate* 41-43.
47 *Fose* par 60.
48 Above par 69.
49 2006 4 SA 478 (SCA).
50 Above par 33.
51 Above.

monetary yardstick against which to measure a loss of this kind.[52] In this case, the approach of the court was conservative in the sense that the court was mindful to award damages actually suffered and not as a punishment to the state.

In the matter of *Modder East Squatters v Modderklip Boerdery (Pty) Ltd; President of the Republic of South Africa v Modderklip Boerdery (Pty) Ltd*,[53] the Supreme Court of Appeal had to entertain the issue of how to protect the property rights of a private land owner whose land had been unlawfully occupied by approximately 40,000 homeless people after they were evicted by the state. The court also had to balance this issue with its duty to protect the housing rights of the unlawful occupiers. A side issue which arose was whether the court may order an organ of state to expropriate property. The Supreme Court of Appeal and subsequently the Constitutional Court left this issue undecided and applied the novel remedy of constitutional damages.[54]

Regarding constitutional damages, the court highlighted the advantages of this remedy as it compensates the property owner for the unlawful occupation of its property in violation of its rights on the one hand. On the other hand, it ensures that the unlawful occupiers will continue to have accommodation until suitable alternatives are found. In addition, it relieves the state of its urgent duty to find such alternatives. The court in addition held that the difficulty in quantifying the compensation may be met by employing the provisions of section 12 of the Expropriation Act 63 of 1975.[55] The court in this matter as well did not award punitive damages to the property owner but compensated the owner in terms of existing legislation relating to expropriation.

In the *Life Esidimeni* matter, the arbitrator held that the actions of the state and its officials violated the constitutional rights of the mental health care users who had died, the patients who survived and the family members of these patients, who were powerless to prevent it.[56] Not only did the treatment of the mental health care users during the transfer and thereafter violate their constitutional right not to be treated in a cruel, inhuman or degrading way, it also impacted on the right to life, freedom and security and the rights to access to adequate health care and sufficient food and water. As for the families of the mental health care patients, the arbitrator held that they entrusted the government to take care of their loved ones but were denied the opportunity to participate or to be informed of decisions made in respect of them. This violated the right to family life as it deprived the family of an opportunity to take decisions in the best interests of the health of their loved ones.[57]

---

52   Above.

53   2004 3 All SA 169 (SCA).

54   Above par 59. See also Dugard *"Modderklip* revisited: can courts compel the state to expropriate property where the Eviction of Unlawful Occupiers in not Just and Equitable? 2018 21 *PER/PELJ* 1.

55   This section determines how the amount of compensation for expropriation of land should be calculated.

56   Award par 185.

57   Award par 196.

In *Komape v Minister of Basic Education*,[58] a five-year-old boy, Michael Komape, was attending his third day of primary school, when he fell into a dilapidated pit toilet at school and died as a result of suffocation.[59] This matter was decided after the delivery of the *Life Esidimeni* award. The plaintiffs instituted a delictual claim for emotional shock and trauma experienced by the family as a result of Michael's gruesome death.[60] In the alternative, they claimed punitive damages as a penalty and deterrence for the wrongful conduct that caused the death of Michael.[61] The plaintiffs contended that the court should develop the common law as they do not have an effective remedy for compensation and that compensatory damages in view of the facts of the matter are integral to vindicate them for the breach of their constitutional rights and duties.[62]

The court referred to the case of *Jones v Krok*[63] where an award for punitive or exemplary damages was described as "contrary to public policy". The court pointed out that the rationale of a claim for delictual damages is not to enrich a claimant, but to serve as compensation for the loss suffered. In the court's view, the constitutional damages claimed by the plaintiffs amounted to nothing short of a claim for punitive damages.[64] The court was of the opinion that a successful claim for punitive damages would over-compensate the Komape family, which would not be in the interests of society.[65] In the court's opinion, a structural interdict would be a just and equitable remedy which would effectively vindicate the Constitution. The best interests of all learners at school where pit toilets are still in use will have to take preference. Such an interdict will compel the state to comply with its obligations in terms of the Constitution.[66]

The matter was taken on appeal to the Supreme Court of Appeal[67] where the court again addressed the issue of constitutional damages and held that this type of damages is awarded in respect of financial loss which would otherwise not have been catered for at common law.[68] The court further indicated that there is no reported decision in South Africa where constitutional damages were awarded as compensation for a breach of a right not resulting in direct or indirect financial loss, or where compensation of this kind was awarded for a physical or psychiatric

---

58 [2018] ZALMPPHC 18 (23 April 2018).

59 *Komape* par 17–19.

60 Above par 10.

61 Above par 7.

62 Above par 9.

63 1995 1 SA 677 (SCA) 696 C-H.

64 *Komape* above par 67.

65 Above par 68.

66 Above par 70.

67 *RK v Minister of Basic Education* [2019] ZASCA 192 (18 December 2019). The appellants appealed as the court *a quo* also dismissed their claim for damages for emotional trauma and shock. This aspect is not discussed as only the issue of constitutional damages is relevant to this contribution.

68 *RK* par 58.

injury.[69] Such further damages would amount to a punishment for the breach of a right in addition to the compensation already granted for damages suffered as a result of a physical or psychiatric injury.[70]

The breach of rights involved a failure to provide proper sanitation facilities at a large number of schools which affected the rights of a large number of scholars across the Limpopo province. The public purse should be utilised for the benefit of all the scholars rather than paying the appellants a large additional award in constitutional damages in order to vindicate the rights of all scholars to proper sanitation facilities. The court accordingly held that there was no room for an award of constitutional damages.[71]

The court referred to the award in *Life Esidimedi* and commented that the award recognised the rights of the families of health care users who died and awarded compensation as constitutional damages. In view of the fact that the award was not binding and the facts differed substantially from the facts *in casu*, the award was not relevant authority.[72] Mukheibir and Mitchell[73] correctly suggest that the purpose of the *Life Esidimedi* award is in the nature of an award for aggravated or even punitive damages, although these terms were not used in the award.

Some reservations were, however, levelled against the high amount of the monetary compensation awarded as constitutional damages. Mackie[74] correctly states that no one who is familiar with these tragic and cruel events would begrudge the survivors or their families their award. He however cautions that if one looks beyond the circumstances of this tragedy, the details of the award could be a cause for concern. He submits that the large monetary amount and symbolism of the award is problematic for the reasons listed below.

Almost any shocking or outstanding delict committed by the state or its officials may be moulded as a violation of constitutional rights. Remoulding a delict in this way should not be a reason why the existing common law remedies should not be used to vindicate the rights of the claimant. The argument that shocking, appalling or very complicated delicts cannot be properly vindicated within the common law remedies is in his opinion not convincing. The claims are delicts and compensation should be calculated within the rubric of the common law.[75]

---

69   Above.

70   Above par 59.

71   Above par 63.

72   Above par 62.

73   Mukheibir and Mitchell "The price of sadness: comparison between the Netherlands and South Africa" 2019 22 *PER/PELJ* 18.

74   Mackie "The problem with the Esidimeni arbitration award" http://www.fp7-frame.eu/wp-content/uploads/2016/08/Deliverable-11.3.pdf (2019-02-04).

75   Above.

He views the arbitrator's disregard for the going rate for general damages by the courts as "damaging" and argues that no amount of money can ever compensate a claimant for the grief and trauma associated with losing a loved one. Courts are bound by judicial precedent and accordingly do apply a going rate based on established quantification principles in order to promote consistency and fairness, leading to a fair result. The magnitude of the award places it far above the amount that a claimant could reasonably expect to be awarded in a court of law. This factor risks distorting the perception of the public of what constitutes fair compensation for delicts. Although the award, as an arbitration award, is not binding or precedent setting, it will in his opinion have an inflationary effect on similar claims which the state can hardly afford.[76]

He views it as troubling when high-profiled victims of high-profile wrongdoings are disproportionately compensated as a symbol of collective disgust at a particular incident. This has the result that other victims of similarly serious wrongdoings are largely ignored by the public eye and receive considerably less compensation for similar wrongs, even if they do get the opportunity to vindicate their rights.[77]

Constitutional damages were *inter alia* awarded by the arbitrator to promote the values of the Constitution and to punish the state in an effort to prevent or deter future infringements. The actual effect of the award, in his opinion, was that a very sizeable amount of money, to the tune of R135 million, in constitutional damages was taken from an already financially strained health budget and paid over to relatively few individuals.[78]

The arbitrator held that the claimants' claim for compensation arising from the "invasive and pervasive" violation of constitutional rights by the state cannot readily be couched in common law terms. He came to the conclusion that there is no equivalent common law claim based on the state's breach of the right to access to health care, the right to food and water, freedom from torture and protection from cruel and degrading and inhumane treatment. There is also no common equivalent for a claim breaching the rule of law or its obligations in respect of mental health users in terms of international law or domestic legislation. All these breaches let to "agonising devastation" for the families of the deceased, surviving mental health care users and their families.[79]

The arbitrator decided that the going rate for compensation for psychological injury and shock, which might be R180 000, is insufficient viewed in light of the massive proportions of this case.[80] The "narrow and dated structures" of the common

---

76 Above.
77 Above.
78 Above.
79 Award par 217.
80 Award par 219.

law only, was, in his opinion, not sufficient to address the uniqueness and full complexity of the case at hand.[81] He also decided not to differentiate between classes of claimants as such a differentiation would lead to an uneven and unjust outcome and accordingly decided on a uniform award.[82]

The common law relief available to the families of the mental health care users was very limited as their claim did not include a claim for loss of support which, in most cases, forms the largest part of a dependent's action.[83]

Whittaker[84] notes that there is no actuarial formula prescribed by actuarial practice notes or established South African case law for the calculation of constitutional damages. Section 27, the NGO assisting some of the claimants, prepared an actuarial report which was presented at the arbitration proceedings as expert evidence. He comments that the claim of the families of the deceased was not a straightforward loss of earnings claim and it was therefore not necessary to use an actuarial calculation to formulate the value of the claim. He points out that there is "no manual for calculating the monetary value of life; nor of the price-tag of the grief and trauma that the families have endured".[85]

He correctly argues that it was critical that whatever method was going to be employed to quantify this loss had to be deeply rooted in the constitutional values of equity and fairness. The only monetary measure that was available to apply to the health care users was the costs of their maintenance in the Life Esidimeni facilities or alternative facilities for the remainder of their lives. At the time of the transfer of the mental health care users, the state was paying subsidies to Life Esidimeni, which would have been paid as long as the users lived. The calculation of the amount that would have been spent on the deceased as dependants of the state, had the transfer not occurred and the deceased survived, can be viewed as an unlawful saving to the state.[86]

He suggests that the following guidelines should be applied when a stand-alone claim for constitutional damages is considered judicially. In certain cases, the common law remedies may not provide an adequate remedy for the breach of constitutional rights. The granting of constitutional damages should not be awarded to avenge the death of a person but to affirm rights. The claimants should display a persistency in their efforts to end the unlawful infringement of a constitutional right. It is not necessary that the loss should be a direct financial loss. Other forms of loss, such as the reduction of a person's human dignity, are also an empirical monetary standard

---

81   Above.

82   Award par 220.

83   Whittaker "The Life Esidimeni arbitration and the actuarial quantification of constitutional damages" 3 https://www.actuarialsociety.org.za/wp-content/uploads/2018/10/2018-Whittaker-FIN.pdf (2019-02-05).

84   Above 3.

85   Above 13.

86   Above 3-4.

against which a claim may be assessed. Factors that will play a role in this assessment include the multitude and seriousness of the constitutional breaches and the presence of arbitrary state power. Punitive damages do not form part of South African law but the role of the vindication of the right and the deterrence of future violations of the right in question can serve as justification to award compensation. In conclusion, he argues that the actuarial calculation of constitutional damages should be structured so as to be fair to the claimants and the state; be limited to an amount not more than what the state would have expended had the violation not occurred and have the result that a uniform award across various categories of claimants be awarded so as to treat each affected life the same.[87]

Other facets of the award, such as those relating to responsiveness and accountability of the state and its officials, will be addressed in the next section.

6.7   RESPONSIVENESS AND ACCOUNTABILITY

Responsiveness can be defined as the degree to which governments are attentive to what people want and their willingness to act on it. It also reflects on those public policies and institutions which respond to the needs of citizens and uphold their rights.[88] Accountability refers to the ability of citizens, civil society and the private sector to scrutinise the policies and actions of government and its institutions and to hold them accountable thereto.[89]

The arbitrator accurately alluded to the fact that the Constitution holds public officials to be responsive to the plight and reasonable requests and demands of citizens. The officials responsible for the closure of the Life Esidimeni facilities insinuated in their evidence that they were entitled to "empty" the facility as the families had abandoned the mental health care users. Because of this abandonment, they did not have to give anyone notice of the closure of the facility. He accepted that there may have been family members who had not visited their loved ones at the facility over an extended period. However, he rejected these claims as without merit as the claimants in the arbitration relate to a fraction of the total number of mental health care users with who died or survived the ordeal.[90]

The commitment of the claimants is evident from their persistent steps to commence the arbitration proceedings, their protests over the planned transfers, their negotiations and pleas not to move their loved ones, their engagement with public interest litigators of section 27, their involvement in organised public protest marches at which they tendered memoranda to public officials and alerted the print

87   Above 27.

88   Van Donk and Williams "In search of responsible and responsive local governance" 11 https://www.ggln.org.za/images/solg_reports/SoLG_2015.pdf (2019-02-12).

89   "The contribution of government communication capacity to achieving good governance outcomes" 2 http://siteresources.worldbank.org/EXTGOVACC/Resources/BriefGovCommCapacity.pdf (2019-02-12).

90   Award par 197.

and electronic media to make their plight public. After the blind transfer of their loved ones, the families searched for them. Some families whose loved ones died went and retrieved their bodies and buried them at their own cost.[91]

The arbitrator also correctly indicated that the inquiry is not about what the families of the users did, but rather about what the officials refused or neglected to do, namely to stop the mass transfer of users to NGOs not fit for the purpose. After knowing all the facts and risks, they elected not be responsive to the reasonable and lawful requests and demands of the claimants.[92]

The Constitution proscribes a public service motto of *Batho Pele* which requires public servants who are responsive to the reasonable grievances of citizens and others within our borders. This includes the readiness to respond and alleviate these concerns, as well as the protection and promotion of the rights afforded to them. This did not happen in the present case.[93]

As to the accountability of the officials in question, the arbitrator indicated that the answers of Ms Mahlangu to questions put to her in the provincial legislature were "objectively inaccurate and misleading".[94]

The arbitrator referred to the "larger question of accountability for the entire Marathon Project and its toxic aftermath". He indicated how the officials acknowledged the pain caused to the families and the torture endured by the survivors. They apologised in a tearful or near-tearful way but, despite their position of power and authority, they refused to take full responsibility for the administrative and political decision which led to this tragedy.[95]

The arbitrator commented that Ms Mahlangu had resigned from her position as a member of the Executive Council after the publication of the findings of the Ombud. By doing so, she had at least taken political responsibility for the woeful failing of the Department she headed.[96]

From this section, it is clear that the arbitrator evaluated the actions of the various officials against the requirements of responsiveness and accountability. It is submitted that he correctly held that the officials failed both requirements as stipulated in sections 1 and 195 of the Constitution miserably.

It is clear that from the outset that the arbitrator viewed the mental health care users as "utterly vulnerable".[97] As indicated above, Fineman argues that factors such as

---

91   Award par 198.

92   Award par 199.

93   Award par 200.

94   Award par 201.

95   Award par 202.

96   Award par 206.

97   Award par 1.

dependence or pathology, as well as persons confined to state institutions, like the health care users in this case, qualify them to be classified as a vulnerable population.[98]

The Department of Health and its officials are empowered by the state to provide care to the health care users as a result of their vulnerability. The families of the health care users entrust their loved ones into the care of the state and its officials. These officials have a pivotal role to play in addressing the vulnerability of the health care users. As pointed out above, Fineman correctly argues that state-empowered institutions are capable of being captured or becoming corrupt and in the process they can become ineffective.[99] These institutions can also fail in their caring mission as a result of bad or incorrect decisions by its leadership. The decay and ineffectiveness of these institutions which may harm the rights of vulnerable groups may take place unintentionally, but it is submitted that the arbitrator correctly held that the actions of the officials involved and the state acted in a reckless and uncaring manner and contrary to the statutory provisions aimed at protecting mental health care users. Despite the fact that the state attempted in a "blatantly unlawful and life-threatening way" to outsource these duties to ill-equipped and under-prepared NGOs, the state still owed a continued duty of care and other constitutional duties to the health care users and their families.[100] Under such circumstances, Fineman argues that the state would have to rectify the position by acting positively by adjusting the institutional arrangements.[101]

One way of adjusting institutional arrangements is for a court to issue a structural interdict to effectively vindicate the constitutional rights of vulnerable groups.[102] Government and its officials attached to government institutions can in this manner be held accountable for institutional corruption. Another method to ensure that government institutions fulfil their constitutional mandate is for a court to appoint a special master or curator to oversee court-supervised institutional transformation.[103]

6.8   CONCLUDING REMARKS

Section 27 noted that the arbitration process was set up in order to provide information as well as to provide redress and closure to the mental health care users and their families. The award handed down by the arbitrator has generally been welcomed and was hailed as a major step towards a new culture of accountability in the civil service. Section 27 applauded the fact that MEC Mahlangu had resigned and that Dr Selebano and Dr Manamela followed suit by resigning as well.[104]

---

98   Fineman (n 30) 8.
99   Fineman (n 30) 10.
100   Award par 79.
101   Fineman (n 30) 8.
102   *Komape* par 70.
103   See in this regard Erasmus and Hornnigold "Court supervised institutional transformation in South Africa" 2015 18 7 *PER/PELJ* discussion of this aspect falls outside the scope of this contribution.
104   http://section27.org.za/2018/03/section27-welcomes-life-esidimeni-arbitration-award/ (2019-02-03).

The award and the actual hearings may be viewed as a restorative justice process for the claimants and starting point of obtaining closure. The effect of the arbitration process had extended effects apart from the award itself. It touched on issues such as the responsibility and responsiveness of the state towards the people of this country. It highlighted the constitutional values and duties of legality and accountability. It clearly put the spotlight on structural problems and bad decision-making within the South African mental health care governance. In conjunction with the Ombud's report, it lays the foundation for future action to hold government officials and NGOs who act on behalf of the government accountable.[105]

The award is seen as a major step towards a new culture of state accountability.[106] The process, in addition, emphasises the pivotal role NGOs such as section 27, the South African Depression and Anxiety Group, the South African Federation for Mental Health and the Society of Psychiatrists play in advancing and protecting the rights of vulnerable groups.

The role of Legal Aid South Africa should also be commended as this organisation funded the representation of the claimants. In this regard, the Chief Legal Executive, Patrick Hundermark, remarked that "funding precedent-setting matters that promote the rights of communities is a key part of the delivery of Legal Aid South Africa's mandate to ensure access to justice for all. Such impact litigation matters affect many people; in this instance, a large number of vulnerable mental health care users who desperately needed justice to be upheld".[107]

The criticism levelled against the high amount of monetary compensation awarded as constitutional damages is not without merit. The total sum paid to all 134 claimants amounted to R159.46 million. Such an amount could have contributed considerably towards the improvement of mental health care in South Africa.[108] The Democratic Alliance reported that it obtained information that the Gauteng Department of Health has received an additional 200 new claims for financial compensation from families of health care users who survived the Marathon Project move. If successful, the payments that will be made to these claimants would amount to almost R236 million.[109]

---

105 Toxopeüs "Life Esidimeni arbitration: The legal basis for granting the award" https://hsf.org.za/publications/hsf-briefs/the-life-esidimeni-arbitration-the-legal-basis-for-granting-the-award (2019-02-03).

106 http://section27.org.za/2018/03/section27-welcomes-life-esidimeni-arbitration-award/ (2019-02-10).

107 Above.

108 The basis for the granting of constitutional damages and the amount involved is also not in line with the principles laid down by the courts as set out in par 6 above.

109 "DA says 200 new Life Esidimeni compensation claims received" https://www.iol.co.za/news/south-africa/gauteng/da-says-200-new-life-esidimeni-compensation-claims-received-16852842 (2019-02-20).

One can only trust that Government and its officials will indeed adopt a culture of responsiveness and accountability. Although health minister Aaron Motsoaledi apologised for the ordeal, he did not accept political responsibility by tendering his resignation.[110]

In September 2018, the Eastern Cape Department of Health published a R120-million tender to outsource chronic mental health care in the province. Seven hundred adult and 180 paediatric mental health care users are being cared for in Life Esidimeni facilities in Kirkwood and Bethelsdorp. In the tender, emphasis was placed on the reintegration of mental health patients back into their communities. In addition to chronic care, prospective service providers were required to tender for community-based initiatives to achieve the proposed integration.[111] This proposed action has distinct undertones of the Marathon Project of the Gauteng Department of Health.

When cross-examined by the legal counsel for Legal Aid during the arbitration process, former MEC for Health, MS Qedani Mahlangu, was asked whether human rights considerations were taken into account during the implementation of the Marathon Project. She responded as follows: "I am not a prophet. Now I know that the human rights of patients were violated, but it was not intentional and that's important. If I were a prophet, maybe I would have seen and had the foresight, but I am not a prophet."[112]

The former MEC did not need prophetic foresight. It would have sufficed for her and her department to be responsive and accountable towards the human rights of utterly vulnerable mental health care users.

---

110 "The R159-million Life Esidimeni bill has been paid" https://www.timeslive.co.za/news/south-africa/2018-06-13-the-r159-million-life-esidimeni-bill-has-been-paid/ (2019-02-15).

111 "Mental health to be 'outsourced' in Eastern Cape" https://www.timeslive.co.za/news/south-africa/2018-09-24-mental-health-to-be-outsourced-in-eastern-cape/ (2019-02-20).

112 "#LifeEsidimeni: I am not a prophet, says former MEC" https://www.iol.co.za/news/south-africa/gauteng/lifeesidimeni-i-am-not-a-prophet-says-former-mec-12929128 (2019-02-20).

7

THE RELATIONSHIP BETWEEN
THE AFRICAN COURT OF JUSTICE AND
HUMAN AND PEOPLE'S RIGHTS AND REGIONALISM

Sabreen Hassen*

7.1   INTRODUCTION

Sudanese President, Omar Al-Bashir, was the first sitting head of state to be indicted by the International Criminal Court (ICC). This has resulted in tension between the African Union (AU) and the ICC. The AU's initial bone of contention with the ICC was that directly after the Al-Bashir warrants, African states became the sole focus of the ICC's investigations and prosecutions.[1] Other African states which have been the focus of the ICC include Kenya, Central African Republic, Libya, Republic of Côte d'Ivoire, Democratic Republic of Congo and Uganda.[2] The ICC has been accused as having a Western or Northern concept of justice as opposed to an African concept of justice.[3] Professor Dire Tladi, an expert in Public International Law in Africa, questions how the quest for international justice by the ICC can be regarded as imperialistic, colonial or even racist, when the respect for human rights is a common goal for all states.[4]

---

1   Swart and Krisch "Irreconcilable differences? An analysis of the standoff between the African Union and the International Criminal Court" 2014 *AJICJ* 38-40.

2   See generally *The Prosecutor v Francis Kirimi Muthaura, Uhuru Muigai Kenyatta and Mohammed Hussein Ali* ICC-01/09-02/11; *The Prosecutor v Jean-Pierre Bemba Gombo* ICC-01/05-01/08; *The Prosecutor v Muammar Mohammed Abuminyar Gaddafi, Saif Al-Islam Gaddafi and Abdullah Al-Senussi* ICC-01/11-01/11; *The Prosecutor v Laurent Gbagbo and Charles Blé Goudé* ICC-02/11-01/15; *The Prosecutor v Germain Katanga* ICC-01/04-01/07; *The Prosecutor v Joseph Kony, Vincent Otti, Raska Lukwiya, Okot Odhiambo and Dominic Ongwen* ICC-02/04-01/05.

3   Slye "Reflections on Africa and international criminal law" in Slye (ed) *The Nuremburg principles in non-western societies: A reflection on their universality, legitimacy and application* (2016) 232.

4   Tladi "The African Union and the International Criminal Court: The battle for the soul of international law" 2009 *SAYIL* 57-58.

*   LLB, LLM; Lecturer in the Department of Practical Business Law, Faculty of Law, University of Johannesburg.

As a direct result of the tension between the AU and ICC, African States have mobilised towards creating a regional court with international criminal law jurisdiction. The African Court of Justice and Human and People's Rights (ACJHPR), initially only had jurisdiction over human rights violations and any disputes regarding the AU's treaties or Constitutive Document. The ACJHPR was then granted jurisdiction over international crimes. As a result of the expansion of the courts' jurisdiction, the ACJHPR will be the first regional court with jurisdiction over international crimes. To date, regional courts are only used to regulate human rights in Europe and South America and not to prosecute international crimes.[5]

Shortly after Al-Bashir's controversial visit to South Africa in 2015 – for the AU Summit – South Africa gave notice of its intention to withdraw from the Rome Statue,[6] but was subsequently ordered, by the South African High Court, to revoke the notice of withdrawal because it was unconstitutional.[7] This decision of the South African High Court was later confirmed by the ICC's Pre-Trial Chamber.[8] To date, South Africa has no yet withdrawn from the Rome Statute and therefore remains within the ICC's jurisdiction.

Burundi was the first African state to successfully withdraw from the Rome Statute.[9] Neither South Africa nor Burundi have signed the Protocol on Amendments to the Protocol on the Statute of the African Court of Justice and Human and People's Rights (Malabo Protocol). Assuming South Africa had successfully withdrawn from the Rome Statute, like Burundi, a lacuna would have been created. This is because South Africa and Burundi would have – in part – excluded themselves from the ICC's jurisdiction and would not have included themselves in the ACJHPR's jurisdiction. The new ACJHPR could have the potential to close this gap and ensure that international crimes within the African region do not go unpunished.

The ACJHPR has been severely criticised,[10] but has the potential to transform and develop international criminal law in multiple ways. The Malabo Protocol includes 14 international crimes in the court's jurisdiction. In addition to Crimes Against Humanity, Genocide, War Crimes and the Crimes of Aggression are 10 international

---

5   European Court of Human Rights, Inter-American Court of Human Rights and the African Court on Human and People's Rights.

6   South Africa: Withdrawal Depository Notification C.N.786.2016.TREATIES-XVIII.10, 19 October 2016.

7   *Democratic Alliance v Minister of International Relations and Cooperation and Others* (Council for the Advancement of the South African Constitution Intervening) case no 83145/2016 (ZAGPPHC) (unreported).

8   ICC-02/05-01/09.

9   Burundi: Withdrawal C.N.805.2016.TREATIES-XVIII.10, 28 October 2016.

10   See generally Du Plessis "A new regional international criminal court for Africa?" 2012 2 *SACJ* 286; Viljoen "AU Assembly should consider human rights implications before adopting the Amending Merged African Court Protocol" http://africlaw.com/2012/05/23/au-assembly-should-consider-human-rights-implications-before-adopting-the-amending-merged-africancourt-protocol/ (2016-08-15); Du Plessis "Implications of the AU decision to give the African Court jurisdiction over international crimes" *Institute for Security Studies* 2012 1.

crimes which plague the African continent on a daily basis.[11] The inclusion of these quotidian crimes is just one example of how international criminal law will be developed through this court.

Regional courts have managed to regulate areas such as piracy, environmental pollution, money laundering and human rights successfully. With this is mind, one should consider that international criminal law may be able to be effectively managed at a regional level as well.

This chapter will examine the relationship between the ACJHPR and regionalism. The first part of this chapter will provide the reader with a background to the current regional court system which protects human rights in Africa. This will be followed by an outline of the process in which the ACJHPR was created; how this regional court with human rights jurisdiction ultimately acquired its international criminal jurisdiction.

The second part of this chapter will examine the role of regionalism in international criminal law as a whole. Part two will determine the effect that this new court will have with special reference to an intensification of the regime complex already present within international criminal law, as well as the creation of a regime shift within international law.

In considering regionalism, a *grossraum* has been identified as a model of regionalism which has used previously by Western states. A *grossraum* is described as a "political idea with which other member states broadly identify, and which they accept as generally legitimate on the basis of their overlapping cultural traditions and aspirations".[12] By creating the ACJHPR, African states are identifying with a political idea based on their cultural traditions. The last part of this chapter will explain how the ACJHPR could be described as a *grossraum* model, with specific reference to the characteristics a *grossraum* should have, for example the political idea, geographical links in territory and a leading power.

7.2   BRIEF BACKGROUND OF THE REGIONAL COURT SYSTEM PROTECTING HUMAN RIGHTS IN AFRICA

Before we can explore the ACJHPR, it is necessary to familiarise oneself with the human rights court system in Africa. The Organisation of African Unity (OAU) was established in 1963.[13] A number of factors forced the OAU to take its human rights protection more seriously. Amongst these factors was a pressure on Africa to create

---

11   Crime of unconstitutional change of government, piracy, terrorism, mercenarism, corruption, money laundering, trafficking in persons, trafficking in drugs, trafficking in hazardous wastes and illicit exploitation of natural resources.

12   Schmitt "Grossraum versus universalism: The international legal struggle over the Monroe Doctrine" in Legg (ed) *Spatiality, sovereignty and Carl Schmitt: Geographies of the nomos* (2011) 101.

13   Organisation of the African Union Charter.

a regional human rights protection mechanism, the importance given to human rights on an international level, the fall of many dictatorships within Africa,[14] as well as the human rights violations being committed on the continent itself.[15]

The African Charter on Human and People's Rights (African Charter) was adopted by the OAU in 1981.[16] However, it only entered into force in 1986. The African Charter, also referred to as the Banjul Charter, established the African Commission on Human and Peoples Rights (African Commission).[17] The African Commission is primarily tasked to promote and protect human and people's rights.[18] The African Commission is a quasi-judicial body and may only issue recommendations, which are not formally binding.[19]

In 1988, the OAU adopted the Protocol to the African Charter on Human and People's Rights on the Establishment of an African Court on Human and People's Rights (African Human Rights Court Protocol).[20] The African Human Rights Court Protocol established the African Court on Human and People's Rights (ACHPR),[21] which would complement the African Commission in protecting human rights.[22] The African Human Rights Court Protocol required 15 ratifications to enter into force.[23] Ratification was slow and, as a result, the African Human Rights Court Protocol only entered into force in 2002. In the four years between the adoption and entry into force, the OAU was dissolved and replaced by the African Union (AU).[24]

In 2003, the AU sought to create the African Court of Justice,[25] which would be tasked with adjudicating any disputes arising from any AU related treaty or document.[26] Before the Protocol of the Court of Justice of the African Union received the 15 ratifications required to enter into force,[27] the AU decided to merge the African

---

14 Bekker "The African human rights system: An uphill struggle" 2009 *German Yearbook of International Law* 46-48.

15 Heyns "The African regional human rights system: The African Charter" 2004 *Penn State Law Review* 679-685.

16 The African Charter on Human and People's Rights.

17 A 30 The African Charter on Human and People's Rights.

18 A 45(1) & 45 (2) The African Charter on Human and People's Rights.

19 A 53 The African Charter on Human and People's Rights.

20 Protocol to the African Charter on Human and People's Rights on the Establishment of an African Court on Human and People's Rights.

21 A 1 Protocol to the African Charter on Human and People's Rights on the Establishment of an African Court on Human and People's Rights.

22 A 2 Protocol to the African Charter on Human and People's Rights on the Establishment of an African Court on Human and People's Rights.

23 A 34(3) Protocol to the African Charter on Human and People's Rights on the Establishment of an African Court on Human and People's Rights.

24 Constitutive Act of the African Union.

25 A 2 The Protocol of the Court of Justice of the African Union.

26 A 19 The Protocol of the Court of Justice of the African Union.

27 A 60 The Protocol of the Court of Justice of the African Union.

Court on Human and People's Rights and the African Court of Justice.[28] The merged court would be the African Court of Justice and Human Rights.[29]

7.3   CREATION OF THE ACJHR[30]

The thought of an African regional court with international criminal jurisdiction is not a new concept. There are two periods of time which must be distinguished: the first being the mere notion of a regional criminal court, the second being an actual movement towards the creation of such a court.

A regional court that would have international criminal jurisdiction was initially suggested by Guinea during the drafting of the African Charter on Human and People's Rights in 1980.[31] The idea lay dormant for two decades and resurfaced in 2004. While recommending that the ACHPR be merged with the African Court of Justice (ACJ), Nigerian President, Olusegun Obasanjo – the chairperson of the AU Assembly at the time – questioned why the ACJ could not have both a human rights and criminal division as well.[32] 2006 saw a re-emergence of the idea by the committee established by the AU to advise on the possibility of prosecuting Hissen Habre, the former President of Chad. The committee recommended that the proposed African Court of Justice and Human Rights (ACJHR)[33] should be enabled to hear international crimes.[34] International criminal jurisdiction was again suggested in the 2007 African Charter on Democracy, Elections and Good Governance, which stated, "perpetrators of unconstitutional changes of government may also be tried before the competent court of the Union",[35] thus hinting at the creation of a court with international criminal jurisdiction in the future.[36]

From 2009 onward, there was now a concerted effort to create this regional court with international criminal jurisdiction. In 2009, under the direction of the African Union Commission, the Pan African Lawyers Union (PALU) began an enquiry

---

28   A 1-3 The Protocol on the Statute of the African Court of Justice and Human Rights.

29   A 2 The Protocol on the Statute of the African Court of Justice and Human Rights.

30   While the protocol establishing the ACJHPR is called the Protocol on Amendments to the Protocol on the Statute of the African Court of Justice and Human Rights, article 8 specifically states "In the Protocol and the Statute wherever it occurs "African Court of Justice and Human Rights" is deleted and replaced with "African Court of justice and Human and People's Rights".

31   Ouguergouz *La Charte Africaine des droits de l'homme et des peuples* (1993) 72.

32   Report on the Decision of the Assembly of the Union to merge the African Court on Human and Peoples' Rights and the Court of Justice of the African Union, Executive Council, Sixth Ordinary Session, EX.CL/162 (2005).

33   The merged ACHR and ACJ.

34   Report of the Committee of Eminent African Jurists on the Case of Hissene Habre www.hrw.org/legacy/justice/habre/CEJA_Report0506.pdf (2016-08-05).

35   A 25(5) African Charter on Democracy, Elections and Good Governance (2012).

36   Amnesty International *Malabo Protocol: Legal and institutional implications of the merged and expanded African Court* (2016) 7.

into putting forward proposals to amend the ACJHR Protocol.[37] PALU was also tasked with investigating the consequences that would ensue if the court is granted jurisdiction over crimes against humanity, genocide, war crimes and other international crimes.[38] PALU submitted a draft for the amendments to the Protocol, as well as a report on its findings in this regard in 2010.[39] African Ministers of Justice met in 2012 and endorsed the Draft Protocol suggested by PALU.[40] The AU Assembly refused to adopt the 2012 Draft Protocol. The AU Assembly instructed the AU Commission and ACHR to submit a definition for unconstitutional change of government as a crime, as well as conducting an investigation into the financial and structural repercussions of including criminal jurisdiction to the ACJHR.[41]

African leaders met in early 2014 to discuss the 2012 draft. The aim of this meeting was, amongst others, to define the crime of 'unconstitutional change of government', as well as to decide whether or not to include the immunity provision.[42] The crime unconstitutional change of government was defined and is contained in Article 28E.[43] The original 2012 Draft Protocol made no provision for Head of State immunity; however, an immunities provision was inserted into the 2014 draft at the First AU Ministerial Meeting of the Specialized Technical Committee on Justice and Legal Affairs.[44] The immunities provision which was already a cause for concern on its own was expanded. Traditionally immunity *ratione personae* (personal immunity), is only awarded to Heads of State and Ministers of Foreign Affairs.[45] The provision in the 2014 draft, was expanded to include not only heads of state and ministers of foreign affairs, but also the undefined category of "other senior state officials".[46] Later that year, the AU Assembly adopted the 2014 draft, which included the contentious immunities provision.[47]

---

37   Amnesty International (n 36) 9.

38   Decision on the implementation of the Assembly Decision on the abuse of the Principle of Universal Jurisdiction Assembly/AU/Dec. 213(XII) (2009); Decision on the implementation of the Assembly Decisions on the International Criminal Court Doc. Assembly/AU/Dec.366 (XVII) (2011).

39   Amnesty International (n 36) 9.

40   See generally The Report, The Legal Instruments and Recommendations of the Ministers of Justice/ Attorneys General on Legal Matters EX.CL/731(XXI) (2012); "Opening statement by HE Mr Erastus Mwencha, Deputy Chairperson of the African Union Commission at the First Session of the Specialized Technical Committee on Justice and Legal Affairs" www.au.int/en/sites/default/files/newsevents/ workingdocuments/13148-wd-dcp-speech.pdf (2016-07-29).

41   Decision on the Protocol on Amendments to the Protocol on the Statute of the African Court of Justice and Human Rights Assembly/AU/Dec.427 (XIX) (2012).

42   Opening statement by Prof Vincent O Nmehielle, legal counsel and director for Legal Affairs of the African Union Commission', 1st Session of the Specialized Technical Committee on Justice and Legal Affairs (Government Legal Experts) www.au.int/en/sites/default/files/newsevents/workingdocuments/13148-wd-lc-opening_statement-stc_meeting-experts-may_2014_0.pdf (2016-07-29).

43   Statute of the African Court of Justice and Human Rights (as amended).

44   Amnesty International (n 36) 11.

45   Dugard *International Law: A South African Perspective (*2011) 253.

46   A 46A*bis* Protocol on Amendments to the Protocol of the African Court of Justice and Human Rights (Malabo Protocol) 2014.

47   Decision on the Draft Legal Instruments Assembly/AU/Dec.529 (XXIII) (2014).

The Malabo Protocol will enter into force once it has received the minimum 15 ratifications.[48] At the time of writing, only 15 out of the 55 African Union states have signed the Malabo Protocol.[49] None of these states have ratified the Protocol as yet.[50] South Africa has not signed the Malabo protocol.

It is important to note that the Malabo Protocol does not create a separate court. It simply adds on international criminal jurisdiction to the jurisdiction of the ACJHR, which the AU created in 2008. The ACHJR will now be known as the ACJHPR.[51] Effectively the ACJHPR will now have three chambers: a General Affairs Section, a Human and People's Rights Section and an International Criminal Law Section.[52]

Amnesty International aptly stated that "the proposal to extend that mandate of the ACJHR to include a criminal jurisdiction would probably be still-born if it were not for specific events that motivated the AU to seriously consider it."[53] This could also be described as an international crisis rationale.[54] Katzenstein explains that an international crisis is "events that challenge an existing legal rule or rules that some seek to protect".[55]

Prior to the indictment and trial of the Kenyan President, Uhuru Muigai Kenyatta and his Deputy, William Ruto, France and Spain had both issued indictments against Rwandan State officials, under the principle of universal jurisdiction.[56] However, it was ultimately the indictment of Sudanese President Al-Bashir[57] that put the final nail in the ICC's coffin for the AU. This is one of the reasons that steered the African continent towards the creation of a regional court with international criminal jurisdiction.

Each of the aforementioned indictments qualify as an international crisis. These indictments all challenge the customary international law principle of immunity. Immunity is the legal rule which is not only being challenged but also being protected by African states.

---

48   A 11 Malabo Protocol.

49   Benin, Chad, Comoros, Congo, Ghana, Guinea-Bissau, Kenya, Mauritania, Sierra Leone, Sao Tome and Principe and Uganda.

50   List of countries which have signed, ratified/acceded to the Protocol on Amendments to the Protocol on the Statute of the African Court of Justice and Human Rights https://au.int/sites/default/files/treaties/7804-sl-protocol_on_amendments_to_the_protocol_on_the_statute_of_the_african_court_of_justice_and_human_rights_5.pdf (2020-06-01).

51   A 8 Malabo Protocol.

52   A 19 Statute of the Court of Justice and Human Rights (as amended).

53   Amnesty International (n 36) 9.

54   Katzenstein "In the shadow of crisis: The creation of international courts in the twentieth century" 2014 *Havard International Law Journal* 151-153.

55   Katzenstein (n 55) 153.

56   African Union-European Union expert report on the principle of universal jurisdiction, Council of European Union 8672/1/09. REV 1 (2009).

57   *The Prosecutor v Omar Hassan Ahmad Al-Bashir* ICC-02/05-01/09.

Some have criticised the AU's initiative to create this 'regional criminal court'. The main points of criticism are that its creation is, firstly in fact a means for protecting African Heads of State that are guilty of perpetrating international crimes, and secondly a hostile backlash against the ICC for focusing on the African continent.[58]

The motivation behind the creation of the court is not the only aspect under scrutiny. Concern has been expressed over the manner in which the Malabo Protocol was drafted. Unfortunately, African governments were not invited to attend the 'validation workshops'[59] which took place in South Africa in August and October–November 2010.[60] These workshops were attended by the AU Commission, legal advisors of various AU institutions and legal advisors of the Regional Economic Communities (RECs).[61] As a result, the African states, which will be most affected by the Malabo Protocol, have had only one year to review it.[62] States from Southern Africa have raised concern that the process did not allow for sufficient time for adequate consideration.[63]

Du Plessis has described the drafting of the Malabo Protocol as "rushed".[64] He believes that the process did not involve sufficient participation from Civil Society Organisations, NGO's and the public. The criticism is justified since the concerns raised by Civil Society Organisations were not addressed, NGOs were not asked for comment, the Malabo Protocol was not posted on the AU's website and it was not posted in other media sources for public comment.[65] Du Plessis is of the opinion that the current human rights protection mechanisms in Africa are at risk of being weakened by the Malabo Protocol – which he describes as a "deeply flawed legal instrument".[66]

Viljoen echoes Du Plessis' sentiment. In a blog post, Viljoen raises the following concerns: firstly, that the focus on human rights has been reduced by including a criminal section and secondly that the Appellate Chamber – who will have the authority to overturn the decisions made by the Human Rights Section – may not

---

58   Amnesty International (n 36) 6.

59   At a validation workshop, key findings are presented to stakeholders, they are given an opportunity to discuss these findings and to ultimately validate the draft being considered.

60   Carter, Ellis and Jalloh *The International Criminal Court in an effective global justice system* (2016) 245.

61   Deya "Worth the wait: Pushing for the African Court to exercise jurisdiction for international crimes" 24 http://www.osisa.org/openspace/regional/african-court-worth-wait (2016-10-02).

62   Du Plessis "A case of negative regional complementarity? Giving the African Court of Justice and Human Rights jurisdiction over international crimes' http://www.ejiltalk.org/a-case-of-negative-regional-complementarity-giving-the-africancourt-of-justice-and-human-rights-jurisdiction-over-international-crimes/ (2016-10-02).

63   Du Plessis (n 62).

64   Du Plessis "A new regional International Criminal Court for Africa?" 2012 *SAJCJ* 286-288.

65   Du Plessis (n 64) 288.

66   Du Plessis (n 62).

have adequate expertise in the human rights field.[67] Du Plessis describes the Malabo Protocol as an example of "negative complementarity".[68]

Negative complementarity, he explains, occurs when efforts are made, supposedly, to advance international criminal justice but "are intended to distract from or undermine those ideals".[69] This could be for example using a mechanism – other than the ICC – which in all likelihood will not be able to succeed, to prosecute international crimes.[70]

7.4   THE ROLE OF REGIONALISM

A preference for universalism is clear in both the Covenant of the League of Nations[71] and the Charter of the United Nations (UN Charter).[72] The Covenant of the League of Nations acknowledged regional agreements like the Monroe Doctrine.[73] The discussion regarding regionalism and universalism with reference to international organisations is a mirror image of the classic argument regarding a preference between centralism and local governance.[74]

The purpose and function of the ACJHPR is comparable to the ICC. Like the ICC, the ACJHPR will have jurisdiction over crimes against humanity, genocide, war crimes, and the crime of aggression. The difference is that the ACJHPR will have jurisdiction over 11 international crimes that the ICC does not.[75] The additional crimes that the ACJHPR will have jurisdiction over are not the classic or traditional international crimes. The ICC is the universal institution and the ACJHPR is the regional institution and it would be better suited to have jurisdiction over international crimes which are prevalent in its region.

The provisions in the Malabo Protocol which grants immunity to heads of state and senior government officials,[76] the additional crimes created and the provision of corporate criminal liability are all examples of how different courts – the ACJHPR

---

67   *AU Assembly should consider human rights implications before adopting the amending merged African Court Protocol* May 2012 https://africlaw.com/2012/05/23/au-assembly-should-consider-human-rights-implications-before-adopting-the-amending-merged-african-court-protocol/ (2018-07-09).

68   Du Plessis (n 62).

69   Du Plessis "African efforts to close the impunity gap: Lessons for complementarity from national and regional actions" 2012 *Institute for Security Studies Paper number 241* 7.

70   Du Plessis (n 69) 2.

71   The League of Nations no longer exists; it was replaced by the United Nations in 1945.

72   Schreuer "Regionalism v Universalism" 1995 *EJIL* 477.

73   A 21.

74   Schreuer (n 72) 477.

75   Unconstitutional change of government, piracy, terrorism, mercenarism, corruption, money laundering, trafficking in persons, trafficking in drugs, trafficking in hazardous wastes, illicit exploitation of natural resources and crime of aggression.

76   A 46A*bis* Malabo Protocol: "No charges shall be commenced or continued before the Court against any serving AU Head of State or Government, or anybody acting or entitled to act in such capacity, or other senior state officials based on their functions, during their tenure of office."

and the ICC – are interpreting the same norms in different and competing manners.[77] If the ACJHPR receives the required ratifications, it will be the first regional court with international criminal jurisdiction to ever be created.

The relationship that the ICC and ACJHPR will share has not been mapped out in the Malabo Protocol but it is hoped that it will be one of complementarity rather than superiority. Ideally the two courts should work together and share the burden of ensuring that those responsible for committing human rights violations and international crimes are brought to justice. Neither court should believe that it is superior to the other, nor should there be any hostility between them. More often than not, the functions of the universal institution are also assigned to the regional institution, as is the case here.[78] These functions must be divided between the institutions in a manner which does not result in an overlap.[79]

Since the Nuremburg Tribunal, international criminal law has mainly been enforced at an international level.[80] This is because states have come together, either because of treaties or the United Nations Security Council's powers and created *ad hoc* tribunals,[81] hybrid tribunals[82] and ultimately the ICC.[83] It is only more recently that international law is being enforced at a national level, either through domestic courts acting under universal jurisdiction or the creation of hybrid international courts like the Special Court for Sierra Leone (SCSL).[84] There has yet to be enforcement of international criminal law at the regional level.[85]

At the international level of enforcement, the concept of a region has been an important characteristic in defining the jurisdiction of the international tribunals.[86] The ICTY was granted jurisdiction over "serious violations of international humanitarian law committed in the territory of the former Yugoslavia".[87] The ICTR's jurisdiction was also confined to crimes committed within Rwanda.[88] The Special Court for Sierra Leone's jurisdiction is also limited to crimes committed within

---

77 Sirleaf "Regionalism, regime complexes and crisis in International Criminal Justice" 2016 *Columbia Journal of Transnational Law* 699-747.

78 Schreuer (n 72) 484.

79 Schreuer (n 72) 484.

80 Burke-White "Regionalization of international criminal law enforcement: A preliminary exploration" 2003 *Texan International Law Journal* 729-730.

81 Such as the International Criminal Tribunal for the Former Yugoslavia (ICTY) and the International Criminal Tribunal for Rwanda (ICTR).

82 Such as the Extraordinary Chambers in the Courts of Cambodia, the Special Tribunal for Lebanon and the Special Court and Residual Special Court for Sierra Leone.

83 Burke-White (n 80) 730.

84 Burke-White (n 80) 730.

85 Burke-White (n 80) 730.

86 Schabas "Regions, regionalism and international law" 2007 *New Zealand Yearbook of International Law* 3-10.

87 SC Resolution 827 S/Res/827 (1993).

88 A 1 Statute of the International Tribunal for Rwanda.

Sierra Leone.[89] The ICC is the only international tribunal which is truly universal in its nature.[90] The Security Council may refer any UN member state to the ICC and as a result its territorial jurisdiction is not subject to any limitation.[91]

International law enforcement at both international and national levels has its respective advantages and disadvantages.[92] It is at the regional level of enforcement that a balance between these advantages and disadvantages of supranational and national law enforcement can be achieved.[93] Supranational tribunals are exceptionally costly[94] and more often than not are located far away from the crime scenes and affected communities.[95] National tribunals are less costly and closer in proximity but are, however, more susceptible to bias and rarely have the necessary judicial resources required for an effective trial.[96] A regional tribunal provides an alternative which is closer to the crime scenes and affected communities, less expensive than a supranational tribunal, less susceptible to bias than a national tribunal because it would have a variety of judges from different states, more likely to have adequate judicial resources,[97] familiar with the underlying factors of the dispute and have a greater interest in resolving the matter.[98] In addition, a regional tribunal will facilitate regional ownership over the crimes.[99]

The increase in international organisations has brought with it the traditional argument between local and centralised governance, but also added some unique features.[100] The universal sector is perceived as being ineffective and has resulted in a move towards regional organisations.[101] The move towards regionalism and away from universalism is as a result of multiple factors.[102] The most important factor is the inability of the UN to perform its duties.[103] Other reasons include the preference to address issues in a smaller forum ensuring greater cooperation, a revival of unity amongst member states and lastly the prohibition of non-member-

---

89   SC Resolution 1315 S/Res/1315 (2000).

90   Schabas (n 86) 12.

91   Schabas (n 86) 12.

92   Burke-White (n 80) 730.

93   Swart "The prospects for regional and sub regional complementarity in Africa" in Slye (ed) *The Nuremburg Principles in Non-Western Societies, A Reflection of their Universality, Legitimacy and Application* (2016) 217.

94   ICTY and ICTR spent a total of $695 000 000 and $1 000 000 000, respectively.

95   Burke-White (n 80) 734.

96   Burke-White (n 80) 734.

97   Schabas (n 86) 19.

98   Swart (n 93) 227.

99   Moghadam "Revitalizing universal jurisdiction: Lessons from hybrid tribunals applied to the case of Hissene Habre" 2008 *Columbia Human Rights Law Review* 471-515.

100   Schreuer (n 72) 477.

101   Schreuer (n 72) 477.

102   Schreuer (n 72) 479.

103   Schreuer (n 72) 479.

state interference.[104] Regional and subregional mechanisms have proved useful in regulating issues such as piracy, environmental pollution, money laundering and human rights.[105] With the international community's waning faith in the Security Council, regional organisations have had no choice but to step up and actively ensure peace and security within their region.[106]

Another concept worth mentioning here is the "regionalization of universal jurisdiction".[107] Jebberger highlights that the exercise of universal jurisdiction in Europe has declined.[108] He explains that this is possibly due to states realising that exercising universal jurisdiction is expensive, difficult and tiring.[109] Universal jurisdiction has been criticised for being a "concept of jurisdictional imperialism" because it is almost always exercised by states in the Northern Hemisphere against states in the Southern Hemisphere.[110] Cases which have arisen as a result of universal jurisdiction tend to lose momentum from political pressure and judges often struggle to navigate international criminal law provisions.[111]

The 'regionalization of universal jurisdiction' is best illustrated by the creation of the Extraordinary African Chambers (EAC). The EAC was created through an agreement between Senegal and the AU to prosecute Hissene Habre, Chad's former Head of State.[112] While the EAC is a hybrid tribunal, it is different from a traditional hybrid tribunal because it is created in a third-party state (Senegal) and exercises universal jurisdiction as opposed international criminal jurisdiction in terms of a treaty.

Enforcement on a regional level is based on two key factors. Firstly, the international legal issue at hand is one that concerns an entire region, secondly because of their geographical proximity to the communities affected by human rights violations and international crimes.[113] Lastly, a regional organisation will be better equipped to enforce the relevant rule in question because of its political relations.[114] Regionalism can therefore be defined as "a voluntary pooling of resources for a common purpose by two or more sets of partners belonging to different states",[115] to address particular

---

104 Schreuer (n 72) 479.

105 Burke-White (n 80) 731.

106 Swart (n 93) 215.

107 Jebberger "On behalf of Africa: Towards the regionalization of universal jurisdiction?" in Werle, Fernandez and Vormbaum (ed) *Africa and the International Criminal Court* (2014).

108 Jebberger (n 107) 167.

109 Jebberger (n 107) 167.

110 Moghadam (n 99) 484.

111 Moghadam (n 99) 484.

112 Agreement between the government of the Republic of Sénégal and the African Union on the establishment of the Extraordinary African Chambers within the courts of Sénégal, 22 August 2012.

113 Burke-White (n 80) 733.

114 Burke-White (n 80) 733.

115 Biswaro *A rhetoric v reality: A comparative study* (2012) 13.

issues at a level between international enforcement and national enforcement. States create regional organisations because they recognise that certain issues are more effectively addressed collectively, rather than individually.[116]

It has also been argued that states are more inclined to accept a regional method of enforcement because the benefits of a regional mechanism are greater than the sovereignty costs of such membership.[117] Moravcsik describes sovereignty costs as a "surrender of national discretion ... to an international authority".[118] African states are particularly inclined to accept a regional mechanism for these reasons.

As a result of international cooperation, political leaders and heads of state are no longer able to control policy variables as freely as they would have been, had they not been a member to the mechanism.[119] For example, the number of members to the Rome State, a supranational mechanism, inhibits the influence that a state can have on the selection of judges which will preside over these international crimes. Whereas in a regional mechanism, such as the ACJHPR, the number of member states are fewer, thereby increasing the possibility that the judge who was nominated by his or her state, will be elected to serve.[120] As the number of members in the mechanism increase, the more difficult it is to manipulate the policy. The membership and sovereignty costs of a regional enforcement mechanism are significantly lower than those of a supranational mechanism because there are fewer members.[121]

There are over 20 regional and subregional organisations within Africa.[122] The creation of these organisations indicates an enhancement of regionalism on the African Continent.[123] The idea of subregional courts acquiring international criminal jurisdiction is not far-fetched. Modern international law academics have acknowledged the co-dependence of International Human Rights Law, International Humanitarian Law and International Criminal Law.[124] It is not inconceivable to assume that the courts of these subregional organisations will be able to acquire

---

116 Mills "Reconstructing sovereignty: A human rights perspective" 1997 *Netherlands Quarterly of Human Rights* 267-274.

117 Burke-White (n 80) 746.

118 Moravcsik "The origins of human rights regimes: Democratic delegation in postwar Europe" 2000 *International Organization* 217-227.

119 Burke-White (n 80) 746.

120 Burke-White (n 80) 747.

121 Burke-White (n 80) 746.

122 Economic Community of West African States, Southern African Development Community, East African Community, African Union, Intergovernmental Authority on Development, African Economic Community, Economic Community of Central African States, Common Market for Eastern and Southern Africa, Arab Maghreb Union, New Partnership for Africa's Development, African Development Bank Group, West African Economic and Monetary Union, Arab League, Community of Sahel-Saharan States, United Nations Economic Commission for Africa, Southern African Customs Union and the African, Caribbean and Pacific Group of States.

123 Sirleaf (n 77) 729.

124 Swart (n 93) 214.

jurisdiction over war crimes and other international crimes as a result of the mutually inclusive relationship between International Human Rights Law, International Humanitarian Law and International Criminal Law.[125]

7.4.1 Regime complexes

Regionalism in this case leads to a regime complex. Regime complexes are "an array of partially overlapping and non-hierarchical institutions governing a particular issue area".[126] These complexes form as a result of an overlapping of jurisdictional areas.[127] The overlap can be caused in two manners.[128] First, "issue areas" which are governed by international institutions are expanded upon and therefore create an overlap with another international institution.[129] This expansion is usually as a result of a change in policy demands and not to deliberately cause conflict between the institutions.[130] The second possibility occurs when a group of states create a new institution which must be integrated within the existing system of institutions.[131] The creation of the ACJHPR would be an example of the second instance.

With regards to international tribunals, the regime complex is intensified because "there is no hierarchy in the international judicial arena".[132] While Alter and Meunier acknowledge that "rule complexity" is present within the domestic context as well, it is more difficult to reconcile within the international arena because there is no overarching international body with the final say.[133] In the domestic context, the hierarchy is constitutionally regulated,[134] whereas within the international arena, no obligation can take preference over another[135] with the exception of *jus cogens* norms. *Jus cogens* norms are "norm[s] that enjoy a higher rank in in the international hierarchy than treaty law and even ordinary customary rules".[136] The lack of a hierarchy in the international regime complex directly affects the cooperation

---

125 Swart (n 93) 214.

126 Raustiala and Victor "The regime complex for plant genetic resources" 2004 *International Organization* 277-279.

127 Gehring and Faude "The dynamics of regime complexes: Microfoundations and systemic effects" 2013 *Global Governance* 119-123.

128 Gehring and Faude (n 127) 123.

129 Gehring and Faude (n 127) 123.

130 Gehring and Faude (n 127) 123.

131 Gehring and Faude (n 127) 123.

132 Giorgetti "Horizontal and vertical relationships of International Courts and Tribunals – How do we address their competing jurisdiction?" 2015 *ICSID Review* 98-99.

133 Alter and Meunier "Nested and overlapping regimes in the transatlantic banana trade dispute" 2006 *Journal of European Public Policy* 362-365.

134 Kelsen *General theory of law and state* (1961) 123.

135 Vidmar "Norm conflicts and hierarchy in international law: Towards a vertical international system?" in De Wet and Vidmar (ed) *Hierarchy in international law: The place of human rights* (2012) 13.

136 *Prosecutor v Anto Furundzija* 1998 ICTY IT-95-17/1 260.

between states and the institutions.[137] This is because a decision made within one institution may be challenged within another institution.[138]

A regime complex in the field of international criminal law will be inherently present because the Malabo Protocol does not explain the relationship that the ACJHPR and ICC will share. This is a perfect example of institutional fragmentation within international criminal law.[139] Institutional fragmentation is caused by a "lack of dialogue between international institutions".[140] The ACJHPR is not the only court that will have caused an institutional fragmentation. Other courts which have contributed to the institutional fragmentation of international criminal law are: The Special Court for Sierra Leone,[141] the Extraordinary Chambers in the Courts of Cambodia,[142] the War Crimes Chamber of the Court of Bosnia and Herzegovina,[143] and the Extraordinary African Chambers.[144] Until the ICC and ACJHPR agree on the type of relationship they will share, the regime complex will continue to be intensified. While regime complexes usually create conflict and competition amongst the various institutions, it is also possible that it could result in dividing the workload amongst them,[145] as was the case with the War Crimes Chamber of the Court of Bosnia and Herzegovina and the ICTY.

The ICTY, ICTR, Special Court for Sierra Leone and the Special Tribunal for Lebanon were all conferred concurrent jurisdiction over international crimes committed within their respective regions within the given times.[146] In addition to this, each of these courts enjoyed primacy over their respective national courts.[147] While the ICC also enjoys concurrent jurisdiction, it does not have primary jurisdiction, but rather complementary jurisdiction.[148] Primary jurisdiction enables

---

137 Alter and Raustiala "The rise of international regime complexity" 2018 *Annual Review of Law and Social Science* 329-331.

138 Alter and Raustiala (n 137) 331.

139 Sirleaf (n 77) 746.

140 Lattanzi "Introduction" in Van den Herik and Stahn (ed) *The diversification and fragmentation of international criminal law* (2004) 5.

141 Security Council Resolution 1315 (2000), S/RES/1315 (2000), 14 August 2000.

142 United Nations Agreement between the United Nations and the Royal Government of Cambodia concerning the prosecution under Cambodian law of crimes committed during the period of democratic Kampuchea, 6 June 2003.

143 Law on Court of Bosnia and Herzegovina, Official Gazette of BiH 49/09.

144 Agreement between the government of the Republic of Sénégal and the African Union on the establishment of the Extraordinary African Chambers within the courts of Sénégal, 22 August 2012.

145 Gehring and Faude (n 127) 120.

146 A 9(1) Statute of the International Tribunal for the Former Yugoslavia; Article 8(1) Statute of the International Tribunal for Rwanda; A 8(1) Statute of the Special Court for Sierra Leone and A 4(1) Statute of the Special Tribunal for Lebanon.

147 A 9(2) Statute of the International Tribunal for the Former Yugoslavia; A 8(2) Statute of the International Tribunal for Rwanda; A 8(2) Statute of the Special Court for Sierra Leone and A 4(1) Statute of the Special Tribunal for Lebanon.

148 A 17(1) Rome Statute.

the international tribunal to "formally request national courts to defer",[149] the proceedings to it whereas with complementary jurisdiction, the national court must be given first option to initiate proceedings.[150] In addition to the Malabo Protocol not specifying the relationship between the ACJHPR and the ICC, it also does not stipulate whether the international criminal law chamber of the ACJHPR will have primary or complementary jurisdiction.

There are three essential characteristics of regime complexes that have an effect on cooperation.[151] Firstly, continuous legal contradictions between the various institutions encourage state parties to 'forum shop', which in turn creates conflicting regimes.[152] If the ACJHPR is created, African states will be able to forum shop between it and the ICC depending on how they feel about immunity at the time. Secondly, regimes which are created independently from each other are more likely to clash with each other than institutions which are created with existing institutions in mind.[153] Lastly, the presence of both the above factors results in the creation of uncertainty within the regime. As a result of the uncertainty within the regime, enforcement becomes highly complicated which, in turn, requires a "greater outlay of resources", further reinforcing the inequalities between various member states.[154]

Regime complexes affect both the enhancement of legal principles and rules as well as politics in general, in several ways.[155] The overlapping rules and institutions within the regime complex mean that, "new rules and institutions are not negotiated on a clean slate".[156] Rule makers are bound not only by the existing rules, but also the political agendas advanced by these rules.[157] Secondly, as the substantive rules increase in number, there is greater conflict as there are more rules that compete with each other.[158] Third, as there is little to no guidance on resolving the conflict between international rules, there is more likely to be a renegotiation of the international rules, rather than adjudication on the conflict.[159]

---

149 A 9(2) Statute of the International Tribunal for the Former Yugoslavia; A 8(2) Statute of the International Tribunal for Rwanda; A 8(2) Statute of the Special Court for Sierra Leone and A 4(1) Statute of the Special Tribunal for Lebanon.

150 Nouwen *Complementarity in the line of fire: The catalysing effect of the International Criminal Court in Uganda and Sudan* (2013) 15.

151 Struett, Nance and Armstrong "Navigating the piracy regime complex" 2013 *Global Governance* 93-95.

152 Alter and Meunier "The politics of international regime complexity" 2009 *Perspectives on Politics* 13-16.

153 Struett (n 151) 95.

154 Struett (n 151) 95.

155 Peter "International enclosure, the regime complex and intellectual property schizophrenia" 2007 *Michigan State Law Review* 1-14.

156 Raustialia "Density and conflict in intellectual property law" 2007 *UC Davis Law Review* 1021-1025.

157 Raustialia (n 156) 1026.

158 Raustialia (n 156) 1027.

159 Raustialia (n 156) 1028.

Leebron has developed the idea of a regime complex into a conglomerate regime. Conglomerate regimes, he explains,

> are regimes that remain somewhat separate, in terms of both norms and institutional structure, within an overarching regime. Like corporate conglomerates, they are marked by important institutional relationships and perhaps common policies among the constituent parts, but also by institutional separation.[160]

In essence, what Leebron is describing is a situation in which international criminal law intersects with other regimes relating to different aspects of law. As a result of globalisation, areas of law which would normally be completely unrelated to international criminal law will end up in this international criminal law regime complex.[161]

7.4.2 Regime shifting

Regime complexes create an opportunity for states to try and "alter the status quo ex ante by moving treaty negotiations, law making initiatives, or standard setting activities from one international venue to another".[162] This is referred to as a regime shift. There are two types of regimes shifts.

An intra-regime shift is a movement to a different venue within the same regime whereas an inter-regime shift which is a movement to not only a different venue but also a different regime area.[163] The creation of the ACJHPR will be an intra-regime shift because the venue would have moved from the ICC, a multilateral organisation, to a regional organisation.[164] For states which have withdrawn from the Rome Statute, the ACJHPR will ultimately replace the ICC.

Some authors believe that "forum shifting [regime shifting] is a strategy that only the powerful and well-resourced can use".[165] Helfer however disagrees. Helfer states that "regime shifting is a game that both strong and weak actors can play."[166] This view is more plausible as African states are generally viewed as being less developed and less powerful than European states, and are creating an intra-regime shift.[167]

Helfer proposes that less developed states, such as African states, can greatly benefit from regime shifting in multiple ways. First, states which have been previously ignored are given the opportunity to change policy objectives to suit them better.[168]

---

160 Leebron "Linkages" 2002 *American Journal of International Law* 5-17.

161 Peter (n 155) 14.

162 Helfer "Regime shifting: The TRIPs agreement and new dynamics of international intellectual property lawmaking" 2004 *Yale Journal of International Law* 1-14.

163 Helfer (n 162) 16.

164 Sirleaf (n 77) 757.

165 Braithwaite and Drahos *Global Business Relation* (2000) 565.

166 Helfer (n 162) 17.

167 This is a prime example of imperialism and colonialism in public international law.

168 Helfer (n 162) 55.

Second, it allows states to evaluate issue areas within the law.[169] Third, it allows these states to "consign an issue area to a venue where consequential outcome and meaningful rule development are unlikely to occur" and thus operating as a safety net for states.[170] Finally, these states are also provided with the opportunity to start creating the political will required for new laws to be made.[171]

Looking at the current regime shift being created by the AU the aforementioned benefits can be seen. African states which have previously been ignored are now able to create their own policy objectives and exercise an African version of justice. They have also begun to evaluate areas within international criminal law which are problematic. By creating the ACJHPR, the AU is generating the political will to create new laws in international criminal law, for example a change with respect to immunity for sitting heads of state. It is also hoped that the crimes included in the Malabo Protocol will be adopted into the domestic law of African states.

While Helfer believes that less developed states can benefit from regime shifting, Benvenisti and Downs believe that regime shifting harms developing states in the following ways. Firstly by creating more institutions, the scope of multilateral agreements is limited, thereby inhibiting the ability of less powerful states to "build the cross issue coalitions", which would in turn grant these states greater influence and bargaining powers.[172] Secondly, the membership costs of states to international courts and tribunals are increased by the overlap in jurisdiction as states attempt to fulfil their obligations under the various agreements.[173] Lastly, powerful states are able to escape their liability for creating the fragmentation if they simply assert that the fragmentation was unintentional.[174] These authors also suggest that powerful states use this approach because they are aware, "that weaker states are not only more numerous than they are, but they are also far more diverse with respect to size, wealth and their level of development".[175] Whether Helfer's view or Benvenisti and Downs' view is a true reflection of the current shift from the ICC to the ACJHPR remains to be seen after – and if ever – the court comes into existence.

7.4.3 *Grossraume*

The term *grossraum* initially referred to a provision of transnational resources in an economic context.[176] This term is now also used in international law and inter-

---

169   Helfer (n 162) 58.

170   Helfer (n 162) 56.

171   Helfer (n 162) 59.

172   Benvenisti and Downs "The empires new clothes: Political economy and the fragmentation of international law" 2010 *Stanford Law Review* 595.

173   Benvenisti and Downs (n 172) 596.

174   Benvenisti and Downs (n 172) 596.

175   Benvenisti and Downs (n 172) 610.

176   Salter and Yin "Analysing regionalism within international law and relations: The Shanghai cooperation organisation as a grossraum?" 2014 *Chinese Journal of International Law* 819-822.

national relations.[177] *Grossraum* is a model of regionalism.[178] Schmittian describes *grossraum* as a "political idea with which other member states broadly identify, and which they accept as generally legitimate on the basis of their overlapping cultural traditions and aspirations".[179] A *grossraum* is made up of a group of adjacent states. As such, the internal borders of the states themselves are called the second-tier borders and the border of the *grossraum* itself is called the first-tier border.[180] A regional organisation can be classified as a *grossraum* if its territory is linked geographically and it has a particular interest in its distinguishing beliefs and key principles.[181]

In terms of the above, the movement towards the creation of the ACJHPR can be seen as a *grossraum*. The 'political idea' with which African states are identifying and accepting as legitimate is twofold. First, the ICC has solely focused on African States as the subject of its prosecutions. Secondly, African states feel a strange sense of ownership over these international crimes and believe they should be prosecuting it themselves. The internal borders of each individual African state will be the second-tier borders and the continental border will be the first-tier border of the *grossraum*. The AU may also be described as a *grossraum*, because the states which are members of the AU are geographically linked and they identify with similar beliefs and principles.

Liberal democracy, social democracy and communism are all examples of *grossraum* principles.[182] The prohibition on "foreign extra regional intervention" is a key *grossraum* principle.[183] This principle is one with which African states, within the AU, strongly identify with and support. The traditional law system, which is largely based on relationships between member states which are all seen as equals, has been replaced with a system which focuses on different, "regional power blocks", known as *grossraume*.[184] The shift is based on a multiple of reasons including military, geopolitical, technological reasons as well as globalisation.[185]

Schmitt asserts that the first *grossraum* characteristics were present in the 1832 Monroe Doctrine.[186] In this doctrine, United States President Monroe declared that "further efforts by European Nation states to colonise land or interfere with American nation states would be viewed as acts of aggression requiring US intervention".[187]

---

177 Salter and Yin (n 176) 822.

178 Salter and Yin (n 176) 827.

179 Schmitt (n 14) 101.

180 Hooker *"Carl Schmitt's international thought: Order and orientation"* (2009) 142.

181 Salter and Yin (n 176) 824.

182 Schmitt (n 14) 101.

183 Salter and Yin (n 176) 824.

184 Schwab "Contextualizing Carl Schmitt's Concept of grossraum" 1994 *History of European Ideas* 185-187.

185 Salter "The return of politicised space: Carl Schmitt's re-orientation of transnational law scholarship" 2012 *Tilburg Law Review* 5-8.

186 Schmitt *Writings on war* (2011) 88.

187 Salter (n 185) 6.

SELECT ESSAYS ON GOVERNANCE AND ACCOUNTABILITY ISSUES IN PUBLIC LAW

The main principle of this declaration was that the idea of non-intervention of extra regional states would be able to be transferred into other situations.[188] This, "short lived *grossraum* principle", was an important moment for US Foreign policy which was used by many United States presidents.[189] While this doctrine provided a guideline as to what a *grossraum* analysis of international law would be, it was not received in the other continents at that time.[190]

Regions which since then have embodied this principle prohibiting extra-regional interventions include the Russian Commonwealth and the United States of America (USA).[191] Africa could possibly be one of the newest regions to embody this principle as well. Apart from the AU repeatedly voicing its disapproval of the ICC's interference within the region, the AU has gone a step further in initialising the creation of the ACJHPR. The creation of this court could be seen as an additional measure in prohibiting extra-regional intervention.

The UN Security Council has been described as a "world government".[192] However, Africa, Antarctica, Australia and South America are all continents which lack representation "in the highest decision making circle", whereas both the European and Asian continents are more than sufficiently represented.[193] The *grossraum* approach would seek to protect regional entities and keep their territorial areas free from extra-regional interference. Each entity will be under the supervision of a "leading power", which will be responsible for the security and development of that particular region.[194] The "leading power" would also take on the responsibility of the region's economic coordination, while still respecting and maintaining the member states' independence and sovereignty.[195] Traditionally the "leading power" in a *grossraum* is a state. Why can the "leading power" not be a representative body of all the *grossraum* states, like the African Union? In the African region, the AU could then be seen as the "leading power" for the African region.

Schmitt believes that the integration of a "*grossraum* analysis" is essential for a workable and practical structure of international law.[196] International law in this sense would be open to "substantive spatial questions" and is able to deal with a demarcated planet that coexists.[197] This form of international law is in direct conflict with the current form, which is ignorant to spatial differences and is

188 Schmitt (n 186) 88.
189 Salter (n 185) 7.
190 Schmitt *The nomos of the Earth in the international law of jus publicum Europaeum* (2003) 231.
191 Salter and Yin (n 176) 824.
192 Salter and Yin (n 176) 824.
193 Salter and Yin (n 176) 824.
194 Carr *Nationalism and after* (1945) 74.
195 Rasch "Enmity as a structuring principle" 2005 *South Atlantic Quarterly* 253-261.
196 Salter (n 185) 8.
197 Salter (n 185) 8.

premised on state equality.[198] Schmitt completely disregards the principle of state equality, because it does not take into account the difference in apportionment of geopolitical power.[199] Other factors which influence international law issue areas include, "spheres of influence, back country, contiguity and propinquity".[200]

It would not be logical to assume the question of whether a state's territory is one continuous piece of land, or could it be broken up into multiple pieces, is not linked to the concept of sovereignty.[201] It would also not be logical to assume that the lines which appear on the world map are a true reflection of the demarcation of geopolitical power.[202] Nor could it be suggested that a state with no military power, be considered as an equal of a state with a sophisticated military base.[203] A *grossraum* approach to international law is able to evolve itself to fit into the new 20th-century setting taking these factors into account.[204]

The Hillebrand Herman Moyer Index measured the power within Africa and has indicated that as a result of Nigeria, West Africa is the most powerful on the continent.[205] Within Africa Algeria, Egypt, Ethiopia, Nigeria and South Africa are known as "the Big Five".[206] These five states have been identified as being the most influential on the continent by measuring their economic, demographic and military strength.[207] Other measures of power may include wealth, trade, investment, technological capability, government capacity and human capital.[208] This illustrates that there is a difference in each state's geopolitical power and not all states are in fact equal.

A *grossraum* can also be described as an "historical and politically contemporary idea" which is connected to foreign relations.[209] A *grossraum* is more of a "historical event" than a "legal concept".[210] Should the states which make up the African region or even a subregion within Africa choose to withdraw from the ICC, it could be considered as a *grossraum* forming event.

---

198 Salter (n 185) 8.

199 Schmitt (n 14) 101.

200 Kruszewski "International affairs: Germany's lebensraum" 1940 *The American Political Science Review* 964 974.

201 Salter (n 185) 19.

202 Salter (n 185) 19.

203 Salter (n 185) 19.

204 Salter (n 185) 8.

205 Cilliers, Schunemann and Moyer "Power and influence in Africa: Algeria, Egypt, Ethiopia, Nigeria and South Africa" 2015 *Institute for Security Studies Paper African Futures Paper number 14* 5.

206 Cilliers, Schunemann and Moyer (n 205) 1.

207 Hughes "IFs interstate politics model documentation" 2014 *Working Paper 2014.02.17* 13.

208 Cilliers, Schunemann and Moyer (n 205) 3.

209 Salter and Yin (n 176) 826.

210 Salter and Yin (n 176) 826.

In order for a *grossraum* to be able to function, member states must follow the *grossraum*'s key principles at all times, irrespective of whether they are directly beneficial to the state's interests.[211] Member states should all have a cultural connection in addition to a resolution to recognise equality and respect amongst themselves and a prohibition on intervention by non-member states.[212] Structuring the organisations in a manner which ensures that public law, including public international law, is administered in a coherent manner and that policy decisions are correctly applied is a problem for all *grossraume*.[213]

7.5   CONCLUSION

In conclusion, we can see that despite there being a clear preference for universalism in the UN Charter, states have naturally gravitated towards a more regionally centred approach. The fact that both the ICTY and ICTR were granted jurisdiction over crimes committed only within a particular region, is indicative of this.

It is possible that regionalism in international criminal law may be achieved through a less controversial manner than the creation of regional court with international criminal law jurisdiction. Other options may include the creation of hybrid international tribunals,[214] the effective exercise of universal jurisdiction and of course the ICC could also sit regionally.[215] The Rome Statute provides for the latter: "The Court may sit elsewhere, whenever it considers it desirable, as provided in this Statute."[216] Unfortunately, the circumstances in which the ICC may sit regionally is not prescribed and ultimately has been left to the court's discretion, providing little to no guidance in this regard. Unsurprisingly, ICC has not made use of this possibility to date.

The creation of the ACJHPR, even if only in theory, will have contributed to the development of regionalism by being the first regional court to have international criminal jurisdiction. Up until now regional mechanisms have been used primarily to enforce human rights norms, a mechanism which has worked fairly well.

The addition of international criminal jurisdiction to the ACJHPR is not without fault. The additional International Criminal Law Section will only intensify the current regime complex which is present in international criminal law. Perhaps this intensification will force both the ICC and the ACJHPR to not only acknowledge the other's presence but also establish a working relationship with each other and ultimately achieve their common goal, ending impunity.

---

211   Salter and Yin (n 176) 832.

212   Salter and Yin (n 176) 842.

213   Salter and Yin (n 176) 832.

214   Such as the Special Court for Sierra Leone, Special Tribunal for Lebanon and the Extraordinary Chambers in the Courts of Cambodia

215   Burke-White (n 80) 748.

216   A 3(3).

The substantive fragmentation of laws, in particular the granting of immunity by the ACJHPR, might even have the potential to foster a working relationship between the ICC and ACJHPR. Effectively, the immunity provision in the Malabo Protocol does not bar prosecution at the ICC; it merely serves as a jurisdictional filter for the ACJHPR. The ICC could then focus on prosecutions of leaders who enjoy immunity at this regional level and the ACJHPR could prosecute other parties who would not be entitled to immunity.

An intra regime shift has the potential to either benefit weaker states or disadvantage them even further. Only after the ACJHPR is functional will we see if these weaker African states have benefited or been disadvantaged. This is also dependent on how the weaker states choose to view the ACJHPR. For example, the AU may believe the ICC is disadvantaging African states by making them the sole focus of their prosecutions, whereas non-African states may disagree. The fate of these weaker states lies not only in the hands of the ACJHPR prosecutors, but also in the hands of the *grossraum*'s leading power.

Previously, scholars thought the *grossraum* model could only be used by Western states as it was not received elsewhere. However, if we accept that the AU can be the 'leading power' in a *grossraum*, the creation of this ACJHPR is the historical event which the model is based on and the principle of non-intervention is the political idea being identified with, this means that the ACJHPR is a prime example of a *grossraum* analysis/model of international law. The model is therefore successfully adopted by African States.

Many are sceptical as to whether the ACJHPR will ever come to fruition. The Malabo Protocol, which includes the international criminal law into the court's jurisdiction, was only adopted in 2014. In the past four years, the Malabo protocol has received 11 signatures, whereas the African Charter received 18 signatures within the first four years. Granted, the African Charter received 17 ratifications in the first four years, but the Malabo Protocol is asking states to submit themselves to the jurisdiction of the court. Given the history with the ICC, many may be hesitant to give up a fraction of their sovereignty. South Africa only signed the African Charter in 1996, 10 years later. Although the ACJHPR has not physically manifested as yet, there is a definite intention amongst the AU to get this court off the ground – both literally and figuratively.

AFTERWORD

This volume, devoted to the field of governance and accountability in Public Law, at both global and domestic levels, contains diverse contributions authored by academics from the Faculties of Law at the University of Johannesburg and Nelson Mandela University.

The contributions in Chapters 1, 2 and 6 focus on issues impacting on governance and accountability in South African law. The current jurisprudence of the Constitutional Court illustrates the importance of statutory interpretation for the development of the law and it is thus fitting that the volume commences with a contribution highlighting the theoretical underpinnings of statutory interpretation, with particular reference to the Constitution and its founding values, which include accountability and democratic governance. The contribution in Chapter 2 moves to the problem of hate crimes in South Africa. A hate-crime regulatory framework is proposed as a means to promote effective governance and protection for all groups of people, including those who are most susceptible to systemic discrimination and harm. Staying with the need to provide legal relief for those who are most vulnerable, Chapter 6 highlights the aftermath of the Life Esidimeni Tragedy and criticises the state for its failure to act in accordance with its constitutional duties, including responsiveness and accountability.

The contributions in Chapters 3, 4, 5 and 7 centre around issues of accountability and governance in international and regional law, but with a specific focus on the African continent. The authors in Chapter 3 address the responsibility framework for heads of state and the various mechanisms at domestic, regional and international levels, which could be implemented to hold heads of state responsible and accountable. The contribution in Chapter 4 turns specifically to post-conflict Burundi and analyses the extent of responsible governance in Africa with reference to the Constitution of 2005 and the presidential term limit as proposed in the Arusha Peace and Reconciliation Agreement of 2000. Chapter 7 reflects on the role of the proposed African Court of Justice and Human and Peoples' Rights, as a regional court with international criminal jurisdiction, and as a means to hold African states accountable for international crimes, including crimes against humanity, war crimes and genocide.

The authors in Chapter 5 tackle the issue of sexual and gender-based violence which, although a pervasive problem in South Africa and on the African continent, is addressed here in the context of the armed conflict in Syria and the need to hold individual perpetrators, as non-state actors, to account.

Overall, the contributions focus on the many challenges of governance and accountability, both in South Africa and further afield, and offer recommendations to improve state responsiveness.

On behalf of the authors and prospective readers of this volume, the editors thank the respective Deans of the Faculties of Law at the University of Johannesburg and Nelson Mandela University for initiating and conceptualising this project.

Prof Hennie Strydom
University of Johannesburg

Prof Joanna Botha
Nelson Mandela University

www.ingramcontent.com/pod-product-compliance
Lightning Source LLC
Chambersburg PA
CBHW080316220326
41519CB00072B/7433